REMEMBERING BOETHIUS

For Ian and Joan.

Remembering Boethius
Writing Aristocratic Identity in Late Medieval French and English Literatures

ELIZABETH ELLIOTT
University of Edinburgh, UK

Routledge
Taylor & Francis Group

LONDON AND NEW YORK

First published 2012 by Ashgate Publishing

2 Park Square, Milton Park, Abingdon, Oxon OX14 4RN
711 Third Avenue, New York, NY 10017, USA

Routledge is an imprint of the Taylor & Francis Group, an informa business

First issued in paperback 2017

British Library Cataloguing in Publication Data
Elliott, Elizabeth, 1979–
    Remembering Boethius: writing aristocratic identity in late medieval French and English literatures.
    1. Boethius, d. 524. De consolatione philosophiae. 2. Boethius, d. 524 – Influence.
    3. Aristocracy (Social class) in literature. 4. Identity (Psychology) in literature. 5. Exile (Punishment) in literature. 6. Imprisonment in literature. 7. English poetry – Middle English, 1100–1500 – History and criticism. 8. Scottish poetry – To 1700 – History and criticism. 9. French poetry – To 1500 – History and criticism. 10. Literature, Medieval – Roman influences.
    I. Title
    809.1'9352621'0902-dc23

Library of Congress Cataloging-in-Publication Data
Elliott, Elizabeth, 1979–
    Remembering Boethius: writing aristocratic identity in late medieval French and English \ literatures / by Elizabeth Elliott.
        p. cm.
    Includes bibliographical references and index.
    ISBN 978-1-4094-2418-5 (hardcover: alk. paper)
    1. Boethius, d. 524. De consolatione philosophiae. 2. Boethius, d. 524—Influence. 3. Identity (Psychology) in literature. 4. Philosophy, Medieval—Roman influences. I. Title.
    PA6231.C8E45 2012
    100—dc23

                                                                          2012014864

ISBN 978-1-4094-2418-5 (hbk)
ISBN 978-1-138-11874-4 (pbk)

Contents

Acknowledgements

I take great pleasure in thanking the many people and institutions whose generosity made this book possible. My colleagues at the University of Edinburgh have been enormously helpful and encouraging, and warmest thanks are due to Sarah Dunnigan, R.D.S. Jack, Greg Walker, David Salter, James Loxley and Suzanne Trill. I have also benefited immeasurably from discussing aspects of the project with other colleagues, friends and students too numerous to name here, but owe particular debts of gratitude to William Calin, Jane Griffiths, Alastair Minnis, Ardis Butterfield, Alastair Fowler, Philip Bennett, Adrian Armstrong, Alessandra Petrina, Ian Johnson, Joanna Martin, Tracey Sowerby, Louisa Hadley, Sebastiaan Verweij and Patrick Hart, for time and trouble taken in providing assistance of various kinds. Special thanks are also due to Whitney Feininger for her support throughout the publication process, and to Seth F. Hibbert and Heather Dubnick for their editorial work. Research for this project was materially assisted by the generosity of the Arts and Humanities Research Council, and by a fellowship at the University of Edinburgh's Institute for Advanced Studies in the Humanities.

A portion of Chapter 6 has appeared in J. Derrick McClure and Janet Hadley Williams (eds), *Fresch Fontanis: Studies in the Culture of Medieval and Early Modern Scotland* (Newcastle: Cambridge Scholars Press, 2012). I would also thank the British Library for granting permission to use the image of Boethius and Philosophy from MS. Harley 4339, f.2 as a cover illustration.

Elizabeth Eva Leach's valuable study, *Guillaume de Machaut: Secretary, Poet, Musician* (Ithaca: Cornell University Press, 2011) appeared after this book was completed, though I have been able to add some footnotes acknowledging this important addition to Machaut scholarship.

My greatest debts are to my parents, to whom this book is dedicated, and to Kevin, for their unstinting patience, support and affection. If this book has strengths, they reflect the assistance and advice of others; all remaining errors and inadequacies are my own.

Introduction
Remembering Boethius

This book explores the part Boethius's *Consolation of Philosophy* plays in the making of medieval identities, through its adaptation within texts that evoke the *Consolation* as a means to articulate and interpret contemporary experiences of exile and imprisonment. Distinguished by their investment in particular social and historical contexts, these narratives unsettle conceptions of the *Consolation* as unequivocally endorsing a radical rejection of temporal things and the active life that entails a turn towards asceticism. Conventionally framed in erotic terms, such texts have sometimes been described as parodies or subversions of *De Consolatione Philosophiae*.[1] In reexamining the significant conjunction of the political and the erotic within these works, this study brings the social import of these forms, and the interpretative practices they embody, into focus. Locating the role of the *Consolation* in mediating the representation of lives at once political and personal in relation to medieval techniques of memory training, I argue that these works reflect an engagement with conceptions of ethical and textual authority that has an agency of its own, defining an idealised nobility as it reinterprets the Boethian text.

In using the *Consolation* as a narrative model for textual forms that address contemporary political life, these writers establish correspondences between the experience constructed within Boethius's autobiographical narrative and the life histories they reimagine. Eluding the categorical distinctions between history and fiction that inform modern generic expectations of autobiography, these forms of life writing reflect the priorities of cultures that recognise and value modes of subjectivity founded upon likeness. Their shared methodology conceives both texts and selves as the products of intertextuality, and stands in sharp contrast to modern conceptions of selfhood that emphasise the unique qualities of character and experience; like the early modern commonplace books analysed by Adam Smyth, these texts 'reveal the degree to which a compiler's identity might be constructed through a process of alignment with other figures, narratives, and events; through

---

[1] I follow Tim Machan in distinguishing between *De Consolatione Philosophiae*, as written by Boethius, and the *Consolation*, reflecting the diverse forms in which it proliferated within the Middle Ages, Tim William Machan, *Techniques of Translation: Chaucer's* Boece (Norman: Pilgrim, 1985), 128–9. For readings of medieval texts as parodies of the *Consolatio*, see Ann W. Astell, 'Visualizing Boethius's *Consolation* as Romance', in Noel Harold Kaylor, Jr. and Philip Edward Phillips (eds), *New Directions in Boethian Studies* (Kalamazoo: Medieval Institute Publications, 2007), 111–24; Katherine Heinrichs, 'Lovers' "Consolations of Philosophy" in Boccaccio, Machaut, and Chaucer', *Studies in the Age of Chaucer* 11 (1989): 93–115 and *The Myths of Love: Classical Lovers in Medieval Literature* (Pennsylvania: Pennsylvania University Press, 1990) 184, 217–18. See also Karin E.C. Fuog, 'Placing Earth at the Center of the Cosmos: *The Kingis Quair* as Boethian Revision', *Studies in Scottish Literature* 32 (2001): 140–49.

a pursuit of parallels; through an interest in sameness, not difference'.[2] Some of the works I examine have been termed pseudo-autobiographies, in studies that cast valuable light on these practices of life writing, yet the label superimposes an anachronistic horizon of generic expectations on texts whose indistinct and mobile forms evince a fluid sense of self.[3] My use of terms such as life writing and autobiography follows recent discussions of pre-modern self-writing, adopting a more capacious definition of these textual forms in seeking to recognise the full diversity of autobiographical practice, and with an awareness of the problematic character of the critical terminology.[4]

The fecundity of the *Consolation* as a model for medieval life writing in part reflects the cultural sanction it offers for autobiography: arguing the excuse of necessity, Dante identifies Boethius as a paradigmatic example of one of the two principal justifications for such writing, 'since no one else rose to his defence, he sought, under the pretext of finding consolation, to defend himself against the everlasting disgrace of his exile by showing that it had been unjust'.[5] Framed as the author's response to his own political misfortunes, the *Consolation* evokes the experience of exile and imprisonment in literal and figurative terms. Boethius's text establishes a precedent of special relevance to noblemen, for whom political reversals often entailed similar consequences, carrying a marked stigma.[6] The

---

[2]   Adam Smyth, *Autobiography in Early Modern England* (Cambridge: Cambridge University Press, 2010), 5–6.

[3]   On pseudo-autobiography, see Laurence de Looze, *Pseudo-Autobiography in the Fourteenth Century: Juan Ruiz, Guillaume de Machaut, Jean Froissart, and Geoffrey Chaucer* (Florida: University of Florida Press, 1997), and G.B. Gybbon-Monypenny, 'Guillaume de Machaut's Erotic "Autobiography": Precedents for the Form of the *Voir-Dit*', in William Rothwell et al. (eds), *Studies in Medieval Literature and Languages in Memory of Frederick Whitehead* (Manchester: Manchester University Press, 1973), 133–52.

[4]   Notable examples include Smyth, *Autobiography in Early Modern England*; and Meredith Anne Skura, *Tudor Autobiography: Listening for Inwardness* (Chicago: University of Chicago Press: Chicago, 2008). My argument is also indebted to critical discussions including David Aers, 'A Whisper in the Ear of Early Modernists; or, Reflections on Literary Critics Writing the 'History of the Subject,' in David Aers (ed.), *Culture and History, 1350–1660: Essays on English Communities, Identities and Writing* (Detroit: Wayne State University Press, 1992), 177–202; Paul John Eakin, *Fictions in Autobiography: Studies in the Art of Self Invention* (Princeton: Princeton University Press, 1985); Laura Marcus, *Auto/biographical Discourses: Theory, Criticism, Practice* (Manchester: Manchester University Press, 1994); James Olney, *Autobiography: Essays Theoretical and Critical* (Princeton: Princeton University Press, 1980); Sidonie Smith and Julia Watson, *Reading Autobiography: A Guide for Interpreting Life Narratives*, 2nd edn (Minneapolis: University of Minnesota Press, 2010); and Jakki Spicer, 'The Author Is Dead, Long Live the Author': Autobiography and the Fantasy of the Individual', *Criticism* 47.3 (2005): 387–403.

[5]   Dante Alighieri, *The Banquet*, trans. Christopher Ryan (Saratoga: Anma Libri, 1989), Book 1, Chapter 2, 17.

[6]   On the perception of imprisonment, see Jean Dunbabin, *Captivity and Imprisonment in Medieval Europe 1000–1300* (Houndmills: Palgrave, 2002), 162. Dunbabin notes a peculiar absence of prison narratives drawing on the *Consolation* during the period she examines.

text's later reception reflects a particular interest in the specificity of Boethius's experience, in the proliferation of biographical material supplementing the *Consolation*, drawing attention to Boethius's social status and involvement in politics, and explicitly identifying him as a prisoner at the time of writing.[7] Yet, the appeal of the Boethian narrative consists not in a superficial likeness between the social positions and experience of historical subjects, but rather in the symbolic value attached to that experience, its capacity to represent a social ideal.

The reception history of the *Consolation* reflects the identification of the text as a repository of moral wisdom, endorsing universal values considered especially pertinent to the nobility. This logic is anticipated in Philosophy's claim that noble ancestry's only value lies in 'imposita nobilibus necessitudo uideatur, ne a maiorum uirtute degeneret' ['the obligation which rests on noblemen not to fall away from the excellence of their forbears'] (3.pr.6).[8] Virtue is conceived as an idealised standard of behaviour appropriate to the aristocracy, an etymological correlation elaborated within the commentary tradition and texts such as the *Roman de la Rose*: as Jean de Meun argues, 'Gentillece est noble [...] qu'el n'entre pas en queur vilain'['Nobility is noble [...] for she will not enter any base heart'] (6549–50).[9] In seeking to embody this standard of virtue, the nobility thus contribute to the production and maintenance of social distinctions, reinforcing the existing social order in upholding its conceptual basis. Facilitating the *Consolation*'s assimilation to aristocratic tastes, this principle is manifested in the frequency of the text's appearance and citation alongside works in the 'mirrors for princes' genre, and in dedications like that offered by Jean de Meun to Philippe le Bel, of his own French translation, *Li Livres de Confort de Philosophie*.[10]

---

[7]   See Howard Rollin Patch, *The Tradition of Boethius: A Study of His Importance in Medieval Culture* (New York: Oxford University Press, 1935), 9–20; Joanna Summers, *Late-Medieval Prison Writing and the Politics of Autobiography* (Oxford: Oxford University Press, 2004), 13–17.

[8]   Ludwig Bieler (ed.), *Anicii Manlii Severini Boethii Philosophiae Consolatio*, CCL 94 (Turnhout: Brepols, 1957), trans. P.G. Walsh, *The Consolation of Philosophy* (Oxford: Oxford University Press, 1999).

[9]   Guillaume de Lorris and Jean de Meun, *Le Roman de la Rose*, ed. Félix Lecoy, 3 vols (Paris: Editions Champion, 1965–1970), trans. Frances Horgan (Oxford: Oxford University Press, 1994).

[10]   A.J. Minnis, *Fallible Authors: Chaucer's Pardoner and Wife of Bath* (Philadelphia: University of Pennsylvania Press, 2008), 320; on the context of this and similar dedications see Glynnis M. Cropp, 'The Medieval French Tradition', in Maarten J.F.M Hoenen and Lodi Nauta (eds), *Boethius in the Middle Ages: Latin and Vernacular Traditions of the* Consolatio Philosophiae (Leiden: Brill, 1997), 247, 252. Jean de Meun's translation is conventionally numbered III, according to the Thomas-Roques classification, Antoine Thomas and Mario Roques, 'Traductions françaises de la *Consolatio Philosophiae* de Boèce', *Histoire littéraire de la France* 37 (1938): 419–88. *Li Livres de Confort de Philosophie*, in Tim William Machan (ed., with the assistance of A.J. Minnis), *Sources of the Boece* (Athens: University of Georgia Press, 2005), and L.V. Dedeck-Héry, 'Boethius' *De Consolatione* by Jean de Meun', *Mediaeval Studies* 14 (1952): 162–275.

As a narrative that mediates a desire to inhabit an ideal that at once aspires to universality and is marked by particular interests, the *Consolation* frames an engagement with what Sarah Kay has termed the 'complexity of one'. Taking issue with a liberal critical consensus that privileges polyphony, ambivalence and dialogism, Kay draws attention to the radical potential of singularity as it is instantiated within medieval didactic poetry, and to its resonances in current continental philosophy.[11] The didactic practice she examines is founded upon the imaginative constructions of places imprinted within the communal memory through processes of dissemination and renewal played out in textual contexts. Such places facilitate forms of mental gathering, locating arguments in physical and conceptual terms; in doing so, they contribute to the production of consensus, guiding the readers' thoughts to a commonplace that imparts a '*community* of outlook'.[12] Boethius's *Consolation* is instrumental to the construction of the prison house as one such scene, while the text provides a related narrative site of convergence, through its fundamental place within medieval discussions of oneness. Identifying the true end of desire as happiness, consisting in freedom from the bondage of need, in a state of wholeness and self-sufficiency that is the essence of the divine, the *Consolation* reflects on the human potential for attaining that state, sharing in, and coinciding with God.[13] Idealised object of an individual's search for perfection, this state also represents a Utopian aspiration: imagined as a country or city from whence Boethius is exiled, divine unity both redeems and reproaches human society.[14] Manifested in moments of concord that bind nations, friendships and chaste marriages, divine love nonetheless does not rule human hearts, measuring the disjunction between the perfection of the heavenly order and corrupt earthly hierarchies (2.m.8). Yet, in emphasising the responsibility of philosophers to involve themselves in government, the *Consolation* points toward

---

[11]   Sarah Kay, *The Place of Thought: The Complexity of One in Late Medieval French Didactic Poetry* (Philadelphia: University of Pennsylvania Press, 2007). Significant recent engagements with conceptions of oneness include Slavoj Žižek's critique of the repressive function of the notion of totalitarianism, *Did Somebody Say Totalitarianism? Five Interventions in the (Mis)use of a Notion* (London: Verso, 2001), and meditations on community, identity and universality such as Giorgio Agamben, *The Coming Community*, trans. Michael Hardt (Minneapolis: University of Minnesota Press, 1993); Jean-Lucy Nancy, *The Inoperative Community*, ed. Peter Connor, trans. Peter Connor et al. (Minneapolis: University of Minnesota Press, 1991); and Costas Douzinas and Slavoj Žižek (eds), *The Idea of Communism* (London: Verso, 2010).

[12]   Kay, *The Place of Thought*, 2–3, emphasis Kay's.

[13]   See especially 3.pr.2, and discussion in William J. Asbell, Jr., 'The Philosophical Background of *Sufficientia* in Boethius's *Consolation*, Book 3', in Kaylor and Phillips (eds), *New Directions in Boethian Studies*, 3–16.

[14]   1.pr.5; 2.pr.4; 3.pr.9; 4.pr.1; 4.m.1; 5.pr.1, see Astell, *Job, Boethius, and Epic Truth* (New York: Cornell University Press, 1994), 48–9.

the possibility that justice might be realised within the political order, however imperfectly and provisionally.[15]

Recent work in Boethian studies has added to a body of criticism questioning conventional accounts of *De Consolatione Philosophiae*'s meaning.[16] If the *Consolatio* is capable of diverse readings, however, this study seeks to acknowledge the ways in which the desire to preserve textual meaning, and to affirm a universal ethical standard, contribute to textual *mouvance*. As Rita Copeland demonstrates, medieval conceptions of rhetorical invention as 'a hermeneutical performance on a traditional textual source' recognise affinities between the interlinked practices of exposition, translation and composition.[17] Insofar as they engage with authoritative textual sources, such practices at once represent forms of alignment, asserting a relationship of correspondence between texts, and underline disjunctions, in marking temporal, cultural and linguistic difference. In translation and commentary, the work of making a text's meaning readily comprehensible typically entails exposition, through the addition of glosses to elucidate its sense.[18] As Tim Machan observes, here 'meaning, which has as a necessary concomitant interpretation, and the formation of that meaning, have primacy over the fixity of any prior text'.[19] Emphasis on meaning thus lends impetus to the variance inherent in textual production within a manuscript culture, an effect compounded by the conception of *intentio auctoris* in didactic terms, as 'pedagogic purpose, whether explicit or implicit; what was meant in ultimate terms'.[20] Epitomised by the interpretation of Ovid's erotic writings as teaching the morality of love, this tactic assimilates the text to the reader's evaluation of its essential ethical value.

The impact of such interpretative practices is reflected in the diversity of the medieval *Consolation*, its popularity contributing to the development of a Latin

---

[15] On the currency of the Platonic argument reiterated in 1.pr.4 within the Middle Ages, see Pierre Courcelle, *La Consolation de Philosophie dans la tradition littéraire* (Paris: Etudes augustiniennes, 1984), 60–66.

[16] For example, Peter Dronke, *Verse with Prose from Petronius to Dante: The Art and Scope of the Mixed Form* (Cambridge, MA: Harvard University Press, 1994); Mark Miller, *Philosophical Chaucer: Love, Sex, and Agency in the* Canterbury Tales (Cambridge: Cambridge University Press, 2004), 111–51; Joel C. Relihan, *The Prisoner's Philosophy: Life and Death in Boethius's* Consolation (Notre Dame: University of Notre Dame Press, 2007); Jessica Rosenfeld, *Ethics and Enjoyment in Late Medieval Poetry: Love after Aristotle* (Cambridge: Cambridge University Press, 2011), 137–59.

[17] Rita Copeland, *Rhetoric, Hermeneutics, and Translation in the Middle Ages* (Cambridge: Cambridge University Press, 1991), 179.

[18] For example, see A.J. Minnis and Tim William Machan, 'The *Boece* as Late-Medieval Translation', in A.J. Minnis (ed.), *Chaucer's* Boece *and the Medieval Tradition of Boethius* (Cambridge: Brewer, 1993), 172–3; J.D. Burnley, 'Late Medieval English Translation: Types and Reflections', in Roger Ellis (ed.), *The Medieval Translator: The Theory and Practice of Translation in the Middle Ages* (Cambridge: Brewer, 1989), 50–51.

[19] Tim William Machan, 'Chaucer as Translator', in Ellis (ed.), *The Medieval Translator*, 55.

[20] A.J. Minnis, *Medieval Theory of Authorship: Scholastic Literary Attitudes in the Later Middle Ages*, 2nd edn (Aldershot: Wildwood, 1988), xiv.

vulgate tradition, as older readings were gradually and continuously replaced with new ones, and texts supplemented with glosses.[21] The effective function of translation and commentary as forms of substitution, ineluctably reinventing the text even as they seek to expound its perceived didactic value, is attested by the profuse variety of surviving versions. Simund de Freine's late twelfth-century *Roman de Philosophie*, the earliest surviving Romance-language version, offers a precedent for the autobiographical practice of later poets in setting his selective Anglo-Norman verse paraphrase in the context of an account of his own experience of misfortune.[22] While several later translations, including Jean de Meun's influential prose version, are relatively accurate by modern standards, they follow medieval academic practice in their incorporation of material from the commentary tradition.[23]

The context of translation itself marks a further estrangement from Latin authority, as a tendency towards linguistic uniformity in later versions of the *Consolation* disrupts the illusion of succession preserved within the shared context of Lain commentary. In the case of the most copious body of vernacular translations, the French, this effect is compounded by the dynamics of vernacular reception, giving rise to new traditions.[24] Rita Copeland draws attention to the particular role of Jean de Meun's preface to the *Livres de Confort de Philosophie* as a conduit for this process: Jean's dedication to Philippe IV at once positions his patron as heir to the cultural and political authority of the Roman Empire, and

---

[21]   Barnet Kottler, 'The Vulgate Tradition of the *Consolatione Philosophiae* in the Fourteenth Century', *Mediaeval Studies* 17 (1955): 209–14 (211); Minnis and Machan, 'The *Boece*', 173–4. For a concise overview of the variety of the medieval Boethian tradition, see Noel Harold Kaylor, Jr., *The Medieval* Consolation of Philosophy: *An Annotated Bibliography* (New York: Garland, 1992); Glynnis M. Cropp, 'Boethius in Translation in Medieval Europe', in Harald Kittel et al., *Traduction: Ein internationales Handbuch zur Übersetzungsforschung*, 2 (Berlin: de Gruyter, 2007), 1329–37. For a detailed listing of French translations and MSS, see Frédéric Duval and Françoise Vielliard, *Miroir des classiques*, Éditions en ligne de l'École des chartes, 17 (Paris, École nationale des `iillaume de Machaut:ueried here: full citation is given in Chapter 1, note 2.chartes, 2007), http://elec.enc.sorbonne.fr/miroir/boece/traduction/para=françaises.html, consulted 10 July 2011. Also invaluable are the essays collected in Hoenen and Nauta (eds), *Boethius in the Middle Ages* and A.J. Minnis (ed.), *The Medieval Boethius: Studies in the Vernacular Translations of* De Consolatione Philosophiae (Cambridge: Brewer, 1987).

[22]   John E. Matzke (ed.), *Les Oeuvres de Simund de Freine* (Paris: Société des Anciens Textes Français, 1909), 1–60. See Winthrop Wetherbee, 'The *Consolation* and medieval literature', in John Marenbon (ed.), *The Cambridge Companion to Boethius* (Cambridge: Cambridge University Press, 2009), 281.

[23]   For example, the commentary used by Jean de Meun has been identified as that of William of Conches, see A.J. Minnis, 'Aspects of the Medieval French and English Traditions of the *De Consolatione Philosophiae*', in Margaret Gibson (ed.), *Boethius: His Life, Thought and Influence* (Oxford: Blackwell, 1981), 316–34. Similar uses of commentary for amplification are noted in Cropp, 'The Medieval French Tradition'.

[24]   Copeland, *Rhetoric, Hermeneutics, and Translation*, 127–50.

situates the book in relation to his other vernacular works, both translations and the continuation of the *Roman de la Rose*.[25] Itself embodying a form of literary invention that draws upon the medieval tradition of the *Consolation*, the *Rose* is also significant as a text that anticipates Jean's own translation in defining its moral worth:

> Mout est chetis et fols naïs
> qui croit que ce solt ses païs:
> n'est pas vostre païs en terre,
> ce peut l'en bien des clers enquerre,
> qui Boce *de Confort* lisent
> et les sentences qui la gisent,
> donc granz biens aus gens lais feroit
> qui bien leur translateroit. (5003–10)

> [He is a wretched and stupid fool who believes that this is his country: your country is not on earth, as you can learn from the clerks who explain Boethius' *Consolation* and the meanings contained in it. If someone were to translate this book for the laity, he would do them a great service].[26]

Voiced by Reason, this argument establishes the universal value of the text, as the source of a moral sense of place that negates local attachments, and the particular value of the work of translation, whose realisation in the *Livres de Confort* aspires to Jean's material and spiritual advancement. Connecting royal power and vernacular textual production, the logic of *translatio studii et imperii* within Jean's prologue effectively augments the authority of both Jean and his patron, establishing a reciprocal relation between the two.

Jean's preface was later appended to the most widely circulated translation of the *Consolation*, the revised verse-prose version known as *Le Livre de Boece de Consolacion*, in the majority of the 65 surviving manuscript copies.[27] Its circulation in this context allowed the later translation to assume Jean's vernacular authority, annexing the scholarly credentials of his text and the prestige of its royal patronage, in a process that contributes to the construction of a distinctive

---

[25] Copeland, *Rhetoric, Hermeneutics, and Translation*, 133–6.

[26] Horgan's translation slightly altered here, and see Copeland, *Rhetoric, Hermeneutics, and Translation*, 134–9.

[27] See Thomas-Roques VI, for a detailed description of surviving MSS, see Glynnis M. Cropp, 'Les Manuscrits du *Livre de Boece de Consolacion*', *Revue d'histoire des textes* 12–13 (1982–3): 263–352. An updated list is available in Cropp's edition of this version, which is primarily based on Auckland, City Libraries, Med. MS G119, *Le Livre de Boece de Consolacion* (Geneva: Droz, 2006), 22–8. Another MS of version VI is published in Isabelle Bétemps et al. (eds), *La Consolation de la Philosophie de Boèce: dans une traduction attribuée à Jean de Meun: d'après le manuscrit Leber 817 de la Bibliothèque Municipale de Rouen* (Mont-Saint-Aignan: Publications de l'Université de Rouen, 2004). On version VI's relation to Jean's prologue, see Glynnis M. Cropp, 'Le Prologue de Jean de Meun et *Le Livre de Boece de Consolacion*', *Romania* 103 (1982): 278–98.

Boethian tradition with Jean at its head.[28] The dissemination of these and other translations sustain and augment this diverse corpus, as they become the materials for later revisions and adaptations.

The place of French within the wider context of this vernacular assimilation of Latin authority is evinced by the interlingual influence of translations such as the *Livre de Boece de Consolacion*: a Genoese prosimetric translation of the unglossed variant form of this translation survives from the fifteenth century, and Jacob Vilt produced a Middle Dutch version of the most widespread, glossed version in 1466.[29] Chaucer's *Boece* at once mediates and contests the cultural authority of its Latin and French sources, yet the essentially European character of contemporary vernacularity marks a familial resemblance to Jean's *Livres de Confort*, positioning the *Boece* within a tradition both intimate and antagonistic.[30] Such repeated and renewed vernacular engagements with the *Consolation* are perpetuated as the *Boece* influences Chaucer's own Boethian fictions, and itself becomes an object of commentary, in the form of manuscript glosses, and of translation, as a source for John Walton's distinctive rendering, and for the anonymous *Boke of Coumfort of Bois*.[31]

The traditional emphasis on fidelity to the meaning of the authoritative text, conceived in didactic terms, also licensed a degree of innovation reflected in adaptive practices of expansion and revision that include the interpolation of narrative matter, as well as commentary. Typically drawing on the academic resources of exegesis and commentary, these narrative elements serve the interests of textual fidelity as a means to clarify and further substantiate Boethius's meaning. This form of adaptation is represented in a significant number of medieval French translations, including the Dominican monk Renaut de Louhans's widely circulated verse translation, *Le Roman de Fortune et de Felicité*, completed 31 March 1336. Surviving in 37 manuscripts, with a further three now lost, Renaut's translation characteristically enlarges allusions to history and myth into narrative episodes, drawing on sources such as Nicholas Trevet's Latin commentary.[32]

---

[28]   Copeland, *Rhetoric, Hermeneutics, and Translation*, 140–41; Cropp, 'The Medieval French Tradition', 249.

[29]   The Italian translation is discussed in Thomas Ricklin, '…Quello non conosciuto da molti libro di Boezio. Hinweise zur *Consolatio philosophiae* in Norditalien', in Hoenen and Nauta (eds), *Boethius in the Middle Ages*, 277–9, 286, and Glynnis M. Cropp, 'An Italian Translation of *Le Livre de Boece de Consolacion*', in Kaylor and Phillips (eds), *New Directions in Boethian Studies*, 75–82. On the Dutch version, see Mariken Goris and Wilma Wissink, 'The Medieval Dutch Tradition of Boethius' *Consolatio philosophiae*', in Hoenen and Nauta (eds), *Boethius in the Middle Ages*, 121–65.

[30]   Copeland, *Rhetoric, Hermeneutics, and Translation*, 143.

[31]   Copeland, *Rhetoric, Hermeneutics, and Translation*, 143–9; Noel Harold Kaylor, Jr., and Philip Edward Phillips (eds), '*The Boke of Coumfort of Bois* [Bodleian Library, Oxford MS Auct. F.3.5.]: A Transcription with Introduction', in Kaylor and Phillips (eds), *New Directions in Boethian Studies*, 223–79.

[32]   Thomas-Roques IX, discussed in J. Keith Atkinson and Béatrice Atherton, 'Les Manuscrits du *Roman de Fortune et de Félicité*', *Revue d'Histoire des Textes*, 22 (1992): 169–251. A modern edition exists: Béatrice Atherton, 'Edition critique de la version longue

Renaut's narrative method complements the Christianising approach to Boethian material reflected in his suppression of sections addressing Neoplatonic ideas, and is in line with the classicising practice of friars.[33] Expansion of the repertoire of *exempla* associated with the *Consolation* also serves to locate the argument within more familiar conceptual territory: for example, Renaut's citation of romance heroes such as Roland, Oliver and Ogier in the context of the Boethian discussion of tragedy maps the genre onto contemporary textual matter, redefining it in the process (2.pr.2).[34]

The history of the *Roman de Fortune* suggests the impetus form and narrative content lent to the crosspollination of Boethian tradition: Renaut's experimentation with a variety of poetic forms allowed for the incorporation of 165 verses from the prosimetric *Boeces de Consolacion* (Thomas-Roques VI). Arguing for the potential influence of the *Roman de la Rose* on the *Roman de Fortune*, Rita Copeland draws attention to analogic connections between the two made within their reception history. In MS B.N. fr. 812, both texts are copied in the same hand, by a scribe who transplanted elements from Jean's version of the Croesus narrative, itself enlarged within the commentary tradition, into Renaut's expansion of the same Boethian example.[35] Jean's Boethian fiction thus feeds back into, and supplants, the source tradition that informs it. The *Roman de Fortune* likewise has a legacy of its own, as the basis of a revision that grew into a new verse translation. Its popularity witnessed by the survival of 35 manuscripts, this late-fourteenth century revision in turn inspired a further distinct version of the *Consolation* in the fifteenth century.[36]

Yet, the diversity produced by the cumulative proliferation of *exempla* drawn from the sources of scripture, hagiography, myth and history, in repeated processes of revision and expansion, is nevertheless rationalised in the context of an approach that values fidelity to sense above word for word translation. The anonymous producer of a fourteenth-century Picard translation-commentary articulates the principle, in promising to 'expose /Tout ce que Böeces suppose' ['to reveal all that

---

du Roman de Fortune et de Félicité', unpublished Ph.D. Diss. (University of Queensland, 1994). For a study of interpolated narratives within the French tradition of Boethian translation including several edited examples, see Richard Dwyer, *Boethian Fictions: Narratives in the Medieval French Versions of the Consolatio Philosophiae* (Cambridge, MA: The Medieval Academy of America, 1976).

[33] Dwyer, *Boethian Fictions*, 24, 44–5; Beryl Smalley, *English Friars and Antiquity in the Early Fourteenth Century* (Oxford: Oxford University Press, 1960).

[34] Dwyer, *Boethian Fictions*, 39.

[35] Copeland, *Rhetoric, Hermeneutics, and Translation*, 138–9; Dwyer, *Boethian Fictions*, 44.

[36] Classified as X, Marcel Noest (ed.), 'A Critical Edition of a Late Fourteenth Century French Verse Translation of Boethius' *De Consolatione Philosophiae*: the *Boëce de Confort*', *Carmina Philosophiae: Journal of the International Boethius Society*, 8–9 (1999–2000). This version is a source of the version preserved in the unique MS Aberystwyth, National Library of Wales, 5038D, classified as XI, Glynnis M. Cropp (ed.), *Böece de Confort remanié*, MHRA European Translations 1 (London: Modern Humanities Research Association, 2011).

Boethius supposed'].[37] Underlying these practices are pre-modern conceptions of ethical truths as being incapable of any singular expression; instead, they are accessible only through particular and contingent instantiations. The perfection of knowledge in this context entails the accumulation of examples, rather than the achievement of complete factual accuracy, as the accretion of imperfect partial expressions helps to build a fuller sense of an inaccessible universal, a technique manifested in the compilation of *exempla* under topical headings within medieval *florilegia*.[38] In this sense, the copiousness of the Boethian tradition fills out the meaning imperfectly contained within the *Consolation*.

The desire to add to a common store of knowledge also coincides with a moral imperative to internalise it: as Mary Carruthers demonstrates, medieval culture identified memory as the foundation of ethics, and regarded memory training as a means to perfect the faculty of judgement. In assimilating the cumulative wisdom of a community, individuals might edify themselves, amending natural deficiencies through the construction of a disposition or *habitus* towards ethical behaviour, which is mediated by the contents of memory.[39] Through medieval practices of memorisation, the contents of the *Consolation* contribute to the perfection of the self as they are added to the storehouse of memory, mediating aspiration to a shared ethical ideal.

If the use of the trained memory transforms the user, however, it simultaneously alters the text. In this context, memorisation is conceived as an intimate and embodied mode of engagement, a form of incorporation distinct from modern notions of scholarly objectivity. Supplying a link between the grazing of cattle and the murmur that facilitates the meditative process of memorisation, rumination also points toward the function of memorisation as a kind of consumption, where textual matter is digested to nourish the reader.[40] Recollection was recognised as a physiological process, and medieval methods of memory training engage the emotions and bodily senses. As Aquinas argues, since 'human knowledge has more mastery over objects of sense', abstract concepts must be 'tied [*alligentur*],

---

[37]   Thomas-Roques VII, discussed in J. Keith Atkinson, 'A Fourteenth-Century Picard Translation-Commentary of the "Consolatio Philosophiae"', in Minnis (ed.), *The Medieval Boethius*, 32–62. Selections from this translation are published in Dwyer, *Boethian Fictions*, 92–9, 103–8; and in J.K. Atkinson and A.M. Babbi (eds), *L''Orphée' de Boèce au Moyen Âge: Traductions françaises et commentaries latins (XIIe-XVe siècles)* (Verona: Fiorini, 2000), 45–91. Comprising selections from a number of versions of the *Consolation*, this collection offers a valuable illustration of the variety of Boethian interpretation through the particular treatment of the Orpheus myth.

[38]   See Mary Carruthers, *The Book of Memory: A Study of Memory in Medieval Culture*, 2nd edn (Cambridge: Cambridge University Press, 2008), 30, 197–200. The underlying conception of *habitus* derives from Aristotle, *Nicomachean Ethics*, trans. W.D. Ross, in Jonathan Barnes (ed.), *The Complete Works of Aristotle*, 2 vols (Princeton: Princeton University Press, 1984), II, 1742, Book 2.1.

[39]   Carruthers, *The Book of Memory*, 14–15, 81–9, 229.

[40]   Carruthers, *The Book of Memory*, 205.

as it were, to bodily images'.[41] The trained memory forges such ties, translating semantic content into episodic memory, encoding it as a form of personal experience. This process typically begins with seclusion, since the absence of sensory distractions helps the mind to focus in an intense, emotional state of concentration that stimulates the construction and recollection of such encoded memories.[42]

Mnemonic praxis also appeals to embodied experience in ordering information along schematic lines: most evident in the use of familiar and imagined places as backgrounds within the architectural system described in the *Rhetorica ad Herennium*, reliance on a rigid order of locations typifies other, more widely disseminated memory systems.[43] Ordering schemes such as the alphabet, numerical systems and indices engage the bodily senses involved in navigating a physical environment. They evoke the experience of spatial movement from place to place, as modern research suggesting that the use of such mnemonic schemes stimulates areas of the brain associated with spatial memory indicates.[44] The practice of creating *imagines* or mental images to retain information reflects a similar appeal to the corporeal senses: the violent and sexualised motion of the images Thomas Bradwardine describes in his treatise on memory training disturb modern sensibilities, yet their visceral effect is precisely what makes them memorable.[45] Peter of Ravenna's highly popular art of memory illustrates a related technique, in his use of the image of Juniper, a Pistoian whom he 'loved greatly' as a young man, and of various 'fayre maidens', some of them 'all naked'.[46] The effectiveness of this technique, and its potential shortcomings, are suggested by the experience of some modern mnemonists who adapt Peter's technique in their own practice.

---

[41]   Trans. in Thomas Aquinas, *Summa Theologiæ*, Thomas Gilby (ed.), vol. 36 (Cambridge: Cambridge University Press, 2006) 2a2æ. 49. I, 63.

[42]   Carruthers, *The Book of Memory*, 216, 245–9; and *The Craft of Thought: Meditation, rhetoric and the making of images, 400–1200* (Cambridge: Cambridge University Press, 1998), 99–105; 307n122.

[43]   For a critique of the dominance of the *Ad Herennium* in accounts of the history of memory training, in the wake of Frances A. Yates's pioneering work on Renaissance memory, *The Art of Memory* (London: Pimlico, 1992), see Carruthers, *The Book of Memory*, especially 153–4, 172–94.

[44]   Eleanor A. Maguire et al., 'Routes to Remembering: The Brains Behind Superior Memory', *Nature Neuroscience* 6.1 (2003): 90–95. The subjects of this study were competitors from the World Memory Championships; nine out of ten of these subjects employed the classically derived system termed the 'method of loci'.

[45]   Thomas Bradwardine, 'On Acquiring a Trained Memory', trans. Mary Carruthers, in *The Book of Memory*, 361–8, and see 163–72.

[46]   Peter of Ravenna (Pietro Tommai), first published in Venice, 1491, *The Art of Memory, that otherwise is called the Phenix, a boke very behouefull and profitable to all professours of science, grammaryens, rethoryciens, dialectyks, legystes, phylosophes and theologiens*, trans. Robert Copland [1545 (?)] STC 24112, A7ʳ, B2ᵛ. See Paolo Rossi, *Logic and the Art of Memory: The Quest for a Universal Language*, trans. Stephen Clucas (London: Continuum, 2000), 20–22, 254n47.

Impressed with his success in remembering sequences of cards through mental images of familiar figures performing erotic acts, Joshua Foer nevertheless voices the fear that the involvement of family members might constitute 'upgrading my memory at the expense of tormenting my subconscious'.[47]

These examples are clearly emotive, but other schemes, such as the numerical mnemonic Hugh of St Victor employs, also involve the bodily senses, albeit in more subtle ways. Comprising a series of numbered backgrounds resembling a grid, Hugh's scheme enables the storage of text through an attention to the unique visual qualities of the manuscript page, 'the color, shape, position, and placement of the letters [...] in what color we observed the trace of the letter or the ornamented surface of the parchment'.[48] Hugh also emphasises the mnemonic value of incorporating the particular context of memorisation, recollecting the details of the temporal, physical and personal situation in which it occurs. His advice, like other medieval writing on memory, reflects a profound awareness of the extent to which the associative connections that facilitate memory are particular, formed over time through habitual experience and ultimately unique to the individual.[49] Memory training draws on local attachments and engages the subjective sense of embodied experience to turn the public materials of literary tradition into private property.

In producing a more expansive sense of a work's significance and of its personal applications, the mnemonic aspect of reception and the conception of exegesis as a cumulative process contributing to the copiousness of a text's meaning complicate the attempt to define narrative adaptations of the *Consolation* as parody. The trained memory at once facilitates and offers a precedent for such adaptations because it enables the translation of public material into new forms and contexts as a means of conserving and transmitting meaning. Rita Copeland's analysis of *Rhetoric, Hermeneutics, and Translation in the Middle Ages* draws attention to the role of translation in mediating cultural authority, advancing a claim to affinity with, and subservience to, tradition that, however sincere, tends to displace its subject. Copeland argues persuasively for the development of forms of translation that subvert the rhetoric of fidelity to assume their own, vernacular authority. Key to this development is the conception of rhetorical invention as a hermeneutical performance upon common textual matter. Memory training, as Mary Carruthers demonstrates, is not simply a means of storing and recollecting matter: composition is conceived as an act of memory, dependent upon the collation and reformulation of materials held in the composer's mental inventory. In this context, the process of textual composition could be almost entirely memorial.[50]

It is significant that the *Consolation* itself bears interpretation as a literary representation of this form of composition: in the seclusion of his chamber,

---

[47]   Joshua Foer, *Moonwalking with Einstein: The Art and Science of Remembering Everything* (London: Allen Lane, 2011), 185.

[48]   Hugh of St Victor, 'The Three Best Memory-Aids for Learning History', trans. Mary Carruthers, in *The Book of Memory*, 342, and discussion, 100–106.

[49]   See Carruthers, *The Book of Memory*, 80.

[50]   Carruthers, *The Book of Memory*, especially 240–57.

Boethius lies weeping as he composes poetry. His situation reflects the conditions typically associated with mnemonic activity, with its beginnings in a state of anxiety and emotional distress, and his vision can be understood as the product of meditative invention based on the philosophical contents of memory.[51] Through the exercise of memory, Boethius transforms the experience of misfortune into an occasion for writing that affirms an ideal ethical standard. The texts I examine in this study take the *Consolation* as a model for narratives that address similar, contemporary experiences of the political misfortunes of exile or imprisonment. In doing so, they follow the best mnemonic practice in translating the content of the Boethian lesson into familiar terms, and the dissemination of such texts functions as a form of commentary in enlarging the definitional copiousness of the *Consolation*. The production of these texts depends upon an ethics conceived in rhetorical terms: requiring an audience, they generate a commonplace by linking the public memory of a text with a particular, historical experience, bringing the two into a reciprocal relation that develops the meaning of both expansively.[52] They announce an affinity with Boethius, yet, at the same time, in supplying a contemporary version of the Boethian example, they function to displace the authority of the *Consolation*.

Complementing Catherine Léglu and Stephen Milner's recent collection exploring responses to Boethius in medieval writing on desire, consolation and mourning, this study seeks to address the uses of the *Consolation* after the latter half of the thirteenth century, when it ceased to be a part of the university arts curriculum, and to cast light on the process by which it became 'absorbed into aristocratic lay culture to the extent that quotations from it may pretend to be the expression of natural intellect'.[53] As forms of life writing, several of these texts trouble the boundaries between conceptions of the distinction between biography and autobiography: composed by poets responding to the political experience of a patron, and depicting the relationship that links these subjects, they expose the collective aspects of both the self and self-writing, reflecting the ways in which the poet is invested in the construction of his patron's identity. Spanning French, English and Scottish writing, this book seeks to explore the adaptation of Boethius as an ethical model for medieval experience in focusing on a series of texts that explicitly address circumstances of exile or imprisonment, conditions that most closely resemble the medieval sense of the context in which the *Consolation* was composed. One exception to this rule, Guillaume de Machaut's *Remede de Fortune*, is included for its citation within Machaut's *Confort d'ami*, where it is recommended to Machaut's imprisoned patron, Charles of Navarre, as a valuable resource for the aristocratic reader who seeks to apply Boethian philosophy to political practice. In other cases, the precise nature of the relationship linking these texts is ambiguous: the treatment of imprisonment in Thomas Usk's *Testament of*

---

[51]   Carruthers, *The Craft of Thought*, 173–6.

[52]   Carruthers, *The Book of Memory*, 225.

[53]   Catherine E. Léglu and Stephen J. Milner, 'Introduction: Encountering Consolation', in Catherine E. Léglu and Stephen J. Milner (eds), *The Erotics of Consolation: Desire and Distance in the Late Middle Ages* (Houndmills: Palgrave, 2008), 5.

Love and James I of Scotland's *Kingis Quair* potentially reflects a direct familiarity with the poetry of Guillaume de Machaut and Jean Froissart, and is more clearly the product of practices of adaptation manifested across the Boethian tradition of translation, commentary and rhetorical inventions.

The modes of Boethian adaptation I explore here resonate beyond texts that share a particular concern with exile and imprisonment, however: they are felt in the depiction of the experience of loss and mourning within Machaut's *Jugement dou roy de Behaigne* and *Jugement dou roy de Navarre*, in the role of Boethius within Christine de Pizan's *Livre de chemin de long estude* and of Philozophie in Jean Froissart's *Joli buisson de Jonece*, and in the diverse Boethian engagements of Geoffrey Chaucer.[54] The English love lyrics attributed to Charles d'Orleans during his years as a hostage and the autobiographical poetry of Thomas Hoccleve are similarly marked by Boethian influence, but neither poet uses the form of Boethian narrative to represent and redefine literal experiences of exile or imprisonment directly, so they fall outside the scope of this study.

The following chapters trace the ways in which particular experiences of captivity and exile assume the textual form of Boethian narrative, and how that formal alignment impacts upon both Boethian tradition and social life. Chapter 1 examines Guillaume de Machaut's *Confort d'ami* (1357) as the most explicit formulation of the particular value of Boethius and the *Consolation* for those involved in politics. An advisory poem addressed to Machaut's captive patron, Charles of Navarre, the *Confort* fuses matter drawn from scripture and mythology in ways that have troubled critics, and invokes Boethius as a model for emulation, in his capacity as a philosopher who worked for the common good, suffering pain and exile as a result. As I argue, the treatment of Boethius in the *Confort* is informed by a textual tradition in which versions of the *Consolation* might be readily augmented with biblical and mythic narratives. In this context, Boethian allusion works to shift the focus of the text from literal captivity to spiritual imprisonment, and to identify the possibility of redemption as dependent upon the cultivation of a form of self-discipline associated with mnemonic practice.

Chapter 2 takes its cue from the *Confort* in considering the relevance of the *Remede de Fortune* to this ethical practice, exploring the ways in which the *Remede* responds to the *Consolation*, adapting and engaging with mnemonic themes present within Boethian tradition. Drawing most prominently on the *Consolation*'s treatment of Fortune, the *Remede* elides the text's focus on the experience of Boethius, substituting a beleaguered narrator presented in semi-autobiographical terms. This act of substitution serves the transposition of Boethian materials to a fourteenth-century context, substituting the figure of Hope for that of Philosophy, and recasting the interlocutor's trouble as erotic difficulty. Like the *Confort d'ami*, the *Remede* locates the solution to its central problem

---

[54] Especially relevant in this regard are Helen J. Swift, '*Tamainte Consolation / me fist lymagination*: A Poetics of Mourning and Imagination in Late Medieval *dits*' and Sarah Kay, 'Touching Singularity: Consolation, Philosophy, and Poetry in the French *Dit*', in Léglu and Milner (eds), *The Erotics of Consolation*, 21–38, 141–64; Jessica Rosenfeld, *Ethics and Enjoyment*, 135–59, and Kay, *The Place of Thought*, 95–276.

in the cultivation of memory, and it stages an internalised process of therapeutic meditation that is a characteristic feature of mnemonic practice. As I argue, the nature of the learning process the *Remede* depicts is again informed by a reading of the *Consolation* as a work understood to address the themes of memory, literary skill and the education of the nobility.

Chapter 3 traces the influence of Boethian conceptions of the prison-house as a place of moral education, and of the conditions of exile and imprisonment as constitutive to subjectivity, within Machaut's *Fonteinne amoureuse*. The poem's date of composition (*c.* 1360–1361), together with internal allusions to the troubled state of France, and a central focus on a nobleman forced to leave his country as a hostage, invite identification of the aristocratic figure at its heart with Jean de Berry. Identified as a counterpart to the *Confort d'ami* in its provision of consolation for a patron, the *Fonteinne* shapes instruction as the representation of Jean's experience. Blurring the boundaries between chivalric and clerical identities, the *Fonteinne* engages with the possibility that desire might be sublimated through an imaginative practice of image making. Reimagining the situation of Jean de Berry as a paradigmatic instance of how Boethian wisdom might be applied to contemporary political problems, the *Fonteinne* does not simply enlarge the meaning of the Boethian text, but displaces its source in taking on its function for a contemporary audience.

Alternating between narrative verse, prose letters and intercalated lyric, the subject of Chapter 4, Froissart's *Prison amoureuse* (*c.* 1372/1373) is in dialogue with both Guillaume de Machaut's *Voir dit* and with the recent past. Analysis of the *Prison*'s engagement with the imprisonment of Froissart's patron, Wenceslas of Brabant, following the battle of Baesweiler in 1371, reveals a text which is profoundly concerned with processes of representation common to textual composition and mnemonic practice. As in other texts examined in this study, these issues are presented in amatory terms, within a narrative which appears to address private affairs of the heart. Through prominent episodes, such as the theft of letters from the narrator's purse, which suggestively evokes both the recovery of texts from the storehouse of memory and a form of castration, the reader is invited to equate the processes of sexual, mnemonic and textual reproduction. Froissart's use of mythic and pseudo-mythic material functions as a comment on the idea of vernacular authorship, and on culturally sanctioned uses of the instruments of sexual and textual reproduction. Through an examination of the *Prison*'s treatment of the themes of constraint, enclosure and self-discipline, I read the text as a meditation on the issue of controlling the appetitive will, in which the ability to construct an image of the desired object is imagined as a solution to the problem of frustrated desire. The resulting interpretation supplies further evidence that the *Consolation* was perceived as a literary model synonymous with the interrelated themes of memorial craft, artistic making, and the education of the nobility.

The final two chapters engage with texts in which the Boethian subject of imprisonment reimagines his own experience. Thomas Usk's prose *Testament of Love*, written against the background of the political foment of London in the 1380s, demonstrates the currency of the Boethian tradition traced in previous chapters in the context of vernacular English writing. Drawing on the *Consolation*, the *Testament* seeks to reinscribe the notorious shift in Usk's political allegiance, in denouncing his former master and onetime mayor of London, John Northampton, as the expression of a profound commitment to the common good. Much criticism of the text has been influenced by moralising reactions to this apparent act of betrayal, and the *Testament* has often been read as a self-interested plea for political advancement. Yet, however sincere were the intentions of the historical Usk, such readings of his text neglect the *Testament*'s subtle adaptation of the themes and matter associated with the Boethian tradition, and the ideology of public service which it develops. Concluding with the figure of Love taking root in the narrator's heart, and with the inscription of her teachings in 'perdurable letters' within his mind, the text offers a compelling image of an amended memory, and a self to which stability has been restored.

This study concludes with the *Kingis Quair* (*c.* 1423–1424), in which the figure of the prince takes centre stage in drawing on Boethius to refashion himself. Although the authorship of the *Quair* has been subject to question, the poem's meaning is bound up in its veiled articulation of the experience of James I of Scotland. Like the other texts examined here, the *Quair* is profoundly concerned with the status of vernacular authorship, an issue raised in the poem's treatment of the *Consolation*, as its major source. The poem's opening stages the reading of this authoritative text, yet the *Quair*'s narrator declines the position of subservient exposition adopted by many vernacular writers in order to focus on subject matter derived from his own experience. In an adaptation of the conventional use of the dream vision form to signal a process of meditative invention based on traditional sources, the narrator of the *Quair* responds to Boethius by beginning to write. The poem's treatment of the writing process draws on mythographic tradition to identify composition as the final stage of a learning process played out in the narrator's past, the moment when the subject is able to articulate what he has learned. Reflecting a characteristic interest in the exercise of memory in the dream vision at its heart, the *Quair* functions to recast imprisonment as an ideal preparation for government and James I as a type of the model prince.

The vernacular texts I examine in this study are the product of a culture that not only envisions memory training as a means of altering personal character to achieve a moral standard, but also seeks to use its techniques as a means of altering the way an individual is remembered by a community. Invoking a memory of the *Consolation* common to a community of readers, they strive to eradicate the stigma attached to the historical experiences of exile and imprisonment, in recasting their subjects as the counterparts of Boethius himself. In doing so, these texts work to establish literary authority in the vernacular: they do not present themselves as translations or commentaries on the *Consolation*, but instead reformulate its teachings, locating it within the cultural context and current idiom of the later Middle Ages. Effecting the displacement of their authoritative source, these texts insist upon their own origins in the personal experience of the vernacular writer. In doing so, they contribute to the emergence of vernacular authorship and establish a space for the practice of life writing.

Chapter 1
Boethian Counsel:
Guillaume de Machaut's *Confort d'ami*

Et vues tu clerement savoir,
Sans riens enclorre, tout le voir,
Dont viennent richesse et noblesse?
Resgarde eu livre de Boësse,
Que te dira, s'oïr le vues,
Que tous les biens que perdre pues
Sont de Fortune, qui moult tost
Le bien qu'elle a donné tout tost. (1901–8)[1]

And would you know clearly, with nothing omitted, the whole truth of whence prosperity and nobility come? Look at Boethius's book, which will tell you, if you wish to hear, that all goods that can be lost come from Fortune, who very soon takes back the good she has given.

Guillaume de Machaut's *Confort d'ami* bears eloquent witness to the political resonance of *The Consolation of Philosophy* in fourteenth-century culture, establishing a parallel between the experience of Boethius and that of the late-medieval statesman, as it locates Boethius's book within the tradition of advice to princes literature. Framed as an address to Machaut's imprisoned patron, Charles II of Navarre, the *Confort* is not simply a response to Charles's captivity at the hands of his father-in-law, Jean II, lasting from 5 April 1356 to 8 November 1357. Machaut's poem is informed by the knowledge that Charles's allies were working for his release, interweaving the comfort befitting the situation of a prisoner with advice on government appropriate to the position of a prince.[2]

---

[1] *Œuvres de Guillaume de Machaut*, 3 vols, ed. Ernest Hoepffner, SATF (Paris: Firmin Didot, 1908–1921), 3. Unless otherwise noted, all quotations from Machaut are taken from this edition, with my translation. For a complete English translation of the *Confort*, see the bilingual edition, Guillaume de Machaut, *Le Confort d'ami (Comfort for a Friend)*, ed. and trans. R. Barton Palmer (New York: Garland, 1992).

[2] On the occasion of Machaut's text, see Palmer's introduction, xxviii–ix. For a recent analysis of documentary evidence relating to Machaut's life, see Elizabeth Eva Leach, *Guillaume de Machaut: Secretary, Poet, Musician* (Ithaca: Cornell University Press, 2011), 7–33. Significant studies of Machaut's poetry include Kevin Brownlee, *Poetic Identity in Guillaume de Machaut* (Madison: University of Wisconsin Press, 1984), William Calin, *A Poet at the Fountain: Essays on the Narrative Verse of Guillaume de Machaut* (Lexington: University Press of Kentucky, 1974), Jacqueline Cerquiglini, '*Un Engin si soutil': Guillaume de Machaut et l'écriture au XIVe siècle* (Geneva: Slatkine, 1985) and Isabelle Bétemps, *L'Imaginaire dans l'œuvre de Guillaume de Machaut* (Paris: Champion, 1998).

Machaut's ethical purpose is expressed in a practice of self-representation that identifies the poet as a counsellor whose remit encompasses the spiritual and bodily regulation of the prince: 'te dirai que tu feras /Et comment to gouverneras /T'ame, ton corps et ta maniere' ['I shall tell you what you will do, and how you will govern your soul, your body and your conduct'] (1661–1663). The poet's holistic approach to the discipline of his patron is less presumptuous than it might appear to modern eyes, reflecting the contemporary belief that the health of the body politic is intimately linked with the ethical health of its members, especially those who played an active role in public life.[3] Machaut's tone is appropriate to the conception of good counsel as an ideal that at once emphasised the retainer's responsibility to offer candid advice, and identified a willingness to entertain such advice as the mark of a virtuous ruler.[4] Employing the singular form of the second person pronoun, Machaut creates an ambience of Ciceronian friendship, evoking the Latinate tradition of advice to princes literature, and his stance combines a counsellor's authority with a retainer's deference, as he assures Charles, 'soies assez sages /Pour toy garder, sans mes messages /Et sans mes confors recevoir' ['you are wise enough to look after yourself without receiving my messages or consolation'] (11–13). The poet's role in offering comfort and consolation is presented not as a matter of his superior wisdom, but as the fulfilment of a debt owed to his lord: 'sans riens retenir /Sui tiens, quoy qui'il doie avenir', ['I am yours without reserve, no matter what'] (25–6). As Claude Gauvard observes, the significance of such reciprocal bonds of love and friendship in Machaut's social milieu is imaged in the poet's conception of God as a being who 'N'oublie onques ses bons amis /Eins les conseille et les conforte' [Never forgets his true friends, but counsels and comforts them'] (64–5).[5]

In offering consolation and counsel to his imprisoned patron, Machaut plays the part of Philosophy in a contemporary iteration of *The Consolation of Philosophy*. Yet, in giving this role to a particular individual, rather than a personified abstraction, Machaut's adaptation of Boethian philosophy does not remain bound to the contingent world, as Sarah Kay argues.[6] Within the *Confort*, the particular becomes a conduit for the universal, as the poet defines himself as a *compilator* of biblical *exempla*, mediating divine authority for his patron's benefit:

> Par exemples te vueil prouver,
> Qui sont contenu en la Bible
> Et qui sont a nous impossible,

---

[3]   See Lester Kruger Born, 'The Perfect Prince: A Study in Thirteenth- and Fourteenth-Century Ideals', *Speculum* 3 (1928): 470–504; Elizabeth Porter, 'Gower's Ethical Microcosm and Political Macrocosm', in A.J. Minnis (ed.), *Gower's Confessio Amantis: Responses and Reassessments* (Cambridge: Brewer, 1983), 135–62.

[4]   On good counsel, see Greg Walker, *Plays of Persuasion: Drama and Politics at the Court of Henry VIII* (Cambridge: Cambridge University Press, 1991), 58–9.

[5]   Claude Gauvard, 'Portrait du prince d'après l'oeuvre de Guillaume de Machaut: étude sur les idées politiques du poète', in *Guillaume de Machaut, Poète et compositeur*, Actes et Colloques no. 23 (Paris: Klincksieck, 1982), 24.

[6]   Kay, 'Touching Singularity', 33.

Qu'adés cils qui en Dieu se fie,
S'il a raison de sa partie
Et s"il l'aimme, sert et honneure,
Adés son fait vient au desseure. (46–52)

[I shall prove to you by examples, which are contained in the Bible and which
are impossible to us, that he who trusts in God, if he has reason on his side, and
if he loves, serves and honours him, will always triumph at last.]

Machaut's role in interpreting traditional authority is emphasised as the poet
positions himself as a faithful translator, arguing 'Dou latin ou je l'ay veü /L'ay mis
si pres com j'ay peü' ['From the Latin I have seen, I have put it down as nearly as
I was able'] (415–16, cf. 644–6). This posture of fidelity to the source text reflects
a conception of scripture that incorporates those readings accumulated within the
commentary tradition, however, as Machaut's analysis of his own account of the
book of Daniel suggests:

Je n'en say plus ne n'en di el
Fors tant que pluseur docteur dient,
Qui en l'Escripture estudient
Diligemment (430–33)

[I know no more, nor say anything, except that which many doctors say, those
who study scripture diligently]

Machaut's interpretation of his scriptural materials conforms to contemporary
standards of textual fidelity; his approach embraces the common adaptive
methods of abbreviation and expansion, as Palmer's examination of the *Confort*'s
relationship to its sources demonstrates.[7]

The poet's deferential stance and the initial presentation of the *Confort* as a
repository of scriptural authority belie his interweaving of biblical *exempla* with
Boethian philosophy and with secular narratives drawn from pagan mythology.
In the quotation opening this chapter, Machaut invokes the *Consolation* as
complement to the lesson of the *Confort*, implying that the poet perceived no
conflict between his textual materials. For the *Confort*'s most recent editor, R.
Barton Palmer, however, Machaut's incorporation of Old Testament narratives
such as the miraculous survival of Shadrach, Meshak and Abednego in the fiery
furnace is a tactic that 'insists on a justice which will be experienced in history, on
a righting of wrongs in the here and now'; it 'imagines God acting in time, making
sure that the guilty and not the innocent are punished, awarding success to the
righteous'.[8] From Palmer's perspective, the presence of these narrative elements
within the *Confort* not only places a highly favourable construction upon Charles's
own prospective release, but it also prevents the full expansion of the Boethian

---

[7]   Palmer, *Confort*, lix–xx.
[8]   Palmer, *Confort*, xxxiv.

argument within Machaut's poem. As Palmer argues, Boethian logic affirms that 'the pursuit of political success is mistaken since this goal is only partially good, one that cannot help leading to disappointment and ruin', and culminates in the renunciation of worldly power.[9]

Yet Palmer's argument neglects the *Consolation*'s reiteration of the Platonic dictum that philosophers have a duty to pursue civic virtue, involving themselves in government to prevent the ascendance of the wicked, rather than because political power constitutes an end in itself (1.pr.4). As Philosophy's iconographic attribute, the ladder, implies, while contemplative philosophy was more highly regarded than its practical counterpart, the inferior discipline is not worthless, but serves as a basis for further development.[10] The interlocutor's recognition that political power is a contingent good whose pursuit cannot lead to self-sufficiency does not entail a complete repudiation of political activity. Under arrest, and perhaps already condemned to death, Boethius is at liberty to embrace contemplation, but an appreciation of the spiritual and personal hazards attached to public life would not otherwise negate the moral obligation to cultivate civic virtue. Philosophical wisdom might instead be understood as facilitating political action, in fostering the capacity to distinguish true from false values. Such a reading of Boethius is implicit in Machaut's plea to the reader:

> Je te pri que tu te conseilles
> A bonnes gens et que tu veilles
> A faire le commun pourfit,
> Einsi com Boësses le fit
> Et com maint philosophe firent
> Qui mainte doleur en souffrirent
> Et furent chacié en essil.
> L'escripture le dit, mais cil
> Qui ce faisoient, verité
> Destruisoit leur iniquité. (3749–58)

> [I implore you to be advised by good people and aspire to work for common profit as Boethius and many other philosophers did, suffering great pain in doing so, and being hunted into exile. Scripture says that, for those who do so, truth will destroy their iniquity.]

The identification of Boethius and scripture as complementary authorities and models for human behaviour renders explicit the judgement implied in Machaut's assimilation of biblical *exempla* with Boethian philosophy. Boethius's function as an exemplary instance of the active pursuit of common profit, despite the suffering it incurs, suggests the particular value of a Boethian conception of fortune for the politician. The sense that Machaut's version of Boethianism is in sympathy with the *Consolation* perhaps finds a reflection in the manuscript transmission of

---

9 Palmer, *Confort*, xlvii.
10 Represented at 1.pr.1, the ladder is discussed in Courcelle, *La Consolation*, 77–81.

the *Confort*: one of Machaut's most copied narrative poems, in MS A 95, Bern Bürgerbibliothek, the *Confort* is adjacent to the *Livre de Boece de consolacion* by Renaut de Louhans, an arrangement which may indicate a perceived relationship between the two works, as Jacqueline Cerquiglini argues.[11]

Rather than implying that God will intervene in the present time to preserve the innocent from temporal punishment, Machaut's Old Testament narratives are located in the age of miracles, as examples 'qui sont a nous impossible' ['which are impossible to us'] (48). If these instances of divine intercession offer proof 'that loyal servants of God always win in the end', or that, like Balshazzar, 'bad kings are punished', it does not follow that judgement will be enacted in contemporary life, as Palmer maintains.[12] Conscious that Charles was soon to be released by his allies, Machaut compiles biblical narratives that serve as interpretative models for his patron's future experience. By implication, his fate is to be understood as a temporal analogue for the miraculous intercessions found in scripture that foreshadow a heavenly kingdom of perfect justice. As Martha Wallen argues, the Old Testament narratives that Machaut recounts correspond to different possible outcomes of Charles's imprisonment, and their potential significance: the possibility of Charles' innocence is imaged in the unjust persecution and subsequent release of Daniel and Susanna. Balshazzar's destruction reflects the worst consequences of sin, while the experience of Manasseh suggests that repentance has the power to effect liberation from a bondage at once physical and spiritual.[13] Wallen identifies Machaut's insistence upon a correlation between biblical typology and the personal history of Charles of Navarre as atypical, however: as Palmer argues, such a correspondence 'would not have been generally accepted by theologians of the time'.[14] Yet, reading the parallels established between Charles's experience and Old Testament narratives in terms of an extension of typology to secular history is unnecessary: biblical passages were often used as a source of personal guidance, as in the practice of *sortes Biblicae*, where a text selected at random is taken as a source of private direction.[15] In the *Confort*, Machaut makes the selection for Charles, and this biblical material remains available for a similar form of interpretation. If Charles's allies were successful, he would be aware of the temporal origins of this aid, but could still follow Machaut's biblical protagonists in reading his situation as an imperfect reflection of God's providential plan for the faithful in the afterlife. Like Daniel, following his ordeal in the lions' den, the newly liberated Charles might return to public life, but if he fails to recognise the inadequacy of worldly power in contrast to that of the divine, he can expect to endure the permanent destruction imaged in Balshazzar's fate.

---

[11] The *Confort d'ami* survives in twelve manuscript copies, see Lawrence Earp, *Guillaume de Machaut: A Guide to Research,* New York: Garland, 1995), 218. Cerquiglini, *Un Engin si soutil*, 75n40.

[12] Palmer, *Confort*, xxxiv, lx.

[13] Martha Wallen, 'Biblical and Mythological Typology in Machaut's *Confort d'Ami*', *Res Publica Litterarum* 3 (1980): 191–206 (192).

[14] Palmer, *Confort*, xxxvi.

[15] Carruthers, *The Book of Memory*, 203.

   Such a reading is corroborated in the *Confort*, since, despite the significance
the poem invests in an advantageous reversal of fortune as a mark of divine favour,
worldly success is not praised as an object in itself. Machaut warns that all goods
that may be lost are at Fortune's disposal, and that

> [...] n'est homs vivans qui s'extente
> De Fortune, ne qui se vente
> Qu'en ses mains ne soit, qu'extenter
> Ne se'en porroit homs, ne vanter
> Par raison, s'il n'est de vertus
> Et de bonnes meurs revestus.
> Mais qui bien est moriginez
> Et en vertus enracinez,
> Fortune n'a nulle puissance
> De lui faire anui ne grevance
> Quant aus meurs; car s'elle a l'avoir,
> Les vertus ne puet elle avoir. (1927–38)

> [...there is no living man exempt from Fortune, nor any who can brag that he is
> not in her hands, for no man is able to withdraw from her, nor has any reason to
> be proud, if he has not covered himself with virtues and good habits. But over
> the man who is well educated and in whom the virtues have taken root, Fortune
> has no power, to hurt or injure his integrity; for if she has his goods, she cannot
> have his virtues.]

   This Boethian lesson advances the idea that a good education enables the
student to resist the harmful effects that Fortune's influence might otherwise
produce, such as doubt, and foreshadows the assertion that philosophers are
paragons of statecraft, in presenting a rationale for their ability to endure. Riches,
Machaut argues

> N'onques en un point ne se tiennent,
> Se ce ne sont aucun tresor
> De gemmes, de monnoie ou d'or
> Qui sont en prison et en serre.
> Mais quant li homs est mis en terre,
> Avec li pas ne les emporte,
> Qu'autres les a qui s'en deporte
> Et les despent, espoir et gaste
> Et fait grant tourtel d'autrui paste.
> Mais aussi comme les estoiles
> Raidient plus cler que chandoiles
> Et sont mises en firmament
> Pour luire pardurablement,
> Les vertus luisent et luiront.
> Adès furent, adès seront. (1950–64)

> [Never stay in one place, save treasure-troves of gems, money or gold,
> imprisoned or locked up. But when a man is put in the earth, he cannot take them

with him. So others will have them to enjoy, spend, perhaps waste, and make a
great cake out of another's dough. But just as the stars blaze more brightly than
candles, and are set in the firmament to shine eternally, the virtues shine and will
shine. As they were, so they will be.]

The juxtaposition of temporal and eternal wealth evokes the parables of the
pearl of great price, and of the talents, while the allusion to the hoarding of treasures
suggests an echo of Matthew 6.19–21, in contrasting the frailty of earthly troves
with the immutability of their heavenly counterparts (Matt. 13.45–6; 25.14–30).

In presenting his poem as a compilation of biblical *exempla*, and setting the
mutability of Fortune in relation to Christian conceptions of eternity, Machaut
produces a version of the Boethian argument that reflects the Christianising
tendency manifested in late-medieval commentary.[16] Identifying both scripture
and the *Consolation* as authorities bearing witness that the only object truly
worthy of pursuit is one not subject to alteration, Machaut highlights the mutable
nature of earthly goods and their susceptibility to alienation from their possessor
as signs of insufficiency. Rather than recommending the pursuit of worldly objects
such as political success as ends in themselves, Machaut advocates the cultivation
of ethical character:

> Car vertus sont dons que Dieus donne
> A homme qui a bien s'ordonne,
> Et viennent d'acquisition
> Faite en bonne condition
> Par armes ou par grant estude
> Ou par avoir grant multitude
> De meschiés, de labour, de peinne. (1939–45)

> [Because virtues are gifts God gives to the man who seeks the good, and are
> earned through effort in the right circumstances, through the practice of arms or
> keen study, or by enduring a great many misfortunes, labours and afflictions.]

Machaut's Christian readers are to cultivate spiritual wealth rather than its material
counterpart, and will thereby become impervious to Fortune. In this respect, the
Confort illuminates the conception of the *Consolation* as a text whose message
corresponds to both Christian doctrine and an idealised political practice.

Alongside scriptural and Boethian material, Machaut's discussion of Fortune
also includes elements in harmony with the mirror of princes tradition. The
implication that the good ought to ensure that wealth is not wasted, but instead
is used to create sustaining works on a grand scale, like the proverbial 'grant
tourtel', suggests the virtue of *magnificencia*. Praised in popular examples of the
advice to princes genre, such as Aegidius Romanus's *De Regimine Principium*,
magnificencia entails an appropriate detachment from material wealth, 'for he þat
dredeth to luse moneth vndertaketh none grete dedes', and will be incapable of

---

[16]   On the Christianisation of the *Consolation*, see Courcelle, *Consolation*, 29–66.

magnanimity.[17] The advisory tradition thus complements the biblical and Boethian emphasis on the recognition that wealth is an inadequate means to happiness, and underlines the role of action in virtuous behaviour.

Within Machaut's text, however, the primary means of overcoming attachment to material things lies in the proper cultivation of the imaginative faculty. As Sylvia Huot argues, Machaut's poetry draws on *The Consolation of Philosophy* to explore the role of the creative imagination, and its literary expression, in providing solace for the pain of desire and loss.[18] Poetic consolation is generated by *souvenir*, a term whose sphere of reference is not restricted to memory in its modern sense, but encompassed 'any sort of imaginative conceptualization of that which is not accessible outside the mind, be it spatially distant, temporally removed, or simply nonexistent'.[19] Machaut's emphasis on the consolatory powers of imagination reflects the values of a culture in which the faculty of memory was conceived as the foundation of ethics and the basis of literary invention, its development and practice 'a moral obligation as well as a scholarly necessity'.[20] In the *Confort*, the suffering of the imprisoned Charles is initially imagined as an excess of thought:

> [...] quant Souvenir en moy vient,
> Tendrement plourer me couvient,
> Qu'en monde n'a bien qu'i m'aporte,
> Eins me mourdrist et desconforte,
> Et les pointures que je sense,
> Qui sont a milliers et a cens,
> Chacent de moy par leur rigour
> Sanc, couleur, maniere et vigour. (2071–78)

[when Memory wakes in me, it makes me weep piteously, because it does me no earthly good, but gnaws at me and distresses me, and the hundreds and thousands of sharp pains I feel put to flight my blood, colour, bearing and strength.]

Rather than supporting the prisoner, the undisciplined faculty of memory torments him, undermining his health and capacity for self-government.

In this key passage, the experience of political crisis is recast in terms of erotic suffering, a move whose logic reflects the function of the beloved as 'a figure of the absolute',[21] symbolic object of the desire for completion that marks the

---

[17]   John Trevisa, *The Governance of Kings and Princes: John Trevisa's Middle English Translation of the* De regimine principium *of Aegidius Romanus*, ed. David C. Fowler, Charles F. Briggs and Paul G. Remley (New York: Garland, 1997), 19.

[18]   Sylvia Huot, 'Guillaume de Machaut and the Consolation of Poetry', *Modern Philology* 100 (2002): 169–95.

[19]   Huot, 'Guillaume de Machaut', 174, and see Jacqueline Cerquiglini, 'Écrire le temps: Le lyrisme de la durée aux XIVe et XVe siècles', in Yvonne Bellenger (ed.), *Le Temps et la durée dans la littérature au Moyen Âge et à la Renaissance* (Paris: Nizet, 1986), 108–12.

[20]   Carruthers, *The Book of Memory*, 88.

[21]   Huot, 'Guillaume de Machaut', 177.

subject's constitutive lack. Machaut's poem treats erotic longing as an exemplary instance of desire, emphasising the therapeutic power of imagination to relieve the pain of lack, and a source of pleasure:

> […] Douce Pensee
> Est de Souvenir engendree,
> Dont toutes les fois qu'il avient
> Que de ta dame te souvient,
> Se tu n'as pas en temps passé
> Son commandement trespassé,
> Eins l'as servi sans decevoir,
> Tu dois en ton cuer concevoir,
> Ymaginer, penser, pourtraire
> La biauté de son dous viaire (2153–62)

> [Sweet Thought is engendered by Memory, so that each time you happen to remember your lady, if you have not broken her commandment in the past, but have served her without deception, in your heart you should conceive, imagine, envisage and portray the beauty of her sweet face].

Beginning by visualising her physical attributes, Charles should then 'considerer /Dedens to cuer et figurer /Les vertus done elle est paree' ['consider in your heart and imagine the virtues with which she is arrayed'] (2175–6). Through this practice, 'dois en ton cuer une ymage /Faire, a qui tu feras hommage' ['you should make an image in your heart, and pay homage to it'] (2189–90). The product of this mental construction becomes the subject of a secularised form of devotional practice that conflates the physical presence of the beloved with the imaginative proximity of the object of fantasy:

> Present li, les dois tire a tire
> Doucement recorder et dire,
> Et elle te confortera
> A tes besoins et t'aidera.
> Ell adoucira to dolour
> Et refroidera ta chalour;
> Ta famine saoulera
> Et ta grant soif estanchera. (2193–200)

> [in her presence, you should recollect and recite them [good deeds] calmly, one by one, and she will comfort you in need and help you. She will soothe your pain and cool your heat, staunch your hunger and quench your great thirst.]

Performance of a litany before an imagined image actuates a form of intercession that satisfies mental and physical needs.

Machaut's proposed programme for training his patron's memory resembles other medieval treatments of artificial memory both in its methodical movement through individual points on a linked chain in the act of recitation, and in its purpose, the preservation and reinforcement of moral character. Instigating the emotional response identified by mnemonists as crucial to stimulating recollection, the image of the lady is identified with love as an ennobling influence, reflecting the place traditionally attributed to *eros* in the formation of ethical discipline:[22]

> Elle t'ara si anobli
> Que tu mettras tout en oubli
> Et tous les maus et ta grevence
> Penras en bonne pacience. (2205–8)

> [She will ennoble you so much that you will forget everything and bear all your ills and grievances with good grace.]

Affinity between the lover, the image of the lady, and hope combines them into a 'compaingnie amoureuse, /Aussi comme une trinité ['an amorous company, just like a trinity'] (2260–61). The religious tenor of the poet's advice suggests that, as Douglas Kelly argues, in the *Confort*, '"idolatry" would seem to be an essential element in Machaut's notion of ideal love'.[23] Yet, Machaut is also fully aware of the limitations of such love, reminding Charles that he should serve God first and foremost:

> Qu'il n'est amour qui se compere
> A s'amour, foy que doy saint Pere,
> Ne chose, tant soit pure, eu monde,
> Ne que riens contre tout le monde,
> Ou comme une ymage en pointure
> Contre une vive creature. (2767–72)

> [For there is no love that compares to his love, by the faith I owe the Holy Father, nor anything in this world, however pure it might be, nor anything unearthly, as a graven image differs from a living creature.]

Emphasising the incommensurability of earthly and divine love, Machaut's advice identifies this contrast with idolatry as a focus on the products of art, rather than those infused with spiritual life.

Machaut's allusions to pagan myth contribute to this distinction, at once highlighting the importance of love and hope as a stimulus to action, and obliquely hinting at the dangers of a love that lacks moderation: Paris's abduction of Helen is offered as an illustration of the role of hope in achieving an end, rather than of ruinous cupidity (2645–82). Likewise, Machaut argues that Orpheus's abortive journey to the underworld could not have been accomplished without

---

[22]   On the nexus between love and ethical discipline, see C. Stephen Jaeger, *Ennobling Love: In Search of a Lost Sensibility* (Philadelphia: University of Pennsylvania Press, 1999) and Carruthers, *the Craft*, especially 101–5.

[23]   Douglas Kelly, *Medieval Imagination: Rhetoric and the Poetry of Courtly Love* (Madison: University of Wisconsin Press, 1978), 126.

hope (2277–644). Although the consequences of these actions are not the focus of Machaut's narration, however, the reader is offered subtle reminders of their effects: the destruction of Troy, and the degradation of Orpheus (2263–8, 2585–90). Such veiled criticisms suggest an underlying model of correct loving, of a proper response to foci that arouse the emotions, which is more fully developed in Machaut's treatment of imagination within the *Confort*. Imagination, basis of the remedial practice of image making commended to Charles, was understood as a cognitive faculty governing the invention of mental *imagines*, their retention and expression.[24] As Kelly argues, the cultivation of such images is typically differentiated from idolatry in Machaut's work, with *ydole* used to refer to an object worshipped by pagans and sinners in the literal sense.[25] Such idolatry is conceived as the effect of false imagination, which also finds expression in misleading dreams: as *insomnia*, encompassing nightmares and dreams of the satisfaction of frustrated desires, and as *visa*, fantastic images appearing in the liminal state between consciousness and sleep.[26] If Machaut's ideal of love does not involve idolatry in the literal sense, however, it is menaced by its own potential to assume an idolatrous character, as the poet's initial selection from the Bible, the episode of Susanna and the elders, implies.

The elders who attempt to suborn Susanna precipitate their own ruin through voyeurism, conceiving a passion that corrupts their memory and capacity for judgement. Machaut's rendering of the biblical source material develops his meaning, as he describes the effects of the elders' undisciplined desire:

> Si qu'en ordure et en vilté,
> En ardeur, en concupiscence,
> Par desire, par fole plaisence
> Furent puis pour l'amour de li,
> Tant lor pleü et abelly.
> Lors scens et raison oublierent
> Et leurs yeus en terre clinerent,
> Afin que veoir ne peüssent
> Le ciel et qu'en leur cuer n'eüssent
> memorie dou souverain juge
> Qu fait tout par raison et juge (112–22)

> [So that in filth and depravity, in longing and concupiscence, through desire and mad pleasure, they were overcome with love for her, she pleased and delighted them so much. Then they forgot good sense and reason, and turned their eyes to the ground so that they could not see the heavens, and so that in their hearts there was no memory of the sovereign judge who made everything with good reason and sits in judgement.]

---

[24] A.J. Minnis, 'Medieval Imagination and Memory', in Alastair Minnis and Ian Johnson (eds), *The Cambridge History of Literary Criticism. Vol. II. The Middle Ages* (Cambridge: Cambridge University Press, 2005), 239–74, and Kelly, *Medieval Imagination*.

[25] Kelly, *Medieval Imagination*, 54, 278n79.

[26] Kelly, *Medieval Imagination*, 54, 57.

Concupiscence destroys the memory of reason, and the judges' action represents a conscious decision to turn away from the moral responsibilities entailed upon the conception of divine authority. Machaut's poetic adaptation underlines the emphasis on memory and free will present in the Latin text: 'et everterunt sensum suum, et declinaverunt oculos suos ut non viderent caelum, neque recordarentur iudicorum iustorum' ['And they perverted their own mind and turned away their eyes that they might not look unto heaven or remember just judgements', Daniel 13.9].[27] Allusion to the judges' hearts gives expression to the association between memory and heart reflected in Latin etymology, the verb *recordari* containing *cor*, identifying the heart as the site where memory is imprinted.[28] The elders' choice is a restriction of their own vision, producing a form of amnesia that obliterates reason and divine law.

Machaut's version of the Susanna narrative not only highlights the idolatrous character of a passion that replaces the divine with a human object, it resonates with his other sources in a reflection of the problem he seeks to refine and resolve in the *Confort* at large. Where the Latin text finds the judges turning their eyes from heaven, their counterparts turn their eyes towards the ground, an alteration that creates a resemblance between the spiritual state of the judges and that of Boethius as interlocutor. As Glynnis M. Cropp argues, the opening of the *Consolation* expresses the complexity of the transformation the text seeks to enact in its audience, the central problem of how 'the individual bowed down by the cares of the world' is to 'transcend reality and pursue the sovereign good'.[29] This dilemma is articulated through the development of a metaphor of descent and ascent, reflecting the prisoner's transformation from sufferer to 'serene individual standing tall, looking up, and directing prayers and hopes towards heaven'.[30] This metaphor functions as a unifying theme in the *Consolation*, emerging in discourse attributed to both Boethius and Philosophy, as the action of casting one's eyes to the ground is identified with an unhealthy preoccupation with worldly things. Most prominent is Philosophy's description of her former pupil's degraded state:

> nunc iacet effeto lumine mentis
> et pressus gravibus colla catenis
> declivemque gerens pondere vultum
> cogitur heu stolidam cerere terram (1.m.2)

---

[27]   *Biblia Sacra Iuxta Vulgatem Clementinam*, ed. Alberto Colunga and Laurentio Turrado (Madrid: Bibliotheca de Autores Christianos, 1985); trans. *The Holy Bible Translated from the Latin Vulgate and Diligently Compared with Other Editions in Divers Languages (Douay, AD 1609, Rheims, AD 1582)* (London: Washbourne, 1914). I follow Palmer in using the Clementine Bible as a simple measure of Machaut's adaptation, whilst acknowledging the complexity of the textual tradition available to the poet (see Palmer, *Confort*, lix).

[28]   Carruthers, *The Book of Memory*, 59–60.

[29]   Cropp, 'The Medieval French Tradition', 255.

[30]   Cropp, 'The Medieval French Tradition', 255.

[Now prostrate, mental vision dulled,
His neck with chains close bound,
Perforce he trains his downward gaze
Upon the insensate ground.]

Although a brief examination of the treatment of this passage in medieval French translations leads Cropp to conclude that some translators failed to perceive the unifying function of this theme, the descent-ascent metaphor maintained a presence in the vernacular French tradition, and especially in prose versions.[31] Acquaintance with the Boethian tradition in its vulgate or vernacular French manifestations might therefore have prompted Machaut's adaptation.

A resemblance between Boethius' mental state and that of the judges of the *Confort* is further established by the description of the elders as subject to an amnesia that prevents their retention of any 'Memoire dou souverain juge'. Boethius depicts himself as suffering from 'lethargum patitur, communem illusarum mentium morbum', a disease of forgetfulness and lethargy common to deluded minds (1.pr.2). Later, Philosophy introduces another key theme of the *Consolation*, in defining his condition as one of self-imposed exile:

Sed tu quam procul a patria non quidem pulsus es, sed aberasti ac, si te pulsum existimari mavis, te potius ipse pepulisti; nam id quidem de te numquam cuiquam fas fuisset. (1.pr.5)

[But this distance you have travelled from your native land is the outcome not of expulsion, but of your going astray; if you wish to regard it as expulsion, such expulsion was self-induced, for no other person could lawfully have imposed such exile.]

The idea of wandering accompanied by forgetfulness suggests the psychological vice of *curiositas*, the tendency to mental distraction that prevents the practice of arts of memory, in undermining the sustained attention upon which the construction and use of mental pathways in recollection depends.[32] If the affective quality of an image facilitates recollection, however, an image provoking too intense a reaction might divert the subject's train of thought. The advice offered by Peter of Ravenna in his highly influential treatise on memory illustrates the point: while Peter himself finds that images of his former lover Juniper, and of naked, beautiful women are a valuable source of mnemonic prompts, 'for they excite greatly my mynde and frequentation', he warns that the method is inappropriate for those who despise women.[33] *Curiositas* might also manifest itself as an inability to focus on the mnemonic task, shutting out distractions: in a monastic context, this

---

[31]   Cropp, 'The Medieval French Tradition', 255–65.

[32]   On *curiositas*, see Carruthers, *Craft*, especially 82–91, and Giorgio Agamben, *Stanzas: Word and Phantasm in Western Culture*, trans. Ronald L. Martinez (Minneapolis: University of Minnesota Press, 1993), 3–10.

[33]   Peter of Ravenna, *The Art of Memory*, sig. A7r–A7v, B2v.

failing sometimes inspired a form of iconoclasm, since images created by painters and sculptors might be used by practitioners in preference to *imagines* of their own making, disrupting concentration and hindering mental reflection by their physicality.[34] Adornment of the cloister might prevent the proper furnishing of the mnemonist's mental space, or might frustrate the purpose of contemplation, as the practitioner seeks to make an imaginative record of details irrelevant to the cognitive function of the image.[35]

The sensual character of this vice, termed *fornicatio* by John Cassian, is reflected in the explicit visual puns appearing in the margins of some medieval texts, which have been read as a warning to guard against such mental wandering.[36] Aspects of both the *Consolation* and the *Confort* suggest that a similar sensibility is at work. Philosophy expels the poetic Muses from the interlocutor's bedside as 'scenicas meretriculas', who 'infructuosis affectuum spinis uberem fructibus rationis segetem necant himinumque mentes assuefaciunt morbo, non liberant' ['harlots of the stage', 'with their thorns of emotions choke the life from the fruitful harvest of reason'] (1.pr.1). This depiction of the Muses reflects their association with a sensuality that undermines the use of reason, and their association with the theatre suggests an intriguing link to the art of memory, since the mnemonist's animation of abstractions and words as 'visualized images-in-action upon an imaginary stage' has been considered as a form of protodrama.[37] Portrayed as theatrical strumpets, the poetic Muses appear as a source of verbal images that frustrate the attempt to build useful mental associations, stimulating an affectivity that yields self-indulgence rather than ethical development. Their activity aggravates the effects of misfortune and renders the interlocutor unable to reflect on nature's secrets (1.m.2). Likewise, in its effects, the judges' lust for Susanna resembles *curiositas*, as it deprives them of the will to contemplate the heavens, the mnemonic cue that kept them in mind of the divine order and the prospect of judgement, and which should have regulated their behaviour. As forms of sensual impulse, the judges' lust and the seductions of the poetic Muses carry cognitive associations resembling those of the marginal images of fornication in manuscripts, and arguably serve a similar purpose, in identifying the underlying problem in each case as one of *curiositas*.

The relationship between the *Consolation* and the *Confort* suggests that Machaut's emphasis on the potential distortion of human love into idolatry specifies a cognitive problem rather than a purely libidinal one. Sensual transgressions such as lust and fornication serve as metaphorical signifiers of the worldly preoccupations that frustrate the development of an ethical character impervious to the vicissitudes of Fortune. If the focus is on intellection rather

---

[34]   Carruthers, *Craft*, 84–7.

[35]   Carruthers, *Craft*, 209.

[36]   Carruthers, *Craft*, 164.

[37]   Jody Enders, 'Memory, Allegory, and the Romance of Rhetoric', *Yale French Studies* 95 (1999): 49–64; *Rhetoric and the Origins of Medieval Drama* (Ithaca: Cornell University Press, 1992).

than the nature of lover, the other biblical *exempla* compiled in the *Confort* harmonise with one another, and with the argument of the text. With the exception of Susanna's narrative, each of Machaut's examples turns explicitly upon idolatry: Shadrach, Meshak, and Abdenego are condemned to the fiery furnace for their refusal to worship Nebuchadnezzar's golden statue; Balshazzar is punished for the proliferation of idolatry within his kingdom; and the order that Darius' subjects should worship him alone precipitates Daniel's consignment to the lion's den (*Confort*, 481–646, 671–954, 955–1282). Machaut's final example, that of Manasseh, is prefaced by a discussion of idolatry derived from Wisdom:

> Q'un entailleur fait une ymage
> De corps, de membres, de visage;
> Et quant faite l'a gente et bele,
> Son signeur et son dieu l'apelle.
> Il scet bien qu'il est plus grant mestre
> Qu l'image ne porroit estre,
> Car il l'a fait comme soutis
> A ses mains et a ses outis,
> Et si la porroit bien deffaire,
> Mais l'image ne puet riens faire,
> Car vie n'a ne sentement,
> Mouvement, scens n'entendement.
> Si ressamble Pymalion
> En meurs et en condition
> Qu fist l'image et tant l'ama
> Qu'amie et dame la clama.
> Aussi ressamble il Manassés
> Qui ne faisoit feste qu'a ses
> Fausses ymages et ydoles.
> Moult avoit or pensees foles,
> Qui laissoit le dieu de Nature
> Pour servir une tele ordure. (1289–311)

[That a sculptor makes an image with a body, limbs and face, and when he has made it fine and fair, he calls it his lord and his god. He is well aware that he is a greater master than the image could be, because he made it skillfully, with his hands and his tools, and could well destroy it by those means, but the image can do nothing, because it has no life nor feeling, movement, reason, nor understanding. Thus he resembles Pygmalion in his behaviour and situation, the man who made an image and loved it so much that he called it beloved and lady. He is also like Manasseh, who honoured only his false images and idols. He had many foolish thoughts then, he who abandoned the god of creation to serve such filth.]

The resemblance to Wisdom 13.11–9, describing a carpenter's fabrication of a lifeless image to worship, is marked, and the implication that the maker has greater powers than his image echoes 15.15–19. As Douglas Kelly notes, this is one of the only instances in Machaut's work where 'ymages' are equated with 'ydoles', and the association implies that the warning against idolatry relates to a concern with the workings of the imagination.[38] Jacqueline Cerquiglini goes further, arguing that Machaut's preoccupation with idolatry reflects a concern with the proper use of images: in this context, false imagination and idolatry emerge as comparable delusions.[39]

This association is enhanced by Machaut's allusion to Pygmalion, an example that translates the sin of idolatry into amatory terms; its effect is to underscore the link between the behaviour of the biblical idolaters and the elders' lust for Susanna.[40] Characterisation of Manasseh's gods as 'ordure' echoes Machaut's description of the spiritual state in which the elders succumbed to concupiscence (311, 112). Once these examples are connected, the allusion to Wisdom lends new resonance to the Boethian and biblical character of the judges' action in turning their eyes to the ground. Wisdom 15.8 depicts the making of a clay idol by a potter, who 'paulo ante de terra factus fuerat, [e]t post pusilum reducit se unde acceptus est' ['a little before was made of earth himself, and a little after returneth to the same out of which he was taken']. Against this background, the earthward gaze becomes synonymous with a focus on humanity and its productions that neglects the duty to the divine required by Christian teaching.

The Ovidian myth of Pygmalion also carries with it the weight of meaning accumulated during its medieval reception history: retold in Jean de Meun's continuation of the *Roman de la Rose*, its intertextual function in fourteenth-century poetry has been the subject of considerable critical interest.[41] Prefaced by a discussion of idolatry, Machaut's allusion to Pygmalion evokes the *Rose*, since Jean's retelling of the myth serves to develop a comparison between Pygmalion's statue and the enshrined silver image that represents the object of Amant's erotic desires. Yet, as Sylvia Huot argues, Pygmalion also occupies an important position within the *Rose* as symbol of a poetics in conflict with that represented by figures of sterile desire, such as Narcissus and, especially, Orpheus.[42] The sermon of Genius

---

[38]   Kelly, *Medieval Imagination*, 278n79.

[39]   Cerquiglini, *Un Engin si soutil*, 207.

[40]   See Renate Blumenfeld-Kosinski, *Reading Myth: Classical Mythology and Its Interpretations in Medieval French Literature* (Stanford: Stanford University Press, 1997), 147.

[41]   The retelling begins at *Rose* 20787. On the myth's role in the reception of the *Rose*, see Pierre-Yves Badel, *Le 'Roman de la Rose' au XIV siècle: Étude de la reception de l'œuvre* (Geneva: Droz, 1980), 91. Other notable treatments of the myth's French reception include Kevin Brownlee, 'Pygmalion, Mimesis, and the Multiple Endings of the Roman de la Rose', *Yale French Studies* 95 (1999): 193–211; Daniel Poiron, 'Narcisse et Pygmalion dans le *Roman de la Rose*', in Raymond J. Cormier and Urban T. Holmes (eds), *Essays in Honor of Louis Francis Solano* (Chapel Hill: University of North Carolina Press, 1970), 153–65.

[42]   Huot, *From Song to Book: The Poetics of Writing in Old French Lyric and Lyrical Narrative Poetry* (Ithaca: Cornell University Press, 1987), 96–9; see also Kevin Brownlee, 'Orpheus Song Re-sung: Jean de Meun's Reworking of *Metamorphoses*, X', *Romance Philology* 36 (1982): 201–9.

alludes to Orpheus' mythical status as the originator of homosexual practices, and compares male genitalia to hammers, ploughs and styluses. Orpheus is described as one who 'ne sot arer ne escrivre /ne forgier en la droite forge' ['could not plough or write or forge on the right forge', *Rose* 19622–3). Huot interprets these lines as polyvalent, since they also characterise Orpheus as a master of song, rather than writing, whose history embodies the deferment and denial of sexual passion that typifies the lyric tradition.[43] As frustrated lover and *virtuoso* musician, Orpheus is the emblem of an eroticism articulated through a transient lyric performance that is without issue, generating neither progeny nor textual artefact. In contrast, Pygmalion's desire generates an object: his hammer and chisel encompass both penis and stylus, and as a record of sexual longing, his beloved Galatea represents the concrete productions of a poet whose performance is now enacted primarily in writing, rather than song. Huot further reads the unique fecundity of Pygmalion and Galatea amongst Jean's cast of mythical figures, as an allegory that identifies the artist's treatment of the artefact as an autonomous reality, independent of its progenitor, as a precondition for generation.[44] Within the *Confort*, Machaut's allusion to the myth of Pygmalion serves to develop and complicate this model of aesthetic production, in exploring the benefits and risks of imagination.

In depicting Pygmalion's love as futile, the *Confort* suggests a reference to the poet's state prior to the animation of Galatea, although the popularity of narrative's medieval iterations would have ensured that Machaut's readers were familiar with the myth's conclusion. The intertextual context lends further significance to Machaut's interpolation of the myth of Orpheus within the *Confort*, and it is significant that this account emphasises Orpheus' skill as a musician, adept in both theory and practice, 'plus souverein mestre /Qu'homme né ne qui fust a nestre' ['a more consummate master than any man born or to be born'] (2311–12). The sterility of Orpheus' love is reflected in his failure to regain his bride, and in allusions to the subsequent direction of his desires:

> Et devint homs de tel affaire
> Que ne le vueil mie retraire,
> Car li airs corront et empire
> De parler de si vil matyre.
> Mais onques puis ne volt clamer
> Dame amie, ne femme amer. (2585–90)

> [Becoming a man of such conduct that I do not wish to tell of him at all, because it would corrupt and spoil the air to speak of so vile a matter. Never again did he call a lady beloved, nor love a woman.]

These elements of the mythical narratives potentially evoke the significant opposition between Orpheus and Pygmalion constructed within the *Rose*, yet the *Confort* frustrates the effect of this pairing. Here Pygmalion is not only

---

[43]   Huot, *From Song to Book*, 96–9.

[44]   Huot, *From Song to Book*, 144.

characterised as sterile, but the allusion to Wisdom links the narrative to the biblical claim that '[i]nitium enim fornicationis est exquisitio idolorum; [e]t adinventio illorum corruptio vitæ est' ['For the beginning of fornication is the devising of idols: and the invention of them is the corruption of life'] (14.12).

The iconoclastic implications of Machaut's treatment of the myths of Orpheus and Pygmalion are nevertheless complicated by their relationship to the advice offered to Charles, that he should remedy his suffering through the creation of an image of his beloved in his heart (2189–90). Machaut's poem does not finally endorse a position analogous to negative mysticism, which privileges active forgetfulness, resisting the imaginative capacity for image making, and cognition itself, as impediments to communion with an unknowable God.[45] Instead, the *Confort* traces the similarities between the construction of physical images and mental *imagines*, as activities that seek to form likenesses. As Karma Lochrie argues, 'psychology and aesthetics defined images in terms of their twin capacities for *likeness* and *intention*'; the aesthetic thought of Aquinas in particular was dependent on the belief that Christ was made in God's image, so that the perfect nature of his likeness to God 'represents the very property of beauty'. Accordingly, as the 'human faculty of remembrance constructs a region of images or similitudes', it also 'enacts an imitation of Christ'. If the intention is faulty, however, imagination generates deceptive images that pervert the quality of likeness.[46] In this respect, acts of creation necessarily entail interpretation, both because the products of imagination must be subjected to evaluative judgement, and in determining the particular form of likeness the image is to body forth.

Insofar as making and reading signs are complementary activities, it is significant that several of Machaut's biblical *exempla* establish a telling contrast between the sin of idolatry and successful instances of the reading of divine signals. Machaut's poem characterises the prophet Daniel as the only man capable of interpreting Nebuchadnezzar's dream, and while the poet does not recount this narrative, which appears in his *Remede de Fortune*, Machaut identifies this achievement as the rationale for his presence within the *Confort*:

> [ ] Pour ç'a parler propos
> De sa vie et de sa maniere
> Pour continuer ma matiere. (444–6)

> [For this reason it is fitting to speak of his life and his deeds in order to enlarge upon my theme.]

In the episode of Balshazzar's feast, Daniel is once again represented as the possessor of a unique ability to interpret divine messages (737–954). The theme is also implicit in Susanna's narrative, since familiarity with Daniel's biblical

---

[45]   On negative mysticism, see Karma Lochrie, *Margery Kempe and Translations of the Flesh* (Pennsylvania: University of Pennsylvania Press, 1991), 30.

[46]   Lochrie, *Margery Kempe*, 73.

reputation as interpreter enables the reader to perceive a contrast between his ability and that of the elders who, like Boethius, are blinded to divine immanence in nature by worldly cares (*Consolation* 1.m.2; *Confort* 112–22).

Machaut's final biblical example, that of Mannasseh, underlines the significance of the capacity to read natural signs for the subject who hopes to find grace. Imprisoned for his idolatry, Manasseh is depicted in chains, as scripture suggests, yet his release is not dependent on a transformation of his material circumstances, but of his state of mind:

> Si muse, pense et se retourne
> Et sa pensee en maint tour tourne,
> Mais reiens n'i vaut le retourner:
> Il li couvient son cuer tourner
> Et sa pensee en autre tour,
> S'il vuet issier de ceste tour.
> Einsi pense, muse et tournoie,
> Mais il couvient au'a ce tour noie
> Les ydoles qui bestourné
> Ont son scens et si mal tourné
> Que ja sans mort n'en tournera,
> Se sa pais a ce tour ne ra.
> Adont vers le ciel se tourna
> Et devotement s'aourna
> Pour cognoistre son creatour
> Qu'est signeur dou munde et actour,
> Qui les mauvais einsi chastie. (1427–43)

[So he muses, thinks and revolves, and turns his thoughts many a turn, but nothing serves to restore him: he must turn his heart and thoughts in another direction, if he would leave that tower. Thus he thinks, muses and turns it over, but he must at this turning point deny the idols that have warped his senses and twisted them so badly that, barring death, he will not turn away from them, but he will not have his peace again without this turn. He turned to the heavens and devoutly made himself ready to recognise his creator, who is lord of the world and author, who thus chastises the wicked.]

The figure of *annominatio* at once emphasises the mental and physical confinement Manasseh endures,[47] and the action he must take to ensure his freedom. While divine power can and does enact physical release in response to this mental revolution, the privileging of intellectual reform as the efficient cause of change implies that it is not the material, but rather the spiritual dimension of Manasseh's imprisonment that is important. He is portrayed, not as the captive of the Syrian king, so much as of the illusions to which he has fallen victim.

Manasseh's action in turning to the heavens resembles the appeal to the divine made by Pygmalion in Ovidian myth and its medieval iterations, in order to free

---

[47]   Didier Lechat, *'Dire par fiction': Métamorphoses du je chez Guillaume de Machaut, Jean Froissart et Christine de Pizan* (Paris: Champion, 2005), 113.

himself from fruitless desire for Galatea. It also serves as a reminder of the failure
of the elders, whose sin prevents them from looking heavenwards (119–20). Like
the elders, Manasseh's mental captivity reflects a materialistic approach to the
world, as a source of things to be desired in themselves, rather than of objects
signifying the divine. The distinction is comparable with that made by Augustine
in *De Doctrina Christiana*, which likewise identifies slavery as a consequence of
faulty reading:

> Sub signo enim servit qui operatur aut veneratur aliquam rem significantem,
> nesciens quid significet. Qui vero aut operatur aut veneratur utile signum
> divinitus institutum cuius vim significationemque intellegit non hoc veneratur
> quod videtur et transit sed illud potius quo talia cuncta referenda sunt.

> [A person enslaved by a sign is one who worships some thing which is
> meaningful but that remains unaware of its meaning. But the person who attends
> to or worships a useful sign, one divinely instituted, and does realize its force
> and significance, does not worship a thing which is only apparent and transitory
> but rather the thing to which all such things are to be related.][48]

In each case, correct reading is a practice that approaches the sign as an instrument
revealing the divine. Manasseh's spiritual redemption is fittingly expressed in his
recognition of nature as a book inscribed with divine signals: 'Qui en la mer terms
et signes /Has mis par tes paroles dignes [ ] Conclus limité has l'abisme /Et signé
par ton nom saintisme' ['who has fixed boundaries for the sea and set signs in it
through your blessed words [ ] You have enclosed and set limits to the abyss, and
signed it with your holy name'] (1461–2, 1465–6). Manasseh's prayer reflects
a liberating shift in his approach to signification, in using, rather than enjoying,
worldly signs.

The coincidence of material and spiritual imprisonment in the example of
Manasseh draws us back to Boethius the interlocutor, confined and depicted in
chains (1.m.2). As Anna Crabbe argues, the *Consolation* derives its impetus from
the 'paradox involved in the apparently identical nature of [Boethius's] physical
and spiritual situation and the long struggle to establish the unreality of the
physical prison and escape the reality of the mental chains'.[49] Freedom is achieved
through an amended reading practice that interprets physical circumstances
allegorically, as a means of conceptualising the authentic, ontological problem in
order to confront it. This symbolic economy is at work in the images of exile and
imprisonment that serve to characterise Boethius's alienation, privileging it over
the coincident bodily incarceration that functions as its emblem.[50] Identifying the
function of a similar practice within the *Confort* resolves the difficulty Palmer

---

[48]   St Augustine, *De Doctrina Christiana*, ed. and trans. R.P.H. Green (Oxford:
Clarendon, 1995), 144–7.

[49]   Anna Crabbe, 'Literary Design in the *De Consolatione Philosophiae*', in Gibson
(ed.), *Boethius*, 242.

[50]   See 1.m.2, 1.pr.2, 1.pr.3, 1.pr.5, 2.pr.4, and discussion in Crabbe.

finds in Machaut's claim that, if Charles repents as sincerely as Manasseh, 'De s'amour seras si refais /Qu'il te rendra tout ton païs' ['you will be so restored by his love that he will give you back all your land'] (2050–51). At the literal level, this claim implies the material restoration that was to follow Charles' expected release, a sign of worldly success Palmer considers un-Boethian. Allegorically, however, it can be read as an allusion encompassing Philosophy's view of exile and the arguments of Reason in the *Roman de la Rose* (*Rose* 5003–10). If Charles understands Machaut's lesson, he will recognise that his true home is not an earthly territory, but a condition to be regained through the reformation of the self.

This analysis of the *Consolation* as a work addressing the problems of reading becomes more compelling in the light of the work's medieval reception history. Responding to Fortune's claim that Boethius ought to have taken the fate of individuals such as Croesus, king of Lydia, as a token of her ways, commentators such as Remigius of Auxerre, Willliam of Conches and William of Aragon glossed and expanded a reference to Croesus' salvation through a shower of rain (2.pr.2).[51] Although details vary between commentators, these expansions reflect a shared concern with Croesus's fate, following a dream of being washed by Jove and dried by the sun, interpreted accurately by his daughter Phanie as a premonition of her father's exposure to the elements after suffering crucifixion at the hands of his enemy. To this example of a king's failure to heed a divine warning, William of Conches adds an account of Croesus's misinterpretation of an ambiguous Apollonian oracle anticipating the fall of his own kingdom: 'If Croesus crosses the Alys, a great kingdom will fall'.[52] In each case, commentators have expanded the initial argument, blaming the interlocutor for his failure to construe the evidence of Fortune's nature correctly, by matching it with other ineffectual attempts to read divine messages. This expansive method is echoed in the anonymous fourteenth-century Picard Boethius translation-commentary, which not only expands the story of Croesus but also includes a retelling of the Orpheus myth, alongside the story of Balshazzar's feast, offering a further example of a sinner's interpretive failure. Dated approximately 1315–20, the manuscript's synthesis of Boethian material and Old Testament narrative, and the particular *exempla* selected, potentially represent a source for Machaut's poem.[53] If the possibility of direct influence cannot be discounted, however, the appearance of Balshazzar's feast in the context

---

[51] My discussion is indebted to Alastair Minnis, 'Aspects of the Medieval French and English Traditions'.

[52] Minnis, 'Aspects', 329.

[53] VII in the Thomas-Roques classification, surviving in two MSS. B.N. fr. 1543, ff. 1–76 is incomplete. MS fr. 576, comprises ff. 1–82, of which fols. 19–20v and 51–52v are printed in Dwyer, *Boethian Fictions*, 92–9, 103–8. The latter section is a version of the Judgement of Paris, a myth alluded to in *Confort* 2645–82, and developed at greater length in Machaut's *Fonteinne amoureuse*, offering some further support for the hypothesis of influence. The Orpheus section of this translation is published in Atkinson and Babbi (eds), *L''Orphée' de Boèce au Moyen Âge*, 45–91. Atkinson discusses the translator's attempt to harmonize episodes in 'A Fourteenth-Century Picard Translation-Commentary'.

of a translation of the *Consolation* at the least offers compelling evidence that such biblical material was not considered antithetical to the Boethian tradition.

The elaboration of commentators' glosses within the *Roman de la Rose* offers further evidence of the ways in which Boethian reason might be applied to the question of signifying practice. As Alastair Minnis demonstrates, the glosses provided material for Jean de Meun's own retelling of the story of Croesus, in which Jean follows William of Conches in implying that Phanie's ability to interpret dreams derives from good moral character, an inference absent in other commentaries.[54] Phanie's probity is the foundation of a wisdom that contrasts with her father's pride and ignorance, manifested in his stubborn belief that the dream is a good omen. In the *Rose*, her perspicacity is reflected in a sermon on 'gentillece' to her father. Minnis comments that the word 'gentillece', which also occurs in Jean's translation of Boethius, *Li Livres de Confort*, links Phanie's advice to the concept of nobility articulated in *Consolation* 3.pr.6 and 3.m.6. Here, Philosophy argues that a claim to nobility based on ancestry is invalid, since it is based on no quality of the subject's own. True debasement occurs only when sin leads the individual to pursue unworthy objects, and the only laudable quality of nobility is 'imposita nobilibus necessitudo uideatur, ne a maiorum uirtute degeneret' ['the obligation which rests on noblemen not to fall away from the excellence of their forbears'] (3.pr.6). In the *Rose*, Jean expounds this Boethian theme through Dame Nature and through Phanie, who claims that Fortune disregards everything except 'Gentillece' (*Rose* 6538). As Minnis argues, this is 'an obscurely metaphorical statement of the commonplace that the wise man can control Fortune', and Phanie's sermon further illuminates the attraction of Boethius's work for the nobility, as an expression of 'Boethian philosophy [...] in terms of the behaviour appropriate to the ideal king or knight':[55]

> Gentillece est noble e si l'aim
> qu'el n'entre pas en queur vilain.
> Por ce vos pri, mon tres chier pere,
> que vilenie en vous n'apere.
> Ne saiez orguilleus ne chiches;
> aiez, por enseignier les riches,
> Large queur et corteis et gent
> Et piteus a la povre gent.
> Ainsinc le doit chascuns rois fere. (6549–57)

> [Nobility is noble, that is why I love her, for she will not enter any base heart. Therefore, dearest father, I beg you not to let any baseness appear in you. Do not be proud or avaricious, but in order to set an example to the rich, let your heart be generous, noble, and compassionate towards the poor. That is how every king should be.]

---

54 Minnis, 'Aspects', 332; *Rose* 6484–5.
55 Minnis, 'Aspects', 334.

The assertion that true nobility is a spiritual quality is also a feature of the summary of the *Consolation* offered in the *Confort*, where the status accorded to rank becomes a metaphor for moral worth:

> [...] se de ses vices separez
> Estoit et des vertuz parez,
> Uns savetiers nobles seroit
> Et uns rois villains, qui feroit
> Maises ouevres et villonnie. (1909–13)

> [if he were parted from vice and adorned with virtues, a shoemaker would be a noble and a king a peasant, if he did wicked and base deeds.]

As the analogy suggests, the nobility have a duty to behave in a manner appropriate to their rank, since this is the means by which hierarchical order is maintained. Failure to preserve the unity of signifier (noble birth) and signified (noble spirit) endangers the system as a whole. Machaut's lessons in the *Confort* are applicable to humanity as a species but, as the character of his examples suggests, they are imperative for officials, kings and others who exercise power. The importance attached to appropriate conduct as a mechanism of subjugation is also at issue in the example of Orpheus in the *Rose*, since his original failure to employ the stylus on the appointed table has the power to disrupt both writing and the patriarchal order. Unless man impresses his authority on woman, envisaged as a blank surface, the social order this relationship of subjection creates cannot survive. Since the linguistic order was conceived as a manifestation of the political order, both as a vital precursor to civilisation and through the personification of grammatical features such as verbal government, such alterations in behaviour are conceived as a hazard with the potential to destabilise the order of discourse altogether.[56]

In seeking to address the threat failure to conform to accepted standards of noble behaviour poses to the social order, however, Machaut's poem simultaneously highlights the conventional basis on which hierarchy rests. Alexandre Leupin argues that the *Confort* exposes the debt nobles owe to language as the discourse that enables them to claim their position. Yet, the *Confort* undermines this claim to power, in revealing the extent to which the prince himself is subjected to language, to desire and the difficulty of establishing stable distinctions between truth and falsehood. The *Confort* 'is thus a mirror in which the prince sees himself fall because language is the Law from which his power abusively originates'.[57] Moreover, although all are equally subject to the vagaries of this law, the nature of the poet's work renders him more experienced than his patron, authorising his position as advisor.[58] Paradoxically, the poet occupies the positions of both moral

---

[56] On the relationship between linguistic and political hierarchy, see Eugene Vance, *Mervelous Signals: Poetics and Sign Theory in the Middle Ages* (Lincoln: University of Nebraska Press, 1986), 257–63.

[57] Alexandre Leupin, 'The Powerlessness of Writing: Guillaume de Machaut, the Gorgon, and Ordenance', trans. Peggy McCracken, *Yale French Studies* 70 (1986), 137.

[58] Leupin, 'Powerlessness', 137.

arbiter and consummate deceiver, since the act of representation is a process that necessarily distorts its subject. The images representation produces are a means to ethical development, yet inevitably carry the potential to entrap the user into the mindset characteristic of idolatry, approaching them not as tools, but as objects powerful in themselves. The poet, whose art entails an awareness of the implications and techniques of signifying practice, is most aware of the conditional nature of the associations and structures this praxis creates. In consequence, poets possess a highly developed capacity to judge the ethical quality of the images they create, using them as tools, since their art renders them conscious of the distinction between these earthly signs and the true object of desire, 'comme une ymage en pointure /Contre une vive creature' ['as a graven image differs from a living creature'] (2771–2). In this respect, the *Confort* not only adapts Boethian philosophy to the use of contemporary nobles, but it also highlights the need for the prince to develop the skills associated with the poet.

Analysis of the *Confort* reveals a work in which reading is conceived as part of a programme of education whose object is the development of ethical character, and which depends upon the cultivation of the faculty of memory. In this context, the *Consolation* is recommended as a work able to teach the reader how best to live and which, as such, is especially valuable to the nobleman. This approach reflects an interpretive practice that treats textual material as a source of personal guidance, rather than seeking to recover a fixed meaning associated with the moment of its composition. The *Confort*'s adaptation of Boethius suggests that the *Consolation* was perceived as a text that shares its own concern with the art of memory as means to the achievement of a stable identity, of becoming good. Machaut's poem provides a suggestive indication of an idea of the *Consolation* current in the later Middle Ages.

Chapter 2

Consolatory Vision:
Translating Boethius in Guillaume de
Machaut's *Remede de Fortune*

Advising his imprisoned patron, Charles of Navarre, of the sustaining power of hope, Guillaume de Machaut emphasises the value of his own previous work for the politically invested reader, urging him to consult the *Remede de Fortune* (*Confort d'ami* 2241–50). Long acknowledged as the fullest reworking of the Boethian text in Machaut's poetic oeuvre, the *Remede* complements the *Confort* in translating the matter of Boethius's *Consolation of Philosophy* in ways that render it especially meaningful for a courtly audience. Analysis of the *Remede*'s inflection of the theme of consolation reveals further similarities to the later *Confort*, illuminating medieval conceptions of Boethian tradition and their relationship to contemporary ideas of nobility.

Although Machaut's allusion demonstrates that the *Remede* predates 1357, when the *Confort* was composed, attempts to establish its date more precisely remain controversial.[1] Opening with a series of recommendations for the aspiring student, the *Remede* sets out 12 prerequisites for effective learning. Offering his own experience as a model, the narrator identifies his teachers as Love and a lady, who serve as the pattern for his own ethical development. The narrator describes how, afraid to reveal his love, he channelled his emotions into the composition of poetry, and interpolates the product, a *lai*, into the *Remede*. The *lai*'s circulation precipitates a crisis within the narrative as, having asked the narrator to read this poem, his beloved solicits the composer's name. Incapable either of lying or telling the truth, the narrator flees to the park of Hesdin, where he composes a complaint blaming first Fortune and then Love for his sorrow. In a trance, he is visited by Esperance, who works to determine the cause of his distress, refuting the arguments of his complaint through debate and song. The *Remede* shares characteristics with vernacular works in the *Ars Poetica* tradition: Machaut incorporates an example of each of the seven contemporary *formes fixes* in decreasing order of poetic complexity, accompanied by increasingly sophisticated musical settings.[2]

In beginning with a programme for effective learning, Machaut exhibits an interest in educational praxis that encompasses the art of memory, defining the

---

[1]   Earp, *Guillaume de Machaut*, 191–3, 213.

[2]   The importance of musical poetry in producing and articulating internal harmony and the significance of music within the *Remede* are persuasively demonstrated in Leach, *Guillaume de Machaut*.

relationship between mnemonics and poetics as he develops an analogy for the state of innocence:[3]

> Ressamble proprement la table
> Blanche, polie, qui est able
> A recevoir, sans nul contraire,
> Ce c'on y veult paindre ou pourtraire;
> Et est aussi comme la cire
> Qui sueffre dedens li escrire,
> Ou qui retient forme ou emprainte,
> Si com on l'a en li emprainte.
> Ainssi est il certainement
> De vray humain entendement
> Qui est ables a recevoir
> Tout ce c'on veult et concevoir
> Puet tout ce a quoy on le veult mettre:
> Armes, amours, autre art, ou lettre. (27–40)

[like the white and polished tablet that is ready to receive the exact image of whatever one wishes to portray or paint upon it. And it is also like wax that can be written upon, and which retains the form and imprint exactly as one has imprinted it. Truly it is the same with human understanding, which is ready to recieve whatever one wishes and can apprehend whatever one sets it to: arms, love, other art or letter.][4]

Machaut's positioning of love as a discipline equivalent to arms or letters reflects contemporary conceptions of *amor* as a characteristic practice of the nobility, and the extent to which love was distinguished as an aid to education.[5] The passage associates the mental condition most conducive to learning, and the medium of human understanding, with a surface primed for inscription, evoking the metaphor for memory that Mary Carruthers suggestively describes as 'governing model or "cognitive archetype"' in Western cultures.[6] Placing mnemonic practice at the heart of her reading of the poem, Jody Enders makes a persuasive case for the *Remede* as a manual of instruction illustrating 'how to create literary speech and song by conceiving and safeguarding a memory alphabet that keeps love and its poetics alive'.[7] This engagement with the theory and practice of memory training extends to the *Remede*'s treatment of its major source text, the *Consolation*.

---

[3]   For a valuable analysis of the *Remede* and its relationship to contemporary mnemonic praxis, see Jody Enders, 'Music, Delivery, and the Rhetoric of Memory in Guillaume de Machaut's *Remède de Fortune*', *PMLA* 107 (1992): 450–64.

[4]   Guillaume de Machaut, *Le Jugement du roy de Behaigne and Remede de Fortune*, ed. and trans. James I. Wimsatt and William W. Kibler (Athens: University of Georgia Press, 1988).

[5]   See especially Jaeger, *Ennobling Love*.

[6]   Carruthers, *The Book of Memory*, 18, and see 18–37.

[7]   Enders, 'Music, Delivery', 453.

The *Consolation* itself may be understood as the expression of an approach that links reading, the reinterpretation of textual materials and self-construction in ways that suggest the influence of arts of memory. In his study of the *Consolation* in its original Latin form, Seth Lerer characterises it as a work that 'charts a reader's progress through an engagement with poetic and prose texts', and 'consistently "rewrites" earlier portions of its text into new contexts to measure that progress'.[8] Tracing the development of 'a mind reordering itself along the lines of critical reading', this methodology conceives the subject as an entity determined by reading practice, a standpoint resembling that which informs medieval conceptions of memory training as the foundation of character.[9] This reading of the *Consolation* accords well with Lerer's argument that Philosophy's vocabulary draws on a tradition of memory training, and with Mary Carruthers's analysis of the opening of Boethius's text as displaying a familiarity with mnemonic arts.[10] Against this background, Lerer's discussion of Boethius's treatment of his literary sources, and the plays of Seneca in particular, is especially revealing. Lerer contends that Boethius's borrowings and revisions illustrate 'another reader's progressive engagement with Seneca's plays: from slavish imitation to critical reading, to rejection'.[11] This interpretative maturation is articulated in one of the *Consolation*'s key images, emerging in the recurrent use of the verb *respicere*, signifying the literal act of seeing again, or re-vision, and signalling 'the full exercise of rational abilities and the desire to review and interpret past events as guides for present behaviour'.[12] This mode of thought is in sympathy with mnemonic practice: not only is the past to be developed as a guide for present action and a model for apprehension, but it is also to be treated as a textual source, available for interpretation and adaptation.

Boethius's *Consolation* both advocates and exemplifies this transformative practice, as the narrative incorporates the materials of its author's immediate past, rewriting them through literary adaptation. Philosophy introduces *fabulae* that incorporate and transform earlier portions of the *Consolation* itself, using Seneca's plays as the source of these myths.[13] As Lerer argues, Boethius's treatment of the myths of Orpheus, Ulysses and Hercules serves to 'recapitulate the moral education of the prisoner', and is characterised by a tradition of mythological allegory that translates spatial movement into spiritual conflict, reinscribing the lost native land as transcendental point of origin.[14] Boethius focuses on the

---

[8]   Seth Lerer, *Boethius and Dialogue: Literary Method in* The Consolation of Philosophy (Princeton: Princeton University Press, 1985), 3.

[9]   On memory and character, see Carruthers, *The Book of Memory*, 222, 224, 226.

[10]   Lerer, *Boethius and Dialogue*, 238, 105; Carruthers, *The Craft of Thought*, 173–6, and see also A.M. Babbi, 'Introduction' in Atkinson and Babbi (eds), *L'Orphée'*, xii.

[11]   Lerer, *Boethius and Dialogue*, 239.

[12]   Lerer, *Boethius and Dialogue*, 158–9, listing instances of *respicere* in the *Consolation*.

[13]   Lerer, *Boethius and Dialogue*, 159–60. On the myths, see especially 124–202.

[14]   Lerer, *Boethius and Dialogue*, 184–5.

aptitude of his source materials, be they experiential or literary, for adaptation as standards for personal direction, a technique that reflects the moral concern at work in the disciplines of rhetoric and memory training. The *Consolation*'s medieval readers, sharing an educational foundation in rhetoric similar to that of Boethius, would arguably be predisposed to recognise the significance of the text's engagement with educational processes. Although, unlike Nicholas Trevet and Petrarch, not all readers would have appreciated the echoes of Seneca's tragedies present in the *Consolation*,[15] the popularity of texts such as the *Ovide moralisé* would have enabled many to recognise the development articulated in the mythic interpolations within Boethius' narrative. The methodology adopted in later translations and commentaries recognises and extends Boethian practice: as I argued in the previous chapter, the interpolation of episodes such as the dream of Croesus and Balshazzar's feast supplements Boethius's mythic *exempla* with other narratives serving a similar purpose. It suggests a strand of interpretation that stands in complement to that developed by Lerer, in reading Boethian *exempla* as figures illuminating the idea that a form of mental bondage restricts the human subject's ability to decipher the signs of divine immanence.

Machaut's *Remede* engages with these elements of the Boethian text. As is often acknowledged, the poem owes a substantial debt to the *Consolation*, with much of Esperance's discourse drawing on the Latin text, in an approach Wimsatt and Kibler characterise as 'word-for-word translation'.[16] This appraisal works to efface the changes Machaut's source text undergoes, however: as Hœpffner emphasises, Machaut's treatment of the Boethian source material is 'non pas une traduction, mais une adaptation plus ou moins libre de plusiers, chapitres choisis du traité latin'.[17] Machaut's interest lies primarily in the *Consolation*'s discussion of Fortune, so that this element of the source text becomes much more dominant within the *Remede*. Moreover, Machaut ignores those aspects of the work that are exclusively concerned with Boethius's personal circumstances, instead adapting his material to reflect the narrator's situation, from which derives the most significant change made to the *Consolation*, the substitution of Esperance for Philosophy as a guide.[18] Arguing against any simplistic mimetic identification of poet and narrator, Hœpffner associates this change with the protagonist's situation as an unhappy lover, for whom hope is a more appropriate source of consolation.

In identifying Machaut's treatment of Boethius as a form of interpretation that transforms the work for the poet's own purposes, Hœpffner illuminates the *Remede*'s relationship to its source text. Machaut makes no explicit claims to the elevated status of poet, as distinguished in later medieval readings of Horace's *Ars Poetica*, but nor does he adopt the role of faithful servant to the *Consolation*'s authoritative text. Indeed, in setting his borrowed matter within a lyric narrative with a first-person narrator, Machaut locates the text's origin in

---

15   On Petrarch and Trevet, see Lerer, *Boethius and Dialogue*, 236n1.
16   Wimsatt and Kibler, editorial notes to *Remede* lines 1502–5, 502.
17   Hœpffner, ed., *Œuvres de Guillaume de Machaut* , 2. xx, my translation.
18   Hœpffner, ed., *Œuvres de Guillaume de Machaut* , 2, xxiv, xxiii.

personal experience, rather than seeking to assert its value as a vehicle for classical learning. His approach reflects the position of the subject within medieval rhetoric, which associates the ability to compose with the individual's cultivation of a memorial store from which material can be gathered and shaped into new textual forms.[19] Since memory responds most strongly to associative patterns suggested by the subject's own experience and education, it is this personal dimension that determines how the public matter of the *Consolation* is transformed into private property, both in the sense of its accommodation to Machaut's own memorial store, and the poetic transmission that derives from this accommodation, in the production of the *Remede*.

One effect of this tendency to personalise the content of the *Consolation* is arguably reflected in the primacy of amorous concerns rather than pure philosophy in the *Remede*. Machaut writes in a cultural context where the discourse of love and friendship had long functioned to mediate political concerns, a trope whose other manifestations include Machaut's own poetic representation of those adversely affected by the ongoing military conflicts of the Hundred Years war, in *dits* such as the *Fonteinne amoureuse*. In consequence, Machaut's engagement with the *Consolation*, a text whose concerns complement those of the advice-to-princes tradition, in the form of erotic narrative, suggests the use of the amatory as a surrogate for the political. This technique is in sympathy with the Aristotelian understanding of politics as a branch of ethics that, as a form of practical wisdom, is less elevated than theoretical knowledge, since, as Aristotle argues, 'man is not the best thing in the world.' Practical wisdom cannot concern itself with universals alone, 'it must also recognize the particulars; for it is practical, and practice is concerned with particulars'.[20] The *Remede*'s focus on love reflects this necessary concern with the particular, in applying the vocabulary of contemporary politics to Boethian wisdom. In this respect, it complements Machaut's use of a present-day setting as a means to highlight the specific circumstances in which this knowledge might find practical application.

Machaut's reformulation of Boethius reflects good mnemonic practice, since treatises on the art of memory draw attention to the need for matter to be made familiar, personalised or domesticated, so that it might be retained. If the *Remede* reshapes the teachings of the *Consolation* to reflect the cultural associations and values current in Machaut's time, this activity resembles that of the mnemonist who exploits the association between the colour white and milk or snow, in order to create a mental image. Furthermore, as the literary background to Machaut's work suggests, this amatory transposition perhaps also enables the poet to substitute a version of his own experience for that of Boethius. Rather than presenting a fictive reflection of a really existing romantic attachment, however, the *Remede* evokes the relationship of patron and poet. The beloved lady has been identified with Bonne of Luxembourg, whose patronage is acknowledged as an influence on the *Remede* by

---

[19]   See Carruthers, *The Craft of Thought*, 12.

[20]   Aristotle, *Nicomachean Ethics*, 1801–2, Book 6.7.

several critics. The setting of the park of Hesdin, and Machaut's punning play on the word 'bonne' in lines 54–6, a device that complements the poet's characteristic placement of names in acrostics and anagrams, supports this association.[21] In addition, a prominent expression of devotion to the lady corresponds to another made by the poet to Bonne's son-in-law, Charles II of Navarre, in the *Confort d'ami*: the declaration that 'sans riens retenir /Sui tiens, quoy qu'il doie avenir' finds a parallel in the lover's avowal, 'siens sans riens retenir, /Sui, quoy qu'il m'en doie avenir' ['I am hers without reserve, come what may'] (*Remede* 131–2; cf. *Confort* 25–6). The echo of these lines in the later *Confort* locates a similar quality of feeling within these relationships, and hints at the familial bond that links Bonne and Charles. In this sense, the relationship between lover and lady in the *Remede* serves as an aestheticised representation of the poet's circumstances, substituting for the personal history of Boethius inscribed within the *Consolation*. Both texts derive meaning from a putative relation to the social experience of their protagonists, transposed into literary form; again, this coincides with good mnemonic practice, since the method and example offered by the *Consolation* are not treated in the abstract, but instead are applied to the situation of the interpreter.

The influence of mnemonic culture on the *Remede* is also implicit in the poem's emulation of Boethian form, in the interpolation of *formes fixes* that translate the prosimetric structure of the *Consolation* into a variety of poetic forms: the French tradition of interpolated lyric serves as a domestic medium for the Latin source material, exposing an influence perhaps latent in other examples of the genre.[22] Machaut's transposition of the *Consolation* also extends to the *Remede*'s plot: Hœpffner traces this adaptation to the narrator's arrival at the park of Hesdin, where personal adventure yields to allegory. The narrator's complaint evokes the opening of Boethius's work, which likewise depicts a solitary figure lamenting his misfortune although, as Hœpffner stresses, the poems are otherwise substantially different in content. Falling silent, each protagonist perceives a female figure both beautiful and otherworldly, whom he comes to recognise as an avatar: in Boethius, of Philosophy, and in Machaut, of Esperance. These figures' effect on the afflicted protagonists is like that of the sun, banishing darkness and storm clouds (1.m.3; *Remede* 1519–26). Each personified abstraction examines the sufferer's complaints, in a dialogue interspersed with consolatory song and, in their words, the protagonists find comfort and encouragement.[23]

The structural resemblance between these works is perhaps greater than Hœpffner's analysis allows, however: the *Consolation* identifies the author's

---

[21] See Daniel Poiron, *Le Poète et le prince: l'évolution du lyrisme courtois de Guillaume de Machaut à Charles d'Orléans* (Paris: Presses Universitaires de France, 1965), 194, 201n28; Wimsatt and Kibler, 'Introduction', 33–6, and see also Earp's comments, *Guillaume de Machaut*, 213.

[22] On prosimetry and French practices of interpolation, see Hœpffner, *Œuvres de Guillaume de Machaut*, 2.xxi,n1, and, on interpolated verse, see Ardis Butterfield, *Poetry and Music in Medieval France: From Jean Renart to Guillaume de Machaut* (Cambridge: Cambridge University Press, 2002).

[23] Hœpffner, *Œuvres de Guillaume de Machaut*, 2. xxi–xxii.

development with a generic progression towards more prestigious literary forms, a movement in this instance frustrated by the interlocutor's regression into genres such as elegy.[24] Boethius's initial state, as mute amanuensis to the poetic Muses, attests to the spiritual confusion that Philosophy seeks to address.[25] Philosophy herself attributes this change to a causal relation between the prisoner's experience of fortune and his linguistic capacity: although he was capable of attacking Fortune with persuasive arguments when she was favourable to him, in misfortune, he is silent (2.pr.1). Philosophy's critique of Boethius's passive transmission of verse supplied by the Muses evokes a conception of poetics resembling that developed in Horace's *Ars Poetica*, since it implies a failure to modify common matter derived from traditional sources, translating public material into private property. As an outpouring of emotion, the prisoner's poetry also suggests a surrender to forms of non-traditional matter the artist is advised to reject, in addressing personal experience.[26] Philosophy defines the problem further, in lamenting the prisoner's loss of the ability to decipher Nature's secrets; the verb *reddere* literally signifying 'to give back in language, to translate or interpret from one language to another, or from symbols into speech', and including 'the sense of reciting or rehearsing a speech' (1.m.2).[27] This skill is necessary to the making and use of mnemonic images, and that its failure supplies another reason for the prisoner's silence: he is unable to use the faculty of memory to generate speech.

A similar transition from eloquence to incapacity is staged within the *Remede*, as the narrator first demonstrates the apparent success of his apprenticeship to Love and the lady in his composition of songs in various forms, of which the interpolated *lai* is but one example (401–30). Despite these accomplishments, however, his lady's wish to know who wrote the *lai* presents a crisis that renders him incapable of speech: 'Je n'eüsse dit .i. seul mot /Pour toute l'empire de Romme' ['I couldn't have said a word were I offered the whole Roman Empire'] (704–5). Echoed in the lover's complaint against Fortune, the form of the negative is significant, revealing the failure of the project of cultural appropriation that *translatio studii et imperii* represents and, at the same time, the danger such failure embodies for the nobility, whose decisive actions are vital to the health of the body politic (1214–16). Since this problem relates to love, it also suggests a failure to procreate, recalling the image of Orpheus, unable to write or to forge correctly (*Rose* 19622–3). This fault's effect on memory is made explicit in the narrator's assertion:

> L'amoureus mal que je sentoie,
> Me tollirent si le memoire
> Et les .v. sens, que ne puis croire
> Qu'onquez amans fust en tel point,
> Ne de parler si mal a point. (710–14)

---

24 Lerer, *Boethius and Dialogue*, 96–7; Crabbe, 'Literary Design', 246–8.

25 Lerer, *Boethius and Dialogue*, 94–123.

26 See Copeland, *Rhetoric, Hermeneutics, and Translation*, especially 151–78.

27 Lerer, *Boethius and Dialogue*, 103 and n21.

[the amorous malady I felt so stripped me of my memory and five senses that
I cannot believe any lover was ever in such straits, nor so incapable of reply.]

As Enders argues, 'one might say that, at that time, he had been mnemonically
incapacitated'.[28]

The narrator's lady is counterpart to both Philosophy and Esperance, as a
powerful female questioner, and her association with Esperance is strengthened in
the course of the *Remede*, as Esperance's opinion is cited as the deciding factor in
her decision to accept the poet as lover (3799–839). Like Esperance, the lady is a
courtly figure, and this shared appearance of nobility anticipates the representation
of Philosophy in the fifteenth-century manuscript iconography of the *Consolation*,
where she is depicted in the fashionable dress of the court.[29] In focusing on the
role of an authoritative female teacher in exposing the vulnerability of memory
and rhetoric in the face of misfortune, against the grain of her pupil's previous
training, the *Remede* transposes narrative elements from the *Consolation* into a
contemporary courtly setting and idiom.

If amnesia is common to both narrators, memory also lies at the heart of the
new phase of education on which they now embark. For Boethius, the crisis and its
resolution have a shared origin, in accordance with Plato's concept of reminiscence,
which defines intellection as a process that renews knowledge forgotten through the
corrupting influence of the flesh. Philosophy reminds the prisoner of this process,
advising that truth must be sought 'en sa pensee [...] Dedanz son cuer', since 'com
dit Platon, /Autre chose n'est nostre a prendre /Fors ce qui est oblié a entendre' [in
one's thoughts...in the heart...as Plato says, nothing is ours to learn, except what
we have forgotten to understand] (3.m.11).[30] Philosophy's instruction is matched
in Machaut's location of the source of sufficiency within the self, rather than in
the course of worldly events beyond the narrator's control.[31] Yet, this resolution
is already implicit in the opening of the *Remede* which, like the *Consolation*, is
consistent with mnemonic practices of invention. In her analysis of the opening
of the *Consolation*, Carruthers argues that the interlocutor's composition alludes
to memory work, rather than a physical act of transcription, deducing this from
the prisoner's disposition, recumbent on a bed. A supine posture was favoured
as an aid to the exercise of memory; the prisoner's anxious and sorrowful state
carries similar connotations, as distress is often associated with mental invention,

---

28   Enders, 'Music, Delivery', 456.

29   Courcelle, *La Consolation*, 87.

30   *Le Livre de Boece de Consolacion*, ed. Cropp. Completed *c.* 1350, this anonymous
translation is quoted in Chapters 2–4 as it is the most influential medieval French translation,
and represents a form of the text that is, at least, closer to the version or versions familiar
to these poets than modern editions, based on early manuscripts of the Latin *Consolation*
rather than the medieval vulgate tradition. The possibility that Machaut or Froisssart
referred to this translation, apparently cited by Christine de Pizan, cannot be ruled out. See
Glynnis M. Cropp, 'Boèce et Christine de Pizan', *Le Moyen Age* 87 (1981): 387–417. On
the vulgate *Consolation*, see Kottler, 'The Vulgate Tradition'.

31   Huot, 'Guillaume de Machaut', 176.

a correlation reflected in accounts of the writing practice of Anselm, Aquinas and Augustine, and of the visionary experience of several Old Testament prophets. In monastic meditation, this frame of mind was thought to instigate a contemplative journey along cognitive pathways, as the practitioner gathered mental images whose value was partly dependent on their affective quality.[32] Sharing these features, the *Consolation* lends itself to interpretation as the product of a process of meditative invention that draws on texts incorporated within the prisoner's memorial store.

Like the *Consolation*, the *Remede* describes a method of composition that begins with the experience of anxiety and the adoption of a posture favoured by mnemonists, in this case sitting, in the appropriately isolated location of the park of Hesdin (838). The poem further reflects mnemonic practice in the representation of the narrator's condition immediately prior to his encounter with Esperance:

> [...] fui je touse desvoiez
> De sense, de memoire, et de force,
> Et de toute autre vigour. Pour ce
> Estoie je cheüs en transe
> Aussi com cilz qui voit et pense
> Sa mort devant li toute preste. (1490–95)

> [I had wandered far from the way of sense, memory, energy, and every other power. For this reason I'd fallen into a trance, like someone who sees and senses his death fast upon him.]

The narrator's trance anticipates the liminal state he enters in listening to Esperance's *chant royal*:

> Commença son chant delez mi,
> C'un petitet m'i endormi;
> Mes ne fu pas si fermement
> Que n'entendisse proprement
> Qu'ainssi comença par revel
> Jolïement son chant nouvel (1979–84)

> [she began her song with such a melody that soon I fell asleep; but not so deeply that I didn't accurately hear how her new song began beautifully and gaily]

Described by Enders as an example of 'the classic mnemonic state', the narrator's trance accents the focus on memory that permeates Esperance's teaching.[33] In particular, Enders draws attention to the proliferation of words connected with education and recollection in Esperance's speech, and her insistence that the narrator memorise her instruction.

The association with remembrance is a further attribute Esperance shares with the lady, who is characterised by memorable qualities that make her, too, a teacher of the art of memory:

---

[32] Carruthers, *The Craft of Thought*, 173–6.
[33] Enders, 'Music, Delivery', 454.

> Car, sans plus, de leur remembrance,
> Maintieng, maniere, et contenance
> Loing de li souvent me venoit
> Meilleur, quant il m'en souvenoit.
> Si que dont, quant je la veoie
> Vis a vis et que remiroie
> Son port, son maintien, sa maniere,
> Qui plus est estable et entiere
> Que nulle qu'onquez mes veïsse,
> Beien estoit droiz qu'en retenisse
> Aucun notable ensaignement,
> Quant dou souvenir seulement
> Maintez foys par Douce Pensee
> Ma maniere estoit amendee. (203–16)

[Nothing more than the memory of them improved my own comportment, manner, and bearing when I was far from her and remembered them. Therefore, when I saw her face to face and contemplated her demeanor, her comportment, her manner, which were more constant and harmonious than any I have ever seen, it was quite fitting that I retain from them some memorable lesson, since through memory alone Sweet Thought often amended my behaviour.]

The lover's ability to reproduce the effects of the beloved's presence through an effort of mind, in conjunction with the persistent emphasis on memory within the *Remede*, is significant: it supplies a context in which Esperance emerges as an aspect of the narrator's psyche, an interpretation that has also been applied to Boethius's Philosophy.[34] Yet, as evidence of medieval responses to similar visions suggests, recognition that such figures originate in the mind is not synonymous with a denial of their existence. Although a modern audience might typically perceive such apparitions as an indication of mental instability, medieval accounts suggest that these figures could instead be acknowledged as constructions founded upon traditional matter familiar to a reading public. Formed from common matter held within the mnemonist's mental store, such phantasms possess a social existence for a community able to recognise the sources and functions of such an image.[35]

In this context, Esperance can be considered as a mnemonic vision generated by the narrator in a trance achieved through the initial steps of anxiety and withdrawal from social intercourse. Like the apparitions analysed by Carruthers, and the narrator's mental image of his lady, the vision of Esperance has an autodidactic purpose, serving to effect a change in the narrator's behaviour patterns. Her existence, like theirs, is limited to the intellectual plain; this is implicit in indirect allusions to her essence, such as the narrator's assertion that, after the vision

----

[34]   Courcelle cites Abelard's interpretation of the text as Boethius's dialogue with his own reason, *Expositio in Hexameron* 6, *Patrologica Latina*, t. CLXXVIII, 760 C, in *La Consolation*, 54.

[35]   Carruthers, *The Craft of Thought*, 183–8.

Lors en mon estant me dreçay
Et vers le guichet m'adreçay
Par ou j'estoie la venus.
Mais je m'aperchu bien que nus
N'estoit alez par ceste voie,
Depuis que venus y estoie:
Qu'en riens n'i estoit depassee
L'erbe poignant, et las rousee
Clere et luisant sur l'erbe drue
N'estoit pas encore abatue. (2971–80)

[Then I stood up and went toward the small wicket through which I had entered.
I saw clearly that no one had come that way since I'd entered, for the sharp-
bladed grass had not been disturbed and the bright, sparkling dew was still on
the thick grass.]

Esperance evidently does not have a physical existence of the same kind as the
narrator, and the point is reiterated as he leaves the park:

[…] au guichet m'acheminay
Par le chemin qui fu tout vert;
Mais ne le trouvay pas ouvert,
Car ainssi com je le fremai,
Estoit; adonc le deffremai. (3037–42)

[I walked toward the wicket along the lush green path; but I didn't find it open,
for it was closed just as I'd left it; so I unlatched it.]

Esperance's being is composite; she is simultaneously present in the minds of
those who hold the idea in common, and she leaves the lover without leaving him,
dividing herself 'En plus de .c. mille parties /Qui aus amans sont departies' ['into
more than a hundred thousand shares, to be shared among lovers'] (3175–6). She
exists on a conceptual level for the members of this collective group and beyond,
conceived as a distinctively aristocratic value: as the lover argues, her name is

[…] de si noble renon
Qu'au monde n'a païs ne regne,
Et que chascuns ne se resjoie,
Qui de li puet avoir la joie. (3758–62)

[so nobly renowned that there's not a land or kingdom in the world where she
cannot be found, where she does not reign, and where everyone who is capable
of joy through her is not happy.]

The social reality of the concept Esperance represents is reflected in the physical
existence of the ring she presents to the narrator, and its subsequent use to ratify
the bond of love and loyalty between lover and lady (2094–6; 4055–98).

The manifestation of Esperance serves a didactic end in enabling the visionary to overcome the *curiositas* that frustrates effective contemplation: as the narrator comments, 'Car .i. choses font bestourner /Le sense et müer en folour: /Ce sont grant joye et grant doulour' ['there are two things that falsify the senses and cause them to react irrationally: these are great joy and great sadness'] (2994–5). Esperance serves as a fitting reflection of both the content of a memory encompassing texts such as the *Roman de la Rose*, and of the narrator's situation as a lover, just as Philosophy is appropriate to Boethius's circumstances and educational history. Each functions as a focus permitting the subject to rehearse the elements of his interpretative practice, and an orientation point enabling him to regain the memorial pathways from which he has strayed. In this role, Esperance not only summarises the arguments against sorrow as a legitimate reaction to misfortune, but also demonstrates techniques associated with the art of memory, including rhyme and the making of effective mnemonic imagery. These are illustrated in the *formes fixes* interpolated within the *Remede*, and in the prominent example of the ensign of true lovers. Taking the form of a shield emblazoned with a heart pierced by an arrow, the ensign reflects sound mnemonic principles as a composite image summarising the various features desirable in a lover (1863–94). The ensign is coloured, a tactic recommended in treatises on mnemonic art and displayed in rubricated manuscripts that respond to the predominantly visual nature of human memory, and the hues mentioned in the *Remede* have a cultural resonance that extends beyond Machaut's poem. In associating blue with loyalty, and green, which Esperance argues should be absent from the shield, with inconstancy, Machaut evokes meanings attributed to these colours in other texts such as the *Voir Dit* and the *Dit dou Bleu Chevalier*.[36] The significance of the ensign is reflected in the position it occupies within the iconographic scheme employed in two key manuscripts, MSS Paris, Bibliothèque Nationale, fr. 1586 and 1584. As Huot argues, although both of these manuscripts appear to reflect Machaut's personal supervision, the second strengthens the emblematic and visual character of the image, rather than its narrative function, an innovation that accords well with a mnemonic purpose.[37]

As Esperance's instruction draws to a close, the characteristic methods of the art of memory begin to reemerge in the narrator's own practice, and again, this forms part of the *Remede*'s adaptation of the content of the *Consolation*. In each text, linguistic competence is presented as an index of the subject's intellectual development: while, as Lerer argues, Boethius the interlocutor traces a path 'from a lethargic speechlessness [...] through the excesses of rhetoric and the limitations of dialectic before Philosophy can introduce him to the methods of philosophical demonstration', in the *Remede*, this progression through diverse levels of discourse is enacted in the various interpolated *formes fixes*[38] *The earliest*

---

[36]   On the significance of the colour green, see Cerquiglini, *Un Engin si soutil*, 168–9.

[37]   Huot, *From Song to Book*, 274–80.

[38]   Lerer, *Boethius and Dialogue*, 96.

of these, the lai, represents the narrator as a lover satisfied with the pleasures of 'Doulz Penser', 'Souvenir' and 'Espoir', and critical of any desire to seek further comfort (431–44). In this state of equilibrium, he is capable of composition, both literary and musical, falling into silence and dissatisfied complaint only when he is deprived of hope, by the threat both discovery and continued concealment pose to the status quo. Although the narrator's vulnerability to the vicissitudes of fortune is an evident flaw, such a lover has already demonstrated the capacity to disassociate the beneficial qualities of the lady from the woman herself, relocating them to a mental image that reproduces her effects. The potential this mnemonic strategy offers for self-sufficiency is implicit in the wider meaning of the word 'souvenir', in its association with the imaginative realisation of that which is otherwise inaccessible.[39] Neither the behaviour of the object of desire nor other changes in the world need affect the mental state of the subject who develops this skill, so that its value only needs to be reiterated and reinforced through the discourse of Esperance.

The making of mnemonic images such as the ensign of true lovers, as figures that summarise and embody information to be remembered, represents a form of translation, a rhetorical performance of a kind similar to that exemplified by the interpolated *formes fixes*. In presenting a series of compositions linking material on fortune drawn from Boethius with arguments on love, Esperance demonstrates the technique of gathering matter from the memorial store, and its use in composition, and offers texts which the lover is to use in honing the art of memory. The success of this method is rendered explicit as the narrator's mnemonic skills resurface in his response to Esperance's poetic discourse, as he seeks to memorize her speech by rehearsing it systematically, 'De point en point' ['point by point'] (2937). Several lines are devoted to this process of memorisation, which reflects the traditional emphasis on the identification of a text's meaning, in the development and content of its argument, and in the establishment of its schematic order, both implicit in the phrase 'De point en point'. Machaut's description emphasises the role of affection in this process, as a means of fixing knowledge in mind, and the disappearance of Esperance is suggestively linked with this shift in concentration:

> Si mis moult grant paine a l'apendre,
> Et la soz en si poy d'espasse
> Qu'ains qu'elle partist de la place,
> Ne que toute l'eüst pardit,
> Je la soz par chant et par dit.
> Et pour ce que ne l'oubliasse,
> Failloit il que la recordasse;
> Mais si com je l'ymaginoie
> En mon cuer et la recordoie
> De si tres bonne affection,
> Que toute l'inclination

---

[39] Huot, 'Guillaume de Machaut', 174.

Des .v. sense que Dieus m'a donné
(Fors tant au'adés me souvenoit
De celle dont mes biens venoit,)
La dame fu esvanuïe. (2902–20)

[So I made a great effort to learn it, and memorised it so quickly that before
she'd left the place or had even finished singing it, I knew both the words and
the music.
And so I'd not forget it, I had to imprint it upon my memory; but as I fixed its
image in my heart and imprinted it with such ardor, that every disposition of my
five God-given senses was so intent upon it that I had no heart or desire to think
of anything else (except that I constantly remembered her who was the source of
my good), the lady vanished.]

Repeated recollection of Esperance's teaching is represented as a potential defence
against adversity in love (2952–64), and the exercise of memory leaves the narrator
feeling 'trop plus seür, /Plus fort, plus rassis, plur meür' ['much more confident,
stronger, calmer, maturer'] (2969–70). It reinforces his sense of self, and once
this is done, he recovers the ability to compose, producing a poem that transposes
Esperance's lesson into a *ballade* on the role of hope in love, addressed to the lady
(3013–36).

This composition exemplifies the approach to the source text advocated
in rhetorical teaching, responding to it as a work available for transformative
activities ranging from 'faithful' translation to poetic reformulation and
enlargement. Moreover, as the attribution of redemptive powers to the faculty of
'souvenir' in Machaut's poem implies, the active revisionary approach to a source
text exemplified in both the *Remede* and the *Consolation* is not confined to literary
artifacts, but extends to other phenomena. Philosophy points to the interlocutor's
loss of the ability to decipher Nature's secrets as an index of insufficiency,
identifying it as a fault to be cured by the cultivation of an amended reading
practice. The lover of the *Remede* is taught to read the lady and assimilate her
significance to his own memorial store as if she were herself a text, an approach
that reflects the conception of human identity as an artifact shaped by hermeneutic
practice that is central to the medieval theory and practice of the art of memory. As
Huot argues, 'It is this incorporation of the essence of the lady, through memory
and fantasy, into the lover's own sense of self that makes up his lack, heals his
wounds, and redefines him as a figure of wholeness and serenity, fulfilled by Hope
rather than tormented by Desire'.[40] Here Desire and Hope are set in opposition,
the one focusing on absence and lack that torment the lover with external goods
which can never truly belong to the desiring subject; the other looking forward
to a pleasure that originates within the subject himself. If the *Remede* initially
emphasised the text's ability to modify its reader, exemplified in the capacity of
Love and the lady to alter the lover's behaviour, as the poem draws to a close, the
power of transformation is located in the interpreter's ability to modify the object

---

[40] Huot, 'Guillaume de Machaut', 175.

of his attention. This is illustrated in the narrator's response to the lady; although her behaviour does not cease to cause him pain, his belief in her truthfulness remains unshakable:

Comment que puis mainte paour,
Maint dur assaut, et maint estour,
Mainte dolour, mainte morsure,
Et mainte soudaine pointure,
Maint grief souspir, mainte haschie,
Et mainte grant merencolie
M'en ait couvenu soustenir;
Nonpourquant je me vos tenir
De tous poins a fermement croirre
Qu'ell disoit parole voire. (4221–30)

[Although I later had to bear many fears, many harsh assaults and many attacks, many sorrows, many biting torments and many sudden pangs, many sorrowful signs, much anguish, and much deep melancholy, nonetheless I was determined in every respect to believe firmly that she was speaking the truth.]

The recurrence of pain suggests that the state of self-sufficiency can only be temporarily experienced by the fallible human subject, as part of a constantly renewed process that must necessarily fall short of the stable perfection associated with the divine.

Committed to a particular interpretation of his lady's behaviour, the narrator's refusal to allow his perception of the lady to be affected by her actions shows that his attachment is now to an image of his own creation, rather than the living woman. The desired object has been incorporated within the narrator's mental realm through the faculty of memory, and this process of assimilation might be understood as an aggressive act of displacement, like the project of translation whose methods it shares. The very possibility that the object of desire might alter is denied, and the narrator's assurance has a comic resonance, as Machaut playfully implies that the narrator's mental equilibrium may be founded upon a wilfully constructed delusion. Imperfect signs of absolute truth, the inevitable deficiencies of such images entail the inescapable threat of idolatry. If memory enables the subject to overcome the damaging effects of desire and achieve a form of self-sufficiency, its methods are questionable, and draw attention to the involvement of such hermeneutic strategies with repressive mechanisms of power. Yet, in this respect, training in the art of memory appears especially appropriate for those associated with the court, and for an audience of princes whose incapacity in word or act might present a real threat to the stability of empire.

As the previous two chapters have argued, Machaut's *Remede de Fortune* and *Confort d'ami* display a profound concern with the faculty of memory, to the extent that they might be regarded as manuals of instruction in the art of memory. In each text, the systematic exercise of memory is identified as a means to the development of moral character, and special emphasis is placed upon the ability to generate and preserve mental images, commonly cited as one of the essential skills in the mnemonist's repertoire. Machaut highlights this skill as one that enables its possessor to shift the focus of desire from a material object, subject to corruption and vulnerable to fortune, to an image of the mnemonist's own creation, which can never be damaged or lost. Mastery of this skill is associated with virtuous behaviour and an immunity to the risks associated with fortune, both good and bad. In both poems, this skill is represented as being at once beneficial for any human subject, and as a discipline closely linked with nobility, with the courtiers whose political involvement necessarily exposes them to radical shifts in their personal circumstances.

Yet, if the art of memory is appropriate to the prince, it also belongs to the writer, as part of the art of rhetoric on which poetic craft depends. Thus, the poet can take on the role of teacher, as in the *Confort*, or appear in the character of an exemplary student, like the narrator of the *Remede*. As a craftsman, Machaut is able to highlight the dangers of artifice, drawing attention to the possibility that the artist might, like Pygmalion, be seduced by his own creation. Rather than using the image as an instrument, to achieve the end of moral living, mnemonists might fall victim to the sin of *curiositas*, wandering from their true object in enjoying the image as a thing in itself. The proper use of such images demands an aptitude for judging the nature of one's own intentions, an awareness of the danger of self-deception.

The part played by *The Consolation of Philosophy* in both these poems implies that it was regarded not only as a text whose teachings complemented the instruction Machaut seeks to offer his audience, but also as a work already identified with the themes of the mnemonic arts, literary skill, and the education of the nobility. The relationship that exists between these texts and the *Consolation* serves as an indication of the subjects they address. Each bears interpretation as a text that not only demonstrates how Boethian wisdom might find practical application in contemporary society, but which also tends to displace the authority of the *Consolation*, in accruing its functions to itself. The following chapters trace the development of this practice of Boethian adaptation in texts examining how this philosophical approach to misfortune might be experienced by those who have suffered political misfortune.

Chapter 3
Boethian Discipline:
Desire and Restraint in Guillaume de Machaut's *Fonteinne amoureuse*

In Guillaume de Machaut's *Fonteinne amoureuse*, literal and figurative representations of imprisonment intersect in a fluid relation that contributes to the mutual transformation of Boethian philosophy and life history enacted in the text. The interchangeability of the literal and allegorical values associated with imprisonment is reflected in the complaint attributed to Machaut's noble protagonist, who imagines incarceration as a barrier that divides him from the object of his affection: 'aler n'i puis, car je suis en gëole, /Ou bon loisir ay d'apenre a l'escole' ['I cannot go there, because I am in gaol, where I am disposed to learn as in school'] (823–4).[1] Yet the relationship between desire and imprisonment is rapidly transfigured, with the emergence of the familiar literary trope of the prison of love:

> C'est ma dame qui tient en sa prison
> Mon loial cuer; a trop bonne occoison
> Y devint siens maugré li; c'est raison
> Qu'il oubeïsse
> Et qu'il y soit en tele entencion
> Que mis jamais n'i soit a raënçon
> Et qu'il y muire ou qu'il ait guerredon
> Qui le garisse,
> Qu'amez ou mors sera, eins qu'il en isse. (827–5)

> [It is my lady who keeps my faithful he\art in her prison; in too pleasant a time it became hers in spite of itself; it is just that it obey and be of such a persuasion that it will never be ransomed, and will die there or have the reward that will heal it. For it will be loved or dead, sooner than leave.]

In imagining the noble subject's willing acceptance of restraint, the *Fonteinne* at once evokes the historical circumstances of the patron for whom Machaut wrote, Jean, duc de Berry (1340–1416), together with a mode of self-discipline that reflects contemporary interpretations of Boethian philosophy in serving the

---

[1]   Guillaume de Machaut, *Le livre de la Fontaine amoureuse*, ed. Jacqueline Cerquiglini-Toulet (Paris: Stock, 1993), cited by line number, with my translations. For a complete English translation, see the bilingual edition *The Fountain of Love (La Fontaine Amoureuse) and Two Other Love Vision Poems*, ed. and trans. R. Barton Palmer (New York: Garland, 1993).

interests of the state. Under the terms of the treaty of Brétigny, ratified at Calais on 24 October 1360, Jean was pledged to travel to England as one of the hostages offered as surety for the ransom of his father, Jean II, securing the king's return to France.[2] Machaut's poem invites the reader to identify the aristocratic figure at its heart with Jean de Berry, as it describes the mental suffering of a prince obliged to leave his beloved and travel to a foreign land, in exile with no fixed date of return (for example, 200–205, 2248, 1451, 1471). The *Fonteinne* anticipates the recognition of this relationship between literature and life, instructing the reader to find or compose (*trouver*) the names of the author and his subject in deciphering an anagrammatical signature concealed within the text (45–52). Such anagrams both invite and delimit the activity of the reader, since their inherent obscurity and, frequently, the deficiency of the puzzle, demand collusion: the reader must draw upon prior knowledge to generate the solution that authorises the text.[3] In recognising Jean de Berry and Guillaume de Machaut as the *Fonteinne*'s protagonists, readers assent to, and participate in, the re-authorship of these subjects performed within the text.

Perhaps composed as early as 1360, and in circulation by 1362, the *Fonteinne* addresses an issue of vital political importance in envisaging the consolation of a prince obliged to go into exile.[4] The prince of the *Fonteinne* is presented as a model of virtue, and the relationship between this figure and Jean de Berry is implicit in the assertion that he is of such 'bel arroy /Qu'il sambloit estre fils a roy' ['noble demeanour, That he seemed to be the son of a king'] (1157–8). Yet this praise gives way to a critical reflection on rich men, whose failure to fulfil their duties is distinguished as the origin of a contemporary social and economic crisis (1161–200). The idea that the performance of duty has a direct impact upon the health of the state not only carries a particular force for the aristocracy of a country riven by war and suffering the repercussions of the Jacquerie, but is also especially relevant to the situation of a prince pledged to become a hostage under the terms of the treaty of Brétigny. Set at three million *écus*, Jean II's ransom was a debt of such magnitude that timely payment was always a doubtful prospect; historical

---

[2] On the Treaty of Brétigny, see John Le Patourel, 'The Treaty of Brétigny, 1360', *Transactions of the Royal Historical Society*, 5th ser., 10 (1960): 19–39, and Anne Curry, *The Hundred Years War*, 2nd edn (Houndmills: Palgrave, 2003).

[3] On Machaut's anagrams, see Laurence de Looze, '"Mon nom trouveras": a New Look at the Anagrams of Guillaume de Machaut. The Enigmas, Responses, and Solutions', *Romanic Review* 79.4 (1988): 537–57; and Deborah McGrady, *Controlling Readers: Guillaume de Machaut and his Late Medieval Audience* (Toronto: University of Toronto Press, 2006), 72–4. These arguments serve as a corrective to Margaret J. Ehrhart's critique of the traditional identification of the prince with Jean de Berry, which turns on the solution to the anagram and cannot account for the poem's allusions to a literal imprisonment, 'Machaut's *Dit de la fonteinne amoureuse*, the Choice of Paris, and the Duties of Rulers', *Philological Quarterly* 59 (1980): 119–39 (121–3).

[4] A *terminus ad quem* is suggested by an allusion to the poem in letter 4 of the *Voir Dit* (letter 6 in Paulin Paris's edn), see Armand Machabey, *Guillaume de Machault 130?– 1377: La vie et l'œuvre musical*, 2 vols (Paris: Richard-Masse, 1955), 1: 57–8.

evidence reflects an understandable reluctance on the part of the hostages, and suggests that the compliance of the king's sons was of crucial importance in determining the actions of their fellows.[5] Notoriously, the implications of a prince's refusal were to be realised in 1363: frustrated by the continuing failure to satisfy the terms of the treaty, Louis d'Anjou violated an agreement allowing the hostages to serve their time at Calais, and even to absent themselves for up to four days with the permission of Edward III. Rather than return to captivity following a pilgrimage to Notre-Dame de Boulogne, Louis broke the solemn oath required of the hostages and remained with his young wife, Marie de Châtillon. Wishing to avoid the resumption of hostilities with England at a time when Charles II of Navarre posed an imminent military threat, Jean II took his son's place, embarking for England on 3 January 1364, where he was to die a few months later.[6]

Although imprisonment was something of an occupational hazard for medieval noblemen, and did not necessarily entail physical discomfort, it nevertheless carried a stigma; it was typically perceived as 'a demeaning experience to be thrust into oblivion immediately on release [...] lest a man lose status in the eyes of his fellows'.[7] Machaut's prince is not only concerned with the pain he will suffer in leaving his lady and his homeland, but also with the threat incarceration poses to his honour. He grieves that, during his youth, when he ought to be striving to establish his reputation, he is instead 'en cage [...] Ou faire puis moult po de vassalage /Que je repute a moy moult grant dommage' ['locked up ... where I can perform very few gallant deeds, which I consider a very grave injury'] (402–5). Within a culture where chivalry functioned as a distinguishing practice, defining the place of the aristocracy within the social order, this was a serious concern, and one that also finds acknowledgment in another literary depiction of a Brétigny hostage, Jean Froissart's *Dit dou bleu chevalier*.[8] Froissart's knight is assailed by lovesickness and the fear of a double loss of time and reputation, to the point that he no longer knows which of the two pains him more.[9]

The strategic importance attached to these hostages, and the extent to which their captive status was a matter of personal choice, combine to invest the consolations offered in poems like the *Fonteinne* with a political significance that belies attempts to construe them as escapist entertainments, in contrast to openly

---

[5]   Françoise Lehoux, *Jean de France, duc de Berri: Sa vie, son action politique, 1340–1416*, 4 vols (Paris: Picard, 1966–1968), 1. 157.

[6]   On Louis d'Anjou's recusancy, R. Delachenal, *Histoire de Charles V*, 5 vols (Paris: Picard, 1909–31), 2. 346–7; for an analysis of Jean II's actions, see Raymond Cazelles, *Société politique, noblesse et couronne sous Jean le Bon et Charles V* (Geneva: Droz, 1982), 447–2.

[7]   Dunbabin, *Captivity and Imprisonment*, 162.

[8]   On chivalry and social distinction, see Lee Patterson, *Chaucer and the Subject of History* (London: Routledge, 1991), 168–79.

[9]   Jean Froissart, *Dit dou bleu chevalier*, in *'Dits' et 'Débats'*, ed. Anthime Fourrier (Geneva: Droz, 1979), ll. 275–94. Rupert T. Pickens, 'History and Narration in Froissart's *Dits*: The Case of the *Bleu Chevalier*', in Donald Maddox and Sara Sturm-Maddox (eds), *Froissart Across the Genres* (Florida: University of Florida Press, 1998), 119–52.

didactic texts such as the *Confort d'ami*.[10] Rather than being a distraction from
political misfortune, the *Fonteinne* resembles the *Confort*, since it distinguishes
itself as a text concerned with the education of princes through its relationship
to the *Consolation of Philosophy*. It is a relationship that appears all the more
striking because, unlike the *Confort*, the *Fonteinne* does not address itself to an
absent lord. Instead, Machâut emulates Boethius in depicting the pain of political
exile and the process of consolation experienced by an aristocratic subject. The
Fonteinne evokes the memory of the *Consolation* to generate a commonplace,
linking the authoritative text with a particular experience of exile, in a dynamic
relation that enlarges and alters the meaning of both.[11] One effect of this conjunction
of literature and historical life is to endorse the recasting of the prison-house
as a place of education, where one might be disposed to learn. While Boethius
presents his historical situation as that of exile, rather than incarceration, he makes
significant use of the imagery of imprisonment, and medieval tradition elided
the distinction through manuscript iconography, commentary, and other addenda
identifying Boethius as a prisoner.[12] The idea of the prison as the scene of Boethian
education, a place where the subject might repeat the philosopher's performance
in cultivating the wisdom essential to a good ruler, is a key influence on the literary
tradition described by Robert Epstein, in which 'conventions of imprisonment are
constitutive to subjectivity', and especially so for the aristocratic subject.[13]

The currency and significance of prison imagery in late-medieval culture is
not simply an inheritance from the *Consolation*, however; it marks a continuing
engagement with multivalent philosophical and theological traditions theorizing the
relationship between body and soul.[14] In Christian thought, the Platonic metaphor
of the body as a prison for the soul complements the trope of human life as a form
of exile. As Pope Innocent III formulates it in his highly influential *De miseria
condicionis humane*, virtue entails the recognition of this state of affairs, so that

---

[10]   For interpretations which propose a categorical distinction between the *Fonteinne*
and the *Confort*, see Robert Deschaux, 'Consolateur d'illustres exclus: Guillaume de
Machaut', *Exclus et systèms d'exclusion dans la littérature et la civilisation médiévales*.
Actes du colloque organise par le C.U.E.R. M.A. à Aix-en-Provence, les 4–5–6 mars 1977
(Paris: Champion, 1978), 59–67; and Lechat, *'Dire par fiction'*, 137. See also Jean-Claude
Mühlethaler, 'Entre amour et politique: métamorphoses ovidiennes à la fin du Moyen Âge:
la fable de Céyx et Alcyoné de l'*Ovide moralisé* à Christine de Pizan et Alain Chartier',
Cahiers de Recherches Médiévales, 9 (2002): 143–56.

[11]   On the commonplace as a mutually transformative gathering, where text and life
converge, see Carruthers, *The Book of Memory*, 217–27.

[12]   See Summers, *Late-Medieval Prison Writing*, 16–17, and, on manuscript
iconography, Courcelle, *La Consolation*.

[13]   Robert Epstein, 'Prisoners of Reflection: The Fifteenth-Century Poetry of Exile and
Imprisonment', *Exemplaria* 15 (2003): 159–98 (162).

[14]   On these traditions, see Pierre Courcelle, 'Tradition platonicienne et traditions
chrétiennes du corps-prison (*Phédon* 62b; *Cratyle* 400c)', *Revue des études latines*,
43 (1965): 406–43, and 'L'Âme en Cage', in Kurt Flasch (ed.), *Parusia: Studien zur
Philosophie Platons und zur Problemgeschichte des Platonismus. Festgabe für Johannes
Hirschberger* (Frankfurt: Minerva, 1965), 103–16.

'the just man [...] endures the world as a place of exile, confined in the body as in a prison'.[15] In the *Consolation*, Philosophy privileges the experience of adversity as a revelation of the true nature of Fortune: 'Celle qui se cele encores aux autres s'est toute monstree a toy' ['she who still conceals herself to others has revealed all to you'] (2.pr.1). Implicit in both examples is the idea that apprehension of the authentic conditions of human existence relies on corporeal experience, on forms of cognition that make figurative analogies between the material world and spiritual things. A similar conception of the impact of embodiment upon intellection is reflected in Aquinas's arguments on the cultivation of memory as an aspect of the virtue of prudence: 'Lighting on such images and likenesses is necessary, because simple and spiritual ideas slip somewhat easily out of mind unless they are tied [*alligentur*], as it were, to bodily images; human knowledge has more mastery over objects of sense'.[16] Against this background, experience of the conditions of exile or imprisonment might be regarded as an aid to philosophical education, since this form of misfortune not only dispels the perilous illusion of worldly prosperity, but also affords a visceral insight into the terms commonly used to represent the real nature of human life.

Positive law and the prison were themselves theorized as institutions engendered by the relationship between body and soul in a fallen world. For Augustine, prelapsarian humanity was not purely spiritual in nature, but corporeal, and the Fall marks a rupture between body and spirit that originates in the will's perverse rebellion against God. Its effect mirrors its origin: concupiscence opens a fissure in the self, as an obscure appetite that exceeds conscious control. After the Fall, in both the body and human society, the harmonious concord of the members yields to the bitter government of a discipline achieved through coercion.[17] Augustine's formulation of the problem allows for the existence of sex in Paradise and, while he regards continence as a superior means to transcendence in a fallen world, he also conceives marriage and friendship as expressions of a divinely instituted social being, which anticipate the concord of the City of God. Sexual desire was not the most damaging consequence of the Fall in Augustine's interpretation, but his reading shapes the landscape of Christian thought, contributing to what Peter Brown identifies as 'a muted but tenacious tendency to treat sexuality as a privileged ideogram of all that was most irreducible in the human will'.[18]

---

[15] Lothario dei Segni (Pope Innocent III), *De miseria condicionis humane*, ed. and trans. Robert E. Lewis (Athens: University of Georgia Press, 1978), 124.

[16] Aquinas, *Summa Theologiæ*, 2a2æ. 49. I, 63.

[17] Augustine, *The City of God against the Pagans*, ed. and trans. R.W. Dyson (Cambridge: Cambridge University Press, 1998), 14. 23, 623–5; Peter Brown, *The Body and Society: Men, Women, and Sexual Renunciation in Early Christianity* (New York: Columbia University Press, 1988), 404–5. My discussion is also indebted to Lochrie, *Margery Kempe*, 19–47.

[18] Peter Brown, 'Bodies and Minds: Sexuality and Renunciation in Early Christianity', in David M. Halperin, John J. Winkler and Froma I. Zeitlin (eds), *Before Sexuality: The Construction of Erotic Experience in the Ancient Greek World* (Princeton: Princeton University Press, 1990), 481; Brown, *Body and Society*, 402–3.

The idea that the human community is the imperfect expression of a sociality that points towards the unity of the divine, and that loving concord foreshadows a higher form of government, manifests itself in the culture of love and friendship whose impact on medieval Europe has been traced by C. Stephen Jaeger. Privileging erotic discourse as the idiom of political and social interactions, the culture of 'ennobling love' resists the imposition of modern distinctions between the realms of private emotion and public life. It entails the performance of social gestures that systematically invoke the experience of libidinous desire, yet the performative quality of such gestures marks them as spectacles of control, rather than purely impulsive effusions. As Jaeger argues, 'Social gesture displays policy, based on an art of representing intention, and like any other work of art, it is a product of calculation and planning'.[19] Ennobling love is an aspirational practice, which distinguishes its practitioners in casting their interactions as those of subjects in whom the will works in concord with the dictates of reason; its effect is to produce society as a reflection of the divine order.

In framing political consolation in the language of love, Machaut's *Fonteinne amoureuse* contributes to a burgeoning literary tradition which expounds Boethian philosophy in amatory terms. The eroticisation of Boethius is often identified as a late-medieval innovation, however, the convergence of love and politics within these texts speaks to the central concerns of the *Consolation*.[20] Identifying the multifarious forms of human desire as distorted expressions of the fundamental longing for a state of sufficiency that mirrors the essence of the divine, a mode of being complete within itself and untouched by need, the *Consolation* locates the cause of human unhappiness in the disordered will, which is unable to recognise the true object of its appetites. Boethius's analysis coincides with the Augustinian theorisation of the human condition in a postlapsarian world; moreover, the *Consolation* also grants a privileged position to the role of love in governance. This idea is powerfully expressed by Philosophy, who identifies the ordering principle at work in the universe as 'vrayë amour', conceived as a 'souverain seignour', a sovereign lord who reigns in heaven and on earth. Her argument indicates that divine love finds only a limited expression in human society, and imagines the effects of love's dissolution:

> [...] s'il vouloit laschier sa resne,
> Guerres feroient toutes choses
> Qui par lui sont en paix encloses,
> Et si fort se guerroieroient
> Que le monde despeceroient[...]
> Ceste amour lïe les couraiges
> Des saulx et le bons marriages,
> Et touz les vrays amis ralie
> Et tient en bonne compaignie.

---

[19]   Jaeger, *Ennobling Love*, 20.

[20]   See, for example, the arguments of Miller, *Philosophical Chaucer*, 156, and Kay, 'Touching Singularity', 21, both of whom identify Jean de Meun as a key innovator in the eroticisation of Boethius.

Hommes seroient en bon point
Se l'amour, qui les cieulx conjoint,
Les cuers ensemble ralïoit,
Droitte beneürté seroit (2.m.8)

[If he were to let slip the reins, all things that he encloses in peace would
make war, and would war amongst themselves so forcefully that the world
would sunder into pieces…This love binds the hearts of those who are to be
redeemed and good marriages, and joins all true friends, and holds them in noble
companionship. The human condition would be a happy one if love, who unites
the heavens, were to unite our hearts; it would be a blessed ordinance.]

It is significant that while the medieval translation depoliticises the metrum to an
extent, in omitting the claim that such love is at work in treaties between nations,
it retains the idea that concord in marriage and friendship is a manifestation of
divine love.[21] Yet this endorsement of human relations is heavily qualified in the
concluding wish, which serves as a reminder that divine love does not rule the
human heart. As the image of love relaxing the reins of the universe implies, order
is maintained through an effort of will, and the figure is thus an apt expression
of the labour Philosophy requires of Boethius, in curbing and redirecting his
desire as he comes to recognise its true object. The *Consolation* therefore not
only anticipates the political applications of Boethian philosophy, as I have argued
in previous chapters, but its conception of the relationship between love and the
government of both self and state is precursor to the ideology underpinning the
public practice of love in medieval culture.

Machaut's *Fontaine* brings these ideas into alignment as the poet elaborates an
arresting opening image describing his decision to write a work in honour of his
beloved:

Pour moy deduire et sou*lacier*
Et pour ma pensee *lacier*
En loial amour qui me *lace*
En ses *las*, ou point ne me *lasse*
Car jamais ne seroie *las*
D'estre y, ne n'en diroie 'he*las*'
(1–6, my emphasis)

[To divert and solace myself, and to lace up my thoughts in loyal love that laces
me in its laces, of which I do not tire, for I would never grow tired of being there,
nor would I say 'alas!']

The insistent repetition of the syllable 'las' in the figure of *annominatio* evokes
and challenges the perception of constraint as an affliction, as it underlines the
narrator's free choice of subjection as the precondition of pleasure.[22] His poem is

---

21   *Philosophiae Consolatio*: 'Hic sancto populos quoque /iunctos foedere continet'.
22   Cerquiglini-Toulet notes this phonetic play in the introduction to her edition, but
does not comment on its effects, *Fonteinne*, 12.

to inspire joy in both poet and audience: 'Vueil commencier a chiere lie [...] Chose qui sera liement /Věuě' ['I shall begin with a joyful air ... something that will be joyfully received'] (7–10). In its style, the *Fonteinne* is as playful as its opening suggests, not only linguistically, but also in its other effects: the troubles of Jean de Berry are given a positive valuation, and the figure of the narrator in particular is treated as a source of comedy. Yet the poem also insists on a fundamental connection between pleasure and discipline. The conception of writing as an activity which entails the binding of one's thoughts with cords is reminiscent of the image Augustine uses to describe the ordering schemes employed in memory work, the vital instrument of literary composition, and of Aquinas's allusion to the tying of spiritual ideas to bodily images in his discussion of memory.[23] In this respect, the amatory and pleasurable nature of the ties which are to bind thought suggests the importance placed on affectivity in writings on memory, as a response which can stimulate the process of recollection.

The opening of the *Fonteinne* establishes a link between the art of writing and self-discipline that reflects the ethical valuation placed on the exercise of memory, and the morality of the narrator's activity is underscored in the description of his love as 'loial', which also carries the senses 'legal' and 'Christian'. In presenting the narrator's decision to write as a form of self-consolation that inspires pleasure, the poem endorses a connection between bondage and enjoyment. This relationship is significantly reinforced as the narrator introduces the anagram in which he names himself and his patron, contained in lines 40–41, and described as an obligation to which he is constrained by the command of 'Amours fine' and Delight:

> Avec mon cuer y a bon gage
> Car mes corps en est en ostage
> Qui jamais jour ne cessera
> Jusques a tant que fais sera (37, 41–4)

> [With my heart, he has a good pledge, because my body is held hostage to this end, that will never rest a day until it is done]

The conjunction of pleasure and restraint might evoke the psychosexual pathology of masochism for the modern reader, yet the mode of enjoyment envisaged in the *Fonteinne* is precisely non-compulsive. It is defined as instrumental activity rather than spontaneous pleasure, a distinction that identifies this form of satisfaction as a synthetic version of the prelapsarian state, where desire does not elude control.[24] The reception of the *Consolation* as a text illuminating the role of mnemonic exercise as self-administered therapy, traced in previous chapters, identifies

---

[23]   Augustine, *Confessions*, trans. William Watts, 2 vols (London: Heinemann, 1912), Book X.12, 106–9. I follow Carruthers in reading this passage in the context of rhetorical *memoria*, see *The Craft of Thought*, 32–5.

[24]   On the distinction between instrumental activity and spontaneous pleasure, see Slavoj Žižek, *The Plague of Fantasies*, 2nd edn (London: Verso, 2008), 20. My analysis is also indebted to Miller's interpretation of the *Consolation*, *Philosophical Chaucer*, 111–51.

memory work as the pre-eminent form of such instrumental activity, and a means to establish concord between will and reason. The narrator's desire is 'loial amour' because it finds expression in a self-discipline conducive to the spiritual well-being of the subject and the good of society, rather than in cupidity, which endangers both the self and the social order. In signalling his pleasure in submitting to the discipline of writing, Machaut constructs himself as both consummate artist and moral exemplar.

Medieval jurisprudence conceived the moral fetters established by the acceptance of behavioural constraints as being analogous to physical bonds, creating the conditions for forms of detention like that experienced by Jean de Berry and his fellow hostages at Calais.[25] The *Fonteinne* replicates the equation underpinning such arrangements as it simultaneously anticipates the anagrammatical naming of Jean de Berry and hints at the problem of his political situation in casting the poet as hostage. The effect is that of an unsettling motion between literal and figurative conceptions of imprisonment, to be echoed in the interchangeability of these states within the prince's complaint. It is significant that the complaint also produces a temporal disjunction, as the prince sometimes speaks as though he were already imprisoned when his incarceration is still ostensibly a future event, further blurring the boundaries between literal and subjective forms of imprisonment. These literary devices focus attention on the subject's intellectual response to restraint, rather than the contingent circumstances which are its cause, as an ethical problem with serious consequences.

As the example of Louis d'Anjou demonstrates, moral bonds could be broken, but doing so imperils the state as it exposes the consensual basis of the social order, and such actions inflict a corresponding wound on the subject's public image: the terms of the oath taken by the hostages voiced a wish that oath-breakers should be universally held as perjurers and convicted of a lapse of faith.[26] Machaut's poem offers consolation to his patron in framing captivity as a situation that throws the essential problem of humanity's fallen nature into relief, affording the opportunity to recognise the true object of desire and, by this means, to achieve the ability to function in the world without being incapacitated by frustrated longing. Rather than being simply an obstruction to the chivalric and amatory practices of self-definition employed by the aristocracy, the *Fonteinne* constructs the prison as a privileged site of self-fashioning, a place of memory associated with the development of mnemonic skill.

In its role as an instrument used to systematise the workings of the mind, facilitating and optimising its function as storehouse and means of production, memory training can be understood as a form of technology. As Mary Carruthers observes:

> Medieval *memoria* was a universal thinking machine, *machina memorialis* – both the mill that ground the grain of one's experiences (including all that one

---

[25] Dunbabin, *Captivity and Imprisonment*, 43.

[26] Delachenal, *Charles V*, 346–7 and n6.

read) into a mental flour with which one could make wholesome bread, and also the hoist or windlass that every wise master-builder learnt to make and use in constructing new matter.[27]

The conception of memory as a mechanism whose most highly valued product is the ethical subject reflects the sense that human ingenuity might moderate the effects of the Fall.[28] In establishing a predisposition to moral behaviour, the exercise of memory nourishes the health and stability of the social order; it civilises. Yet this function of human invention also serves as a reminder of the lack that necessitates its role: the artificial nature of its products is the mark of the Fall, just as the coercive aspect of discipline recalls the loss of an unforced harmony between will and reason even as it works to establish order.[29] Machaut's *Fonteinne* acknowledges this paradox as it foregrounds the affinity between the rhetorical arts of memory and writing, and other forms of invention.

The *Fonteinne*'s concern with the nature of art is signalled in its title, which takes a duplex form: Machaut calls the poem 'mon livre de *Morpheüs*, que on appelle *La Fontaine Amoureuse*' ['my book of *Morpheus*, called *La Fontaine Amoureuse*'].[30] This doubling is repeated in two of the nine manuscripts in which the *Fonteinne* appears, MSS E and M, both completed after the poet's death.[31] The more familiar title identifies the poem with the fountain upon which it centres, both in its action and spatially: itself named 'la *Fonteinne amoureuse*', its description occurs at the midpoint of the text, and it is the focal point of the poem's garden setting (1413). William Calin astutely comments that, in its essence, the fountain is the embodiment of the poem, an observation borne out by recent work on the cultural significance of fountains.[32] In his study of mechanical culture in the early modern period, Jonathan Sawday draws attention to the ways in which developments in hydraulic science contribute to a fascination with water and the mechanisms used to channel its potentially destructive force. Such technological innovations had a moral dimension: on the one hand, they promised to maximise the value of water to human society, sustaining life and promoting civilisation; on the other, these mechanisms might become an indulgence, serving no purpose beyond the

---

27   Carruthers, *The Craft of Thought*, 4.

28   On this perspective, derived from Cicero and manifested in the work of Duns Scotus and Hugh of St Victor, see Jonathan Sawday, *Engines of the Imagination: Renaissance Culture and the Rise of the Machine* (London: Routledge, 2007), 3, 321n10. See also Jessica Wolfe, *Humanism, Machinery, and Renaissance Literature* (Cambridge: Cambridge University Press, 2004).

29   On the pessimistic view of technology, see Sawday, *Engines of the Imagination*, 4.

30   Guillaume de Machaut, *Le Livre du Voir Dit*, ed. and trans. Paul Imbs, rev. Jacqueline Cerquiglini-Toulet, Lettres Gothiques (Paris: Livre de Poche, 1999), Letter 10, 186.

31   Paris, Bibliothèque Nationale, MS fr. 9221 (E), and MS fr. 843 (M), see Earp, *Guillaume de Machaut*, 92–4, 95, 220.

32   William Calin, '*La Fonteinne amoureuse* de Machaut: son or, ses oeuvres-d'art, ses mises en abyme,' in *L'Or au Moyen Age: monnaie–métal–objets–symbole* (Aix-en-Provence: C.U.E.R. M.A., 1983), 85–6.

provision of a spectacular source of enjoyment. The fountain in particular was a locus of tension between the aesthetic pleasures and practical applications of hydraulic engineering.[33] Against this background, the enduring literary trope of the fountain is invested with new meaning, so that its traditional functions, as an emblem of poetic making and as a feature of political discourse, increasingly converge.[34] Machaut's *Fonteinne amoureuse* anticipates later developments in adopting the fountain as the emblem of a concern with the tensions at work in the imagination, and with their impact upon the human subject and the social order.

In its double form, the poem's title underlines the affinity between material and cognitive forms of invention, as it links the fountain with the figure of Morpheus, emphasising the relationship between these symbols established within the *Fonteinne*. The plot of the *Fonteinne* repeatedly foregrounds artistry, presenting itself as the narrator's account of the consequences of a restless night, during which he overheard and transcribed the poetic complaint composed by a lover in an adjoining room. Separated from his beloved and facing a period of imprisonment, the lover recalls the Ovidian myth of Ceyx and Alcyone. Remembering how Morpheus, son of the god of sleep, appeared to Alcyone in the form of her dead husband, he entreats the god to intervene on his behalf and bear a message of love to his lady. Marvelling at the skill of the poem he has written, the following day the narrator offers homage to the lover, a nobleman who has long desired the poet's company. Together, they walk through a park to a magnificent fountain, mounted on a pillar of ivory carved with the myth of Narcissus. Its marble basin displays scenes from the history of the Trojan War, and at its centre stands a golden serpent with 12 heads, which causes the fountain to play unceasingly, 'par engines et par conduis' ['by means of mechanisms and conduits'] (1345).

Commissioned by Jupiter and Venus and made by Pygmalion, the fountain is famed for its ability to make the drinker amorous, but the nobleman and the poet refuse to drink, because they are already surfeited with love. The nobleman explains the nature of his own erotic trouble, requesting that the narrator compose a poem, since 'la practique /Savez toute, et la theorique /D'amour loial' ['you know all about the practice and theory of loyal love'] (1505–7). The narrator responds by presenting him with the copy of his own complaint, and the pair fall asleep, sharing a vision in which the beloved lady appears in company with Venus to console the nobleman. Her success is measured by the poem's conclusion, as the narrator departs into exile willingly, armed against the assaults of fortune. Yet the *Fonteinne* ends with a question: 'Dites moy, fu ce bien songié?' ['Tell me, was this well dreamed?'] (2848).

As its concluding query suggests, the *Fonteinne* accentuates the ways in which dreaming and the composition of poetry intersect within medieval culture, and as these two experiences bleed into one another within the poem, they open up a space in which the nature of imagination is being negotiated. The implication that

---

[33] Sawday, *Engines of the Imagination*, 31–47.

[34] Hester Lees-Jeffries, *England's Helicon: Fountains in Early Modern Literature and Culture*. (Oxford: Oxford University Press, 2007), 23.

the *Fonteinne* itself is a dream, a form of thought-experiment that explores the potential consequences of Jean de Berry's response to the problem of captivity, evokes the enduring function of the vision as a figure for mnemonic composition. As a practice which entails sustained periods of deep thought, including the mental projection of vivid images, memory work resembles sleep both in the appearance it presents and in the fantastic nature of the experience to which it gives rise. In combination with the mnemonist's typical preference for conditions of solitude and silence, this aspect of memory work informs the cultural shift through which the bedroom becomes a privileged locus for the interaction between readers and texts, as reading is increasingly constructed as a private experience.[35] Dreaming and mnemonic activity also resemble one another as experiences that depend upon the action of the imagination, the cognitive faculty that medieval psychology regarded as including both the unconscious part of the brain that interprets sensory information and turns it into images, and the conscious ability to combine such images to create new ones, of things which do not exist. Imagination might produce useful images, conducive to a better understanding of the world and an enhanced ability to function within it, or misleading ones, whose effects are manifested in idolatry and *insomnia*, dreams of the satisfaction of frustrated desires or nightmares.[36] In drawing attention to the coincidence between memory work, literary invention, and dreaming, the *Fonteinne* poses a question about the utility of the imagination, and the subject's ability to regulate its potential to facilitate or impede function.

The concurrence of dreaming and writing is established from the outset of the *Fonteinne*, as the narrator lies in a state of 'dorveille /Com cils qui dort et encore veille' ['half-slumber, like those who sleep yet are still awake'] (63–4). This liminal state of consciousness is associated with literary composition and reflects the archetypal mnemonic state; the reader might therefore anticipate a vision, representing the labour of invention carried out through memory work.[37] What follows, however, is framed not as invention, but as the transcription of the prince's complaint. Composition is presented as a shared act, in which the patron plays the most significant role, as source of the sentiment that animates the poem, and even of the poetic skill employed therein.[38] Moreover, the nobleman's experience suggests the function of poetry as a form of safety valve, a means to channel a dangerous excess of emotion to a useful end: the poem traces his movement

---

[35] On the conditions of solitude and silence, see Carruthers, *The Book of Memory*, 215–16. On the bedroom as locus of textual reception, see McGrady, *Controlling Readers*, 42–3.

[36] See Kelly, *Medieval Imagination*, 54, 57, and Minnis, 'Medieval Imagination and Memory', 239–74.

[37] Michel Zink, 'The Allegorical Poem as Interior Memoir', trans. Margaret Miner and Kevin Brownlee, *Yale French Studies* 70 (1986): 100–126; Carruthers, *The Craft of Thought*, 171–220.

[38] For an astute reading of Machaut's innovative treatment of patronage, see Deborah McGrady, '"Tout son païs m'abandonna": Reinventing Patronage in Machaut's "Fonteinne amoureuse"', *Yale French Studies*, 110 (2006): 19–31.

from an animalistic state, as a 'creature' who can emit only inarticulate sounds, to consummate expression (70, 195). A parallel between this aspect of poetry and the fountain, as technologies for the management of potentially destructive forces associated with love, is suggested by the terms in which the narrator recognises the prince's poetic skill, identifying him as the possessor of 'l'engin si soutil' ['ingenious intellect'] (1514). The mechanical quality of composition, the extent to which it is the product of calculation, rather than spontaneous effusion, is further underscored by allusions to the technical virtuosity of the complaint, which contains one hundred different rhymes (1021, 1052). This twofold act of textual production, performed in twin bedchambers, is echoed in the dream shared by the side of the fountain, which likewise suggests a mutual act of literary composition.

Insofar as the production of the complaint implies that the prince is already able to sublimate his frustrated desire in poetic labour, and thus displays a familiarity with the mode of discipline envisaged by the narrator at the poem's outset, the *Fonteinne* offers a diplomatic form of consolation: Machaut recognises the prince as a moral authority in his own right. Yet, as Jacqueline Cerquiglini-Toulet argues, these shared acts of literary creation also obscure conventional distinctions between clerical and chivalric identities, constructing an image of the ideal subject as one who unites the qualities of knight and clerk, resolving tensions between the active life of arms and the contemplative occupations of the cleric.[39] This amalgamation furthermore suggests the need for a balance between the spiritual or abstract qualities of art and its practical applications, a message underlined in the treatment of the figure of Morpheus. As Didier Lechat argues, the *Fonteinne* establishes a parallel between Morpheus and the poet, through the prince's analogous commissions to both for labour that will ease the pain of his love, a connection reinforced by the coincidence between Morpheus's name and that of another mythological figure celebrated as a poetic archetype, Orpheus.[40] In this respect, the figure of Morpheus embodies the connections between the imaginative works of dreaming and textual invention in medieval culture, and his significance for the poem is highlighted in Machaut's designation of the work as the 'livre de *Morpheüs*'.

Morpheus's role in the Ovidian myth supplies a model for the method of consolation propounded within the *Fonteinne*, as the protean god appears to Alcyone in the image of Ceyx. Reflection on the image of the absent object of desire is invested with healing power in the discourse of the beloved lady, as she appears in the shared vision of prince and poet. The prince is advised to emulate her example:

Ne la doleur ne la morsure
D'amours, ne chose que j'endure

---

[39] See the introduction to Cerquiglini-Toulet's edition of the *Fonteinne*, 19, and 'Tension sociale et tension d'écriture au XIVème siècle: les dits de Guillaume de Machaut,' in Danielle Buschinger, ed. *Littérature et société au moyen âge*, Actes du colloque d'Amiens des 5 et 6 mai 1978 (Paris: Champion, 1978), 111–29.

[40] Lechat, *Dire par fiction*, 148–9, 176.

Pour toy, tres douce creature,
Ne doubteray,
Car d'Esperance la seüre
Par ton ymage nette et pure
Contre Desire et sa pointure
Me garniray (2263–70)

[neither the pain nor the wound of love, nor anything I bear for your sake, very
sweet creature, will I fear, because I shall arm myself with sure Hope through
your clear and pure image, against desire and its sting.]

Although they are separated, she argues, 'Par pensee te suis procheinne' ['in
thought I am near you'] (2288). The approach to consolation developed here
echoes the strategies advocated in the *Remede* and *Confort*: the satisfaction of
longing is associated with its redirection towards a mental image of the desired
object, rather than the object itself. As I have argued, this methodology of
consolation is in sympathy with a reception history that understood the Boethian
text as an exemplary model illuminating the exercise of memory as a remedy for
the pain of desire. Within the *Fonteinne*, this Boethian tradition undergoes further
development as it is associated with a particular instance of captivity, investing the
experience of imprisonment with new meaning.

In her role as a female figure whose appearance in a vision consoles the
subject through a process of instruction that reconciles him to his fate as an exile,
the lady of the *Fonteinne* resembles Philosophy to an even greater extent than
her counterparts in the *Remede de Fortune*. Her dual function as beloved and
comforter contributes to the eroticisation of Boethian philosophy consolidated
in medieval literature, which entails and develops the use of sexual desire as a
figure for the compulsive agitation of the will. Moreover, within the *Fonteinne*,
the Boethian conception of appetite, as a longing that can afflict and imprison its
subject when it is directed towards goods that are vulnerable to the vicissitudes
of fortune, is thrown into relief by the poem's treatment of the physical condition
of imprisonment. The political situation of Jean de Berry is used to frame the
essential problem of the subject, who is free either to suffer a desire that reflects
and accentuates the deficiency of the human condition, as it defines experience as
a place of confinement where the will cannot be satisfied; or to practise a form of
self-discipline that produces a state of sufficiency, by directing desire towards ends
that the subject can satisfy in and of itself. In this context, the exercise of memory
is conducive to autonomy because it produces images that are under the maker's
control, as an integral part of the subject which cannot be harmed or lost, unlike
the material object of desire.

The *Fonteinne*'s garden setting is appropriate to an exploration of desire and
the implications of its expression: it evokes sexuality and fecundity, by association
with the traditional image of the Virgin's womb as *hortus conclusus*, and in the
phallic connotations of the serpentine fountain, whose flow suggests ejaculation.[41]

---

[41]   Calin, '*La Fonteinne Amoureuse* de Machaut', 82.

Its history as a mythic locus, former rendezvous of Jupiter and Venus, and home of Cupid, further defines it as an erotic space, while the myths displayed and narrated within its borders serve to reinforce the text's focus on the effects of appetite (1381–9). The nature and context of the Trojan narratives adorning the fountain, and the myth of the Judgement of Paris related by Venus, suggest the enlarged significance these tales had acquired within the allegorising tradition represented by works such as the *Ovide moralisé*, one of Machaut's acknowledged sources. Sylvia Huot has observed that Machaut's treatment of these Ovidian narratives underlines the *Fonteinne*'s moral and political concerns. In particular, Huot draws attention to the allegorical interpretation of the marriage of Peleus and Thetis in the *Ovide moralisé* as a figure for sexual reproduction, with bride and groom functioning as the archetypal heterosexual couple; their guests as the members of the human body, and the processes contributing to foetal gestation. The apple of Discord is the original sin that precipitates the Fall.[42] Paris's decision to award this prized object to Venus is glossed as a foolish preference for the voluptuous life: it is a choice that itself reflects the disjunction between will and reason inaugurated by the Fall, since it presupposes a conflict between the objects of contemplation, activity, and appetite. The subject is obliged to form a judgement because it is divided against itself, and the logic of this interpretation is paralleled in Pierre Bersuire's moralisation of the same myth in his influential *Ovidius Moralizatus*. Bersuire glosses the three goddesses as the powers of the soul, whose concord was destroyed by the Fall: in this model, Venus is identified with the will.[43]

Machaut's version of the judgement is in sympathy with such interpretations of the myth, as it emphasises the deliberate nature of Paris's choice. In contrast with the *Ovide moralisé*, where Venus induces Paris to rule in her favour, Machaut renders his verdict as a matter of logic:

> Quant j'ay mestier d'aucun conseil,
> A moy meïsmes me conseil;
> Ne jamais n'iray pain querant,
> Quant je sui fils au roy Priant,
> Einsois aray toudis assez
> Gardés vos tresors amasses,
> Vostre scens et vostre clergie,
> Car l'estat de chevalerie
> Vueil (2125–33)

[When I am in need of any counsel, I advise myself; I shall never go begging for bread, as I am the son of King Priam, but rather will always have enough.

---

[42] Sylvia Huot, 'Reading the Lies of Poets: The Literal and the Allegorical in Machaut's *Fonteinne amoureuse*', *Philological Quarterly* 85 (2006): 25–48 (39).

[43] On Bersuire's gloss, see Margaret J. Ehrhart, *The Judgment of the Trojan Prince Paris in Medieval Literature* (Philadelphia: University of Pennsylvania Press, 1987), 99–101.

Keep your hoarded treasures, your knowledge and learning, because I aspire to
the estate of chivalry]

Against this background, Paris's choice distinguishes him as a member of the
nobility, as Palmer has argued, and is consistent with the idea of love as a cultural
practice that classifies its practitioners.[44] The association of this choice with the
consequences of the Fall suggests that the problem with Paris's judgement is
not that he follows the promptings of desire, but rather that the tendency of his
appetite conflicts with the dictates of reason, causing the downfall of Troy. In this
context, the ideal is the regulation of appetite through a practice of self-discipline
that restores the balance of will and reason within the soul, rather than the total
suppression of the affective response. The *Fonteinne* constructs the nobleman at
its heart as a model of such disciplinary practice by contrasting his experience
of desire with that of Paris. While the nobleman learns to sublimate his desire
for the lady in redirecting it towards a mental image of his own making, and is
therefore enabled to leave his love behind in order to fulfil his political duty, Paris
shows no such restraint. His desire for Helen is expressed in her abduction and
transportation to Troy, a voyage that presents a negative image of the prince's
willing departure into captivity in a foreign land.

Unlike Margaret J. Ehrhart's reading of the *Fonteinne*, which identifies the
points of similarity between Paris and the nobleman as an indication that the love
of princes is essentially detrimental to the health of the state, this interpretation
reads desire as a figure encompassing appetites that are not libidinal, whose
well-regulated expression benefits the social order.[45] The issue is clarified by the
relationship between Machaut's text and Froissart's *Dit dou bleu chevalier*, in
which the object of the knight's desire is identified with France.[46] In this respect,
Froissart's poem is in sympathy with the tradition of political discourse that
identified the body and the household as microcosms of the state: the maintenance
of proper order in the subject and the subject's personal relations will contribute to
the well-being of the realm, enabling him to endure exile, while the indulgence of
affection will be damaging. The pairing evoked within the *Fonteinne* also carries
a political significance elided in interpretations that stress the romantic image
of Jean de Berry and Jeanne d'Armagnac as young newlyweds separated by the
exigencies of war. Their marriage was an alliance arranged in haste by Jean II in
October 1359, to cement relations with Languedoc, under the threat of renewed
hostilities with England. Concluded without the necessary papal dispensation, it
was made legal in June 1360, prior to Jean's departure, most probably to forestall
the possibility of a new alliance, serving the ends of Edward III.[47] The expediency

---

[44]   Palmer (ed.), *The Fountain of Love*, lxii, lxxviii–lxxx.

[45]   Ehrhart expresses this argument most fully in *The Judgment of the Trojan Prince
Paris*, 130–41.

[46]   See Fourrier's introduction to Jean Froissart, *'Dits' et 'débats'*, 57–60.

[47]   See Françoise Autrand, *Jean de Berry* (Paris: Fayard, 2000), 247–53; Lehoux, *Jean
de France*, 1. 140–41, 155–6.

of the match is reflected in Jeanne's young age, eleven to Jean's nineteen at the time of its formalisation. Insofar as it evokes the historical fact of Jean's marriage, the love relationship depicted within the *Fonteinne* is therefore not an entirely private passion, fundamentally at odds with the common good, but instead coincides with the interests of the state.

The idea of a disciplined mode of loving, which enacts a reconciliation between reason and the appetitive will, finds a complement in the *Fonteinne*'s treatment of the prince and the poet. If their association suggests the union of chivalric and clerical qualities in the ideal subject, it also evokes a rapprochement between the active and contemplative lives which restores the harmony of the prelapsarian soul. Yet any such rapprochement remains provisional at best, endangered by the corrupt nature of the will. As Huot observes, acknowledgment of the irreducible ambiguity of the appetite is the province of the poet: when the prince wakes from their vision, the carnal aspect of love is a source of amusement to him, rather than a bodily wrench of longing that disturbs the balance of his soul.[48] The sensual character of desire is exposed in Venus's response to Priapus, the wedding guest whose erection peeks out from under his robe: her gesture in covering her face conceals her enjoyment, and the condemnation offered by others is belied by their laughter. Their reaction is echoed in that of the remembering prince, and this laughter has a subversive quality: like Venus' gesture, the conventional disavowal of complicity in desire may be a performance only, which cannot erase the troubling response of arousal (1675–84, 2594–602).

The efficacy of the trained memory as a remedy for loss is also in doubt: the tale of Ceyx and Alcyone, which functions as the prototype for the imaginative consolation of the prince, offers a bleak prospect. Eliding the suicide of the Ovidian queen, Machaut nevertheless reports the couple's metamorphosis into kingfishers, a transformation glossed in the *Ovide moralisé* as a figure for excessive pleasure in the delights of the material world.[49] Alcyone is not consoled by the image of her beloved, and the action of the imagination exacerbates the pain of her loss, as Helen J. Swift argues.[50] Artifice facilitates the making of signs that can be used as a means to achieve transcendence, restoring the balance of will and reason within the soul, but its products can be abused, when the subject responds to them as things in themselves, rather than using them as instruments. Alcyone is caught up in her affective response to her husband's image, unable to treat it as a sign that might enable her to function in the world. Her problem resembles the mental vice of *curiositas*, which frustrates mnemonic exercise, as an excess of affectivity that causes the remembering subject to react to the sensual character of the sign in inappropriate ways, losing the focus conducive to understanding.[51]

In the context of Machaut's profoundly intertextual poem, the connection between Morpheus and Orpheus suggests a related problem. The *Fonteinne* evokes

---

[48]   Huot, 'Reading the Lies of Poets', 42.

[49]   On the text and its influence on Machaut, see Huot, 'Reading the Lies of Poets', 39–40; and Mühlethaler, 'Entre amour et politique'.

[50]   Swift, '*Tamainte Consolation*, 150.

[51]   On *curiositas*, see Carruthers, *The Craft of Thought*, 164.

the memory of the *Roman de la Rose*, in the centrality of the fountain made by Pygmalion, and its association with Narcissus, whose image decorates the ivory pillar at its heart. In this respect, Machaut's poem, which has already signalled its concern with the ethics and process of literary production, is in dialogue with the *Roman* and its use of myth as the source of a vocabulary for reflection on poetics. As in the *Confort d'ami*, Machaut deploys the figures of Orpheus and Narcissus as emblems of a sterile poetics, which does not achieve material expression. Orpheus is at once the symbol of a transient lyric performance, like the prince's complaint, which must be reified as a textual artefact if it is to achieve circulation, and the symbol of sexual practices that cannot produce issue.[52] The interconnected acts of literary production performed by prince and poet in their bedchambers combine to generate the text of the complaint, yet they also suggest the possibility of an Orphic desire between men that displaces sexual congress, precluding another kind of reproduction. This image foreshadows the possibility that the pleasures of signification, focused in an enjoyment of artifice for its own sake, might disconnect the subject from the material world, preventing the union of the bodily and the spiritual that produces the fruit of knowledge and is the basis of cognition.

Following the *Rose* and the *Confort*, within the *Fonteinne* the possibility of a fruitful poetics is once again imagined through Pygmalion, whose experience of producing a material object that inspires love and is animated with a fecund life of its own serves as a model for human artifice. Machaut's emphasis on the need for a significant union between flesh and spirit finds its counterpart in the valuation placed on the condition of imprisonment as a means to knowledge. Both reflect a philosophy that places an optimistic construction on human sociality, and on the community as a place where political action can have a positive effect and justice can be enacted, in contrast to the pessimistic view of the world as the scene of an intrinsically unjust law, where power is always arbitrary and tyrannical. In this respect, Machaut anticipates Theodor Adorno's telling observation, that 'the human promise of civilisation' entails the recognition that 'humanity includes reification as well as its opposite, not merely as the condition from which liberation is possible but also positively, as the form in which, however brittle and inadequate it may be, subjective impulses are realized, but only by being objectified'.[53]

As Pygmalion's deliverance from fruitless desire by means of an act of prayer suggests, the success of artifice as a means to transcendence ultimately depends upon faith, on the ability to respond to human creations as the sign of a transcendent Other. As Huot argues, Pygmalion responds to his creation as a real and independent object, despite his awareness that Galatea is a thing of his own making.[54] In the *Fonteinne* too, fantasy penetrates reality as the prince awakes to

---

[52]   See Chapter 1, and Sylvia Huot's discussion of Narcissus, Orpheus and Pygmalion in *From Song to Book*, 96–9, 144.

[53]   Theodor W. Adorno, *Prisms*, trans. Samuel and Shierry Weber (Cambridge, MA: MIT, 1981), 106. My understanding of Machaut's philosophy has been refined by Gillian Rose's analysis of the idea of community in *Mourning Becomes the Law: Philosophy and Representation* (Cambridge: Cambridge University Press, 1996), 15–39.

[54]   Huot, *From Song to Book*, 144.

find the ruby ring placed on his hand by his beloved within the vision, exchanged for his own diamond (2504–6, 2523–4). His experience suggests a subjective transition from an awareness of the illusory character of the dream, to a belief that the products of human art have a real significance that can find expression in the world.

The serpentine fountain at the heart of the *Fonteinne* can be understood as the emblem of an active suspension of disbelief that resembles the credence of Pygmalion and the prince, derived from the *Consolation*. Philosophy compares the work of resolving the question of divine providence to the Herculean task of slaying the Hydra, since the resolution of one doubt immediately produces numerous others, incessantly, unless these doubts are restrained by the action of a 'tres vif et ardant engin' ['very lively and ardent intellect'] (4.pr.6). The anonymous translator of the *Livre de Boece* glosses this passage in intriguing terms, with the claim that 'le soutil engin prent legierement les choses fortes' ['the ingenious intellect takes weighty matters lightly']. Intellect or artifice functions as a means to deny troublesome ambiguities, as the subject chooses to interpret signs in the light of faith, rather than seeking to resolve a problem that exceeds human reason. The subtle quality of such an intellect, like the loving practice of Machaut's prince, consists in an ability to deceive oneself, restraining the impulse of an endless curiosity that would undermine faith. The problem of art, and the corrupt quality of the human will that it engages, cannot be resolved, but the subject can elect to read worldly signs as the mark of a benevolent intention. As Philosophy argues, 'combien que tu ne saiches la cause de son ordenement, tu ne doiz pas doubter que toutes choses ne soient bien faictes et droicturierement' ['although you do not know the cause of its ordinance, you must not doubt that all things are made well and justly'] (4.pr.5). Machaut's concluding question frames the problem, and challenges the reader to perform such a faithful act of reading, in deciding whether or not to accept the possibility of a justice manifested in the world: 'Dites moy, fu ce bien songié?'

Chapter 4
Memory, Desire and Writing in Jean Froissart's *Prison amoureuse*

An arresting scene from Jean Froissart's *Prison amoureuse* reveals a complex interplay between desire and the processes of literary production and textual circulation. On discovering that his beloved is outside with a party of women, the narrator hurries to join them and is made welcome. Observing that the purse hanging from his waist is full, the women decide to purloin its contents, but expose their own success through their laughter and lowered voices. A playful fight ensues, as the narrator attempts to recover letters and poems sent to him by his patron, proposing to retrieve his property from its place of concealment in a maiden's bosom. The women respond by assailing his body, as he protests, 'Sans noient espargnier mes draps' ['without sparing my clothes'] (1136).[1] He buys his freedom and the return of his correspondence at the cost of a ballade and a virelay, which his beloved shears away from the letters with her diamond ring. The women read, recite and copy these texts with great pleasure.

At one level, this anecdote, which Deborah McGrady terms 'the purloined letters episode', functions as an elaborate *double entendre*, playfully evoking the euphemistic function of the purse as a metaphor for the scrotum.[2] In this respect, the theft suggests a form of castration, the removal of the testicles in orchidectomy, a figure echoed in the act of cutting that divides the ransom of poems from the letters.[3] For Laurence de Looze, the scene represents an assault in which 'text elides sex', producing 'a textual emasculation', as the women force the narrator to spill 'a distinctly literary seed'.[4] Yet, as McGrady argues, the emphasis on hostility and pain within this reading belies the erotic pleasure the narrator derives from the experience, of which he reports 'Onques depuis si bon tamps n'oi' ['Never

---

[1]   Jean Froissart, *La Prison amoureuse*, ed. Anthime Fourrier (Paris: Klincksieck, 1974), references are by line number; by roman numeral, line number and page number for the prose letters, translations mine. For a complete English translation, see the bilingual edition of Laurence de Looze, ed. and trans., *Jean Froissart: La Prison amoureuse (The Prison of Love)* (New York: Garland, 1994).

[2]   McGrady, *Controlling Readers*, 173. For an example of the purse as scrotum, see *Roman de la Rose*, ll. 7111–13; and Stephen L. Wailes, 'Potency in *Fortunatus*', *The German Quarterly* 59. 1 (1986): 5–18 (9–10). On medieval castration, see A.J. Minnis, *Magister amoris: The* Roman de la Rose *and Vernacular Hermeneutics* (Oxford: Oxford University Press, 2001), 172–3.

[3]   Orchidectomy was the most common form of castration practiced in the Middle Ages, see Wailes, 'Potency in *Fortunatus*', 7.

[4]   De Looze, *Pseudo-Autobiography*, 119–20.

since have I had such a good time'] (1208).[5] Moreover, rather than posing a threat to masculine potency, the theft of this literary seed increases its fecundity, as the poems multiply through copying and recitation, and the experience inspires the narrator to compose a virelay.

The scene plays on an analogy between procreation and writing familiar from Neoplatonic literature and, more immediately, from Jean de Meun's continuation of the *Roman de la Rose*, in which Genius imagines the penis as a stylus whose proper use confers immortality.[6] Within the *Prison*, this model is adapted so that the production and circulation of texts evokes coition, where the beloved's ring functions as symbolic counterpart to the scrotal purse in a bodily encounter that engenders literary offspring. Rather than eliding sexuality, as de Looze argues, however, this episode develops the imagery of textual congress in order to reflect on the materiality of information, upon its embodied nature. In imagining bodily and textual reproduction as coincident actions, the *Prison* focuses on the processes by which spiritual contents, ideas and human souls, come to be embodied, and on the implications of these processes. The idea that sexual reproduction is analogous to textual production relies on the sense that the human subject is in essence a union of body and spirit. Aquinas's observation that human cognition requires the tying of abstract ideas to bodily images, discussed in the previous chapter, underlines this point, as it implies that this activity is both the effect of corporeality, and an act of creation whose products resemble the human subject as a union of the material and the spiritual. This idea of humanity informed conceptions of the incarnation of Christ as a union of matter and spirit, the Word made flesh, in a perfect similitude that inspires human affection.[7] Through its eroticised depiction of textual circulation, Froissart's scene crystallises the sense that the reception and production of verbal signs always involves the body, and that these related activities produce embodiment, in images that link spiritual ideas to objects of sensual experience.

As the *Roman de la Rose*'s version of the figure of sexuality as writing suggests, bodily and textual reproduction each promise a kind of immortality, and a literary afterlife for both poet and patron is anticipated within the *Prison*, as the theft of the letters depicts an erotically charged moment of physical exchange that contributes to both the dissemination of poems originating with a lord and the composition of a new work. Nevertheless, the idea of writing as a form of artifice with the capacity to perpetuate the subject raises questions thrown into relief by present debates surrounding technology. Responding to claims that advances in fields such as artificial intelligence might soon enable the preservation of consciousness in digitally encoded form, N. Katherine Hayles draws attention to the implications of the idea that information can be conceived in isolation from the particular matrix

---

[5]   McGrady, *Controlling Readers*, 180–85.

[6]   *Roman de la Rose*, lines 19599–600, on this analogy, see Huot, *From Song to Book*, 96–9.

[7]   See above, Aquinas, *Summa Theologiæ*, 2a2æ. 49. I, 63; Lochrie, *Margery Kempe*, 29–31.

in which it manifests itself in order to exist, and of the hope that 'if we can become the information we have constructed, we can achieve effective immortality'. As she argues, 'The point is not only that abstracting information from a material base is an imaginary act but also, and more fundamentally, that conceiving of information as a thing separate from the medium instantiating it is a prior imaginary act that constructs a holistic phenomenon as an information/matter duality'.[8] Froissart's *Prison* anticipates the nature of the problem, as the text reflects on the possibilities and implications of the transposition of information into different material forms, of what it might mean for human identity, and of how it might impact upon the human body.

These concerns are encapsulated within the purloined letters episode not only in its sexualisation of textual matters, but also in the violence of the encounter, both explicit and implicit. Insofar as it imagines textual circulation in terms of sexual assault and castration, the scene suggests an inherent brutality in writing, familiar to medieval culture, where the process of book production involves animal skins, whose surfaces must be laboriously broken and pierced in order to make impressions upon them.[9] An instance of violence that inspires pleasure, the episode of the letters reflects a conception of writing that parallels the beginning of Machaut's *Fonteinne amoureuse*. In the *Fonteinne*, Machaut's construction of writing as a discipline conducive to pleasure is informed by the idea of memory as being at once the instrument of literary invention, and the means to achieve the happiness of sufficiency in establishing the proper relation between will and reason that is the hallmark of the ethical subject. The purloined letters episode articulates a similar conception of memory at work within the *Prison*: the 'moult petite aloiiere' ['very small purse'] in which the narrator keeps his letters suggests the symbolic function of the *sacculus* or money-pouch as a common metaphor for the trained memory (803). Although this silken purse presumably lacks the discreet and numerous compartments of the typical *sacculus*, whose function corresponds to that of systematisation in the arts of memory, it nevertheless evokes the role of memory as a place where texts are stored for safekeeping.[10] Read in this light, the theft functions as an allegory of the demands an audience places on a poet's memory in recitation, while the erotic and violent qualities of the episode recall the importance attributed to affectivity as a stimulus to the mnemonic process.[11]

---

[8] N. Katherine Hayles, *How We Became Posthuman: Virtual Bodies in Cybernetics, Literature, and Informatics* (Chicago: University of Chicago Press, 1999), 13.

[9] On the violence of writing, see Carruthers, *The Craft of Thought*, 100–103; Jonathan Goldberg, *Writing Matter: From the Hands of the Renaissance* (Stanford: Stanford University Press, 1990), 70–75; and Sarah Kay, 'Legible Skins: Animals and the Ethics of Medieval Reading', *Postmedieval: A Journal of Medieval Cultural Studies* 2 (2011): 13–32.

[10] Carruthers, *The Book of Memory*, 45–6. On Froissart's interest in memory in the broader sense, see Michel Zink, *Froissart et le temps* (Paris: Paris: Presses Universitaires de France, 1998) and Philip E. Bennett, '*Ut pictura memoria*: Froissart's Quest for Lost Time', *Zeitschrift für französische Sprache und Literatur* 120.3 (2010): 229–44.

[11] Carruthers, *The Book of Memory*, 168, 171; *The Craft of Memory*, 101–3.

The idea that the purse functions in part as a figure for memory finds support in the presence of the ballade and the virelay within the *Prison*, presented as a book compiled by the narrator: despite his claim to have yielded them as ransom, they nevertheless appear at lines 713–44 and 934–62. Their retention suggests memory's ability to give up its contents without suffering their loss, in an exercise that brings pleasure and profit to both audience and mnemonist.

In this respect, memory is conceived as a form of containment that facilitates the circulation of texts, of ideas. Moreover, the purse, in its role as a vessel for poems and letters, is one of a series of such containers whose appearance within the *Prison* reflects a marked preoccupation with the enclosure of texts. The term *aloiiere* (purse) is itself suggestive, implying the 'lien' or tie to which it is etymologically linked. It evokes one of the derivations ascribed to the word *auctor*, from *auieo*, 'to tie', and recalls the idea that mnemonic practice entails binding one's thoughts through the construction of systems for the organisation of knowledge, found in sources from Aquinas to Machaut.[12] The purloined letters episode articulates the sense that different forms of containment, of embodiment, intersect, in a continuum that encompasses the coercion of the human subject, the restraining influence of self-discipline, and the storage of information, whether in memory or on paper or parchment. It expresses the central concerns of the *Prison*, as a text which resembles Boethius's *Consolation* in seeking to revaluate a historically contingent instance of imprisonment, by taking that experience as cue for an exploration of perennial philosophical questions about the nature of embodiment and its impact on human agency.

In contrast to its most immediate Boethian model, the *Fonteinne amoureuse*, the *Prison* does not blur the boundaries between literal and figurative imprisonment overtly: on its surface, the narrative is concerned only with the metaphorical imprisonment of love. Titling the work from within, the narrator signals the importance of this literary trope in defining both the text and the experience it describes, as he offers a rationale for the choice of *Prison amoureuse*. The *Prison* focuses on an exchange of letters between a poet and his patron, a nobleman who writes to him under the pseudonym Rose, seeking his advice on matters of love. Following his example, the narrator adopts an alias of his own, 'Flos'. Since, as Flos explains, Rose is both 'cause et matere' ['cause and subject'] of the book he is making, it is fitting that its title reflect the nature of his experience, which he perceives as a form of imprisonment:

> car coers jolis et amoureus, qui aimme en le fourme et maniere comme vous fetes, ne poet vivre ne resgner sans estre emprisonnés. Or vous est ceste prison jolie et amoureuse, car, Dieu merci, entre vostre souverainne et vous n'a nul

---

[12]   The etymological link between is noted by Jacqueline Cerquiglini-Toulet, who also comments on the significance of containers within the *Prison*, 'Fullness and Emptiness: Shortages and Storehouses of Lyric Treasures in the Fourteenth and Fifteenth Centuries', trans. Christine Cano and John Jay Thompson, *Yale French Studies* (special edition), *Contexts: Style and Values in Medieval Art and Literature* (1991): 224–39. On medieval etymologies of *auctor*, see Minnis, *Medieval Theory of Authorship*, 10.

discort ne soussi, ains sont vo doi coer assés en unite parfet. (XII. 21, 26–32,
p. 171)

[for a kind and amorous heart, which loves in the manner and style you do,
can neither live nor reign without being imprisoned. Yet, to you this prison is
pleasant and amorous since, thanks be to God, between your sovereign and
yourself there is neither discord nor worry, thus your two hearts are quite in
perfect unity]

The image of a heart whose mode of loving entails an experience of constraint that
is not only pleasurable, but conducive to life and, as the verb 'regner' indicates,
to the exercise of sovereignty, once again suggests the influence of the conception
of love as a social practice that signals fitness for government, in displaying an
exemplary ability to control the appetitive will. As in the *Fonteinne*, this sensibility
finds expression in an idyllic social unity, while its function as a distinguishing
characteristic of the nobility is suggested through its association with Rose, and
in the apologetic nature of Flos's own attempt to establish a claim to this mode
of being. Although Flos defines himself as 'rudes et ignorans en tous afaires'
['lacking in refinement and ignorant in all things'], his experience serves, in its
own small way, to corroborate the title (XII. 39, p. 171). As he observes, 'en ceste
prison je languis attendans le grasce de ma dame, se m'en est la vie et li esperance
si joieuse que je le doi bien appeller amoureuse et prison, car je me rench a ma
dame et me tieng son prisonnier' ['I languish in this prison awaiting my lady's
favour, my life and hope are so joyful that I must surely call them "amorous" and
"prison," because I give myself to my lady and hold myself her prisoner'] (XII.
43–47, p. 171).

If Flos's tone suggests a degree of social anxiety, however, his status as the
master to whom Rose appeals for aid reflects the sense that this refined practice of
love is intimately connected with the discipline of writing, as it was in Machaut's
work. Within the *Prison*, the experience of love repeatedly coalesces with the
generation and circulation of texts, a narrative tactic which reaches its zenith in
the purloined letters episode, but is present from the text's outset, where Flos
identifies himself as a servant of Love, the god whose influence is later credited as
inspiring him to compose poetry (273–7). The idea of devotion to love is couched
in feudal terms, as Froissart glosses God's commandment to Moses: 'L'amour
pour le service glose, /Car qui bien aimme, il sert et crient /Et toute obeisance
tient' ['for love read service, for he who loves well serves and fears, and defers
in all things'] (14–16). This conception of love echoes Machaut's 'loial amour'
as a form of affection which accords with Christian duty and contributes to the
maintenance of the social order: it is to bring the subject both worldly glory and
divine favour (*Fonteinne amoureuse*, 3; *Prison* 17–20). The *Prison* articulates the
poet-narrator's willing submission to Love's authority:

Je voel server de franc voloir
Celi qui tant me poet valoir,

A cui j'ai fait de liet corage
Seüreté, foi et homage (23–6)

[Of free will, I wish to serve the one who may profit me so much, to whom I
have pledged my commitment, faith, and homage with a light heart]

This deferent gesture suggests a capacity for self-discipline that will increase the
moral and worldly value of the subject; its position at the opening of the *Prison*
subtly links poetry, morality and the poet's voluntary acquiescence to the service
of a patron as a source of inspiration and profit.

The figure of the patron connects Froissart's *Prison*, with its imagery of
discipline and containment, to a literal and historical experience of imprisonment.
In the course of their literary exchange, Rose sends Flos a book, containing a poem
inspired by a dream, itself conceived under the pleasurable influence of one of
Flos's compositions, the tale of Pynoteüs and Neptisphelé, which Rose has read
and reread several times (VII, 19–27, p. 113). Rose specifies that his vision took
place in 1371, and the text describes an allegorical battle in which he is defeated by
the forces of Avis (Prudence) and Atemprance (Moderation) (2252; Rose's poem
encompasses lines 2252–3420). Rose is subsequently imprisoned in the castle of
Atemprance for 'un yvier et un éste' ['a winter and a summer'], until he receives
word of his imminent rescue by an eagle with a warlike host of birds, whereupon
he wakes (3382). It has long been recognised that the details of this vision suggest
a number of parallels with historical events surrounding the battle of Baesweiler,
also described within Froissart's *Chroniques*.[13] Following the battle, on 22 August
1371, Froissart's patron, Wenceslas of Brabant, was imprisoned in the castle of
Nideggen until the intervention of his half brother, the Emperor Charles IV. He
returned to Brussels on 4 July 1372, and the term of his captivity corresponds to
the period of time during which Flos receives no word from Rose, to his surprise
and consternation (2125–38). Froissart's *Prison* was composed soon afterwards,
not later than 1373, when its relationship to recent events would have been even
more striking.[14]

If the details of the vision suggest that Rose is to be identified with the
historical Wenceslas, the *Prison* also invites its readers to link Flos with Froissart,
as it encompasses other aspects of his public life. For Flos, singing and dancing
at court conjures up the memory of festivities in Savoy, 1368, where the newly
married Lionel, duke of Clarence, and his bride, Violante Visconti, stopped on
their journey to Italy. Froissart was part of the duke's entourage, and gives an

---

[13] For a detailed discussion of these parallels, see Fourrier's edition, 20–28, and
Claude Thiry, 'Allégorie et histoire dans la *Prison amoureuse* de Froissart', *Studi Francesi*
61–2 (1977): 15–29. On Wenceslas as Froissart's patron, see Nigel Wilkins, 'A Pattern
of Patronage: Machaut, Froissart and the Houses of Luxembourg and Bohemia in the
Fourteenth Century', *French Studies*, 37 (1983): 256–84. On the battle and its aftermath,
see Sergio Boffa, *Warfare in Medieval Brabant, 1356–1406* (Woodbridge: Boydell, 2004),
22–4.

[14] On the date, see Fourrier's edition, 28–9.

account of these events in the *Chroniques*. As Catherine Attwood observes, 'the faculty of remembering [...] is a guiding force in the mental activity of Froissart's poetic "I"': in the *Prison*, this subjective chronological movement encourages the reader to accept Flos as a version of Froissart, and to relate the text to lived events, rather than treating it as a purely imaginary construct.[15]

In evoking the sense that Froissart's identity is inscribed within his work, the narrative technique of the *Prison* complements the poet's self-construction in the manuscripts of his poetic corpus, BN MSS fr. 830 and 831. Dated 1393 and 1394 respectively, and ostensibly completed under Froissart's personal supervision, these manuscripts are the sole witnesses for his poetry. Highlighting the correlation between the emergent autobiographical tendency in late-medieval poetry and the development of the single-author codex, Kristen M. Figg argues that the two anthologies project distinctive narratives of Froissart's poetic career, destined for his audiences in England and France.[16] Froissart's own description of one such collection, offered to Richard II, gives a suggestive sense of the overlapping nature of the relationship between the poet and his work: 'I had with me this very fine book, nicely decorated, bound in velvet with studs and clasps of silver gilt, which I meant to present to the King by way of introducing myself [pour faire present et entrée au roi]'.[17] The *Prison* occupies the midpoint of both the surviving manuscripts, so that this narrative of textual making and patronage stands at the centre of Froissart's poetic self-construction.[18]

Despite this, however, the idea that identity can be embedded within texts remains intractable in Froissart's work: if Rose's dream suggests the reality of Wenceslas's imprisonment to the reader, this equation remains obscure within the *Prison* itself. Rose is so mystified by the vision that he requests an exposition from Flos, who develops two detailed interpretations of the dream as an allegory of love in letters IX and XII. By signalling the interpretative difficulty posed by the dream, the *Prison* indicates its own referentiality, as it suggests that the vision requires particular attention and analysis; yet it also disrupts the attempt to forge connections between fiction and history, since the exposition insists on the metaphysical nature of Rose's imprisonment.

The inclusion of prose letters within the narrative has a similarly double effect: the technique recalls the traditional function of interpolated letters as

---

[15] Catherine Attwood, *Dynamic Dichotomy: The Poetic 'I' in Fourteenth and Fifteenth-Century French Lyric Poetry* (Amsterdam: Rodopi, 1998), 126. On Froissart's presence in Savoy, see F.S. Shears, *Froissart: Chronicler and Poet* (London: Routledge, 1939), 26–7.

[16] Kristen M. Figg, 'The Narrative of Selection in Jean Froissart's Collected Poems: Omissions and Additions in BN MSS fr. 830 and 831', *Journal of the Early Book Society*, 5 (2002): 37–55.

[17] Jean Froissart, *Chroniques*, ed. J.A.C. Buchon (Paris: A. Desrez, 1835), 3: 198; trans. Geoffrey Brereton, in Froissart, *Chronicles*, ed. Geoffrey Brereton (Harmondsworth: Penguin, 1978), 403. Several scholars have identified this manuscript with MS 831, see Huot, *From Song to Book*, 241. Figg, 'The Narrative of Selection', 38.

[18] Huot, *From Song to Book*, 302n1, and underlined in the subtitle of her analysis, 311–16. See also de Looze, *Pseudo-Autobiography*, 127.

documentary evidence in historiography.[19] Letters are also a form that carries a particular association with the corporeal, conjuring up an absent speaker through the physical traces of handwriting and in the quality of the voice: within Rose's dream, his lady's letters are one of the signs by which he identifies her messenger (3182). The epistle establishes a particular bond between writer and addressee, establishing an intimate community of readers. Love letters, above all, evoke the physical presence of the absent lover, often substituting for the body as the subject of the loving touch. While critics such as Laurence de Looze regard the *Prison* as a narrative in which the erotic yields to the textual in part because its central correspondence is between two men, such readings underestimate the influence of the ideal of loving friendship between men in medieval culture.[20] Rose and Flos's letters are presented as being born out of the experience of love, and as a mutual consolation for the pains of desire (654–65).[21] Their subject is also intimate in another sense, signalling the rise of a culture of diplomacy founded on epistolary exchange: their correspondence is marked by an anxiety about the security of letters, the possibility of interception and surveillance, given a comic reflection in the theft perpetrated by Flos's lady and her companions.[22] This fear is indicated at the outset, as Rose justifies his action in writing pseudonymously, 'pour eschieuer le peril et l'aventure des lettres [...] je vous envoierai par plusieurs messagiers. Car se celles estoient perdues et mon nom avoec ma devise ens cogneüs, il me tourroit a grant contraire' ['to avoid the peril and risk of letters ... I shall send to you by many messengers. Since if these letters were lost and my name, with my device, were known, it would put me to great trouble'] (I, 49–53, p. 58). In the context of a work that locates itself against the background of contemporary politics, this apprehension suggests something more than the lover's dread of the public exposure of private sentiment. Although the subjects of love and literature appear innocuous on the surface, the desire for secrecy suggests that they are politically sensitive, recalling the function of erotic discourse in the language of public governance.

The possibility that the letters and poems at the heart of the *Prison* are the product of an authentic collaboration between Froissart and his patron has been raised by critics including William W. Kibler and, most recently, Remco Sleiderink.[23] Such a collaboration is witnessed by the *Meliador*, written at Wenceslas's

---

[19]   Cerquiglini, *Un Engin si soutil*, 40–41, 47–9.

[20]   See de Looze, *Pseudo-Autobiography*, 115. On letters, see McGrady, *Controlling Readers*, 41–3. Though addressing a later period, also relevant is Seth Lerer, *Courtly Letters in the Age of Henry VIII: Literary Culture and the Arts of Deceit* (Cambridge: Cambridge University Press, 1997), especially useful is the discussion of letters between men, 90–91.

[21]   Lechat comments on the consolatory aspect of the correspondence, *Dire par fiction*, 277.

[22]   Lerer, *Courtly Letters*, 10.

[23]   William W. Kibler, 'Poet and Patron: Froissart's *Prison amoureuse*', *L'Esprit Créateur*, 19 (1978): 32–46; Remco Sleiderink, *De stem van de meester: De hertogen van Brabant en hun rol in het literaire leven (1106–1430)* (Amsterdam: Prometheus, 2003), 129–30, with thanks to Sebastiaan Verweij for translation.

request and including 79 of his lyrics. Yet, as de Looze observes, references to the *Meliador* elsewhere in Froissart's corpus imply that the Arthurian romance incorporates Wenceslas's complete poetic works, so the poems attributed to Rose are presumably by Froissart, as their inclusion in the two anthology manuscripts of his poetry would suggest.[24] Moreover, if Wenceslas's reputation as a man of letters and patron of the arts invites the reader to identify Rose as a representation of the duke, this impression is simultaneously undermined, since the *Prison*'s narrative of literary correspondence also reflects the influence of Guillaume de Machaut's *Voir Dit*. Itself the subject of a similar controversy, the *Voir Dit*'s role as a literary model lends a double meaning to the traditional function of letters as the sign of authenticity. As Flos adopts the historian's practice of calling attention to the fidelity of his transcription, he recalls the protestations of Guillaume, with an echo that implies the fictive nature of the text, and casts doubt on his assertion: 'Je n'i voel riens oster ne mettre' ['I do not wish to remove or to add anything'] (701).[25] The pseudonymity of the correspondence likewise renders the *Prison*'s relationship to history suspect, as it both invites and resists the attempt to establish identity, in a contradictory movement characteristic of the tradition that de Looze terms pseudo-autobiography.

Through its ambiguous referentiality, the *Prison* invokes the *Consolation*, recasting the experience of Wenceslas of Brabant as a renewal of the Boethian model, as it reimagines a historical instance of imprisonment and develops a remedy for misfortune. In juxtaposing the literary trope of love as imprisonment with the duke's literal incarceration, the *Prison* indicates that the instructive value of Froissart's work is not limited to the particularities of love or politics, but is germane to the human condition. Froissart's text reflects on the role of love as a force that works to establish social bonds and maintain stability, and addresses the problems that can impede its function.

In the prologue, Flos envisages the struggle to maintain this form of affection in military terms:

> [...] je me deffench com vassaus
> Contre toutes temptations,
> Qui voelent mes ententions
> Muer ne tourbler ne cangier. (154–7)

> [like a vassal, I fight back against all temptations that would alter, trouble, or change my intentions.]

---

[24] De Looze, *Pseudo-Autobiography*, 117.

[25] See also *Prison* 745; III. 15–16, p. 68; 932–3; 1999–2000; 2248–51. Cerquiglini draws attention to similar references in the *Voir Dit*, 1239–40, 4805–8, *Un Engin si soutil*, 48. For an overview of the controversy surrounding the authenticity of the *Voir Dit*, and the most recent instance of the claim to its historicity, see the introduction to *Le Livre dou Voir Dit (The Book of the True Poem)*, ed. Daniel Leech Wilkinson, trans. R. Barton Palmer (New York: Garland, 1998), xix–lvii.

This image forges links between the devotion involved in love service and fealty, as it succeeds a historical instance of feudal loyalty that connects material and spiritual bondage. Praising the example set by John of Luxembourg, Froissart describes how the duke's retainers helped their blind lord at the battle of Crécy:

> La li monstrerent grant service
> Li sien, dont ne furent pas nice,
> Car, a fin qu'il ne le perdissent
> Et qu'avoec lui il se tenissent,
> Il s'aliierent tout a li
> Et l'un a l'autre (101–6)

> [There his men did him great service, in which they were not hesitant, for so that they did not lose him and so that they remained with him, they all tied themselves to him and to one another]

Killed in battle, the duke's men are held up as the model of the love and service to which honour constrains the subject, and their bound state offers a material reflection of the social bonds that uphold the hierarchical order (109–15).[26] The courage of John's vassals is the mark of a commitment to an ethic of service that supersedes worldly investments, enabling the subject to courageously offer up 'Corps et biens, avoir et chavance' ['Body and goods, possessions and fortune'] (115). In presenting John as the ideal lord, and focus of an exemplary devotion, Froissart anticipates the connection between Rose, as the nobleman whom Flos will serve, and his own patron, John's son. The narrator's commitment to love is framed to coincide with literary and historical loyalties, and he identifies the greatest threat to this benevolent servitude as Fortune, 'si poissans /Qu'as humles coers obeïssans /Elle poet envoiier discorde' ['so powerful that she can sow discord even in humble obedient hearts'] (195–7).

Necessarily precarious, the narrator's dedication to love is nonetheless reaffirmed by the negative examples of Bellerophon and Narcissus, both of whom refuse the love of women (158–94). In particular, the figure of Narcissus evokes the significance that this myth had acquired as an emblem of poetic practice, suggesting that the rejection of bodily affections results in the barren stasis of an enslavement to artifice for its own sake: 'il enamoura son ombre [...] la fontainne est ses drois lis' ['he fell in love with his shadow ... the fountain is his proper bed'] (179, 182). The role of women within this analogy accords with the traditional characterisation of matter, of flesh, as feminine, and the example points to the need for spiritual intentions to achieve social expression, contributing to the establishment of a community that reflects the promise of divine concord, however transient that reflection might be.

Yet the effort to control desire, rather than attempting to eradicate it, entails problems of its own, and these become the subject of the correspondence at the heart of the *Prison*. In his third letter to Flos, Rose speaks of the pleasure he takes in devotion to his lady, displaying a facility for mental contemplation of the kind

---

[26]   The episode is also recorded in the *Chroniques*, 1: 238.

recommended in the Boethian tradition as a remedy for the pain of desire, as his delight increases in 'regardant et ymaginant sa douce phizonomie' ['looking at and imagining her sweet face'] (V. 18–19, p. 81). Even so, he is troubled by the sting of desire, feeling 'des pointures moult mervilleuses, les queles je ne sçai mie porter si bellement ne si doucement que je vorroie' ['most astonishing wounds, which I do not know how to bear as nobly or as easily as I wish'] (V. 22–4, p. 82). Rose asks Flos to advise him 'comment je m'i puisse gouvrener et a ce metre atemprance' ['how I might govern myself and moderate this (feeling)'] (V. 29–30, p. 82). This plea is coupled with a commission for a new poem, 'sus aucune nouvelle matere qu'on n'aroit onques veü ne oÿ mise en rime, tel com, par figure, fu jadis de Piramus et de Tysbé, ou de Eneas et de Dido, ou de Tristan et de Yseus' ['which treats of some new matter never yet seen nor heard in rhyme, as were once, for example, the subjects of Pyramus and Thisbe, or Aeneas and Dido, or Tristan and Iseut'] (V. 44–8, p. 82). Rose speaks of jealousy, but the essence of his problem is astutely diagnosed by Flos as an excess of feeling: 'le tres grans habondance de corage que vous avés et le desir d'estre amoureus vous ont si ataint et le coer enflame que bien souvent vous en perdés maniere et contenance' ['the very great abundance of sentiment that you have, and the desire to be in love, have so touched you and enflamed your heart that you often lose your bearing and countenance because of it'] (IX. 34–7, p. 151). The juxtaposition of a literary commission with this request for assistance in governing the 'corage', which can also denote 'will', is suggestive, implying the function of writing as a means to control desire. Such a conception of writing is borne out in the part that the commissioned text has to play in the consolation of Flos's patron: in interpreting Rose's dream through its relationship to his own tale, Flos combines literary criticism and practical advice, in developing an analysis of the nobleman's experience of love.

Rose's depth of feeling is a mark of nobility, and his continuing vulnerability to sensation does not signal a culpable failure to become indifferent to worldly things, but instead reflects the conception of Stoicism as a philosophy that teaches the proper management of the affective response.[27] Despite his role as Rose's advisor, Flos exhibits a similar vulnerability, which is both caused and assuaged by writing. Prior to his correspondence with Rose, Flos suffers the pangs of desire as a by product of the anonymous circulation of his poetry, when a virelay he wrote to express his love comes to the attention of the object of his desire. Although initially pleased at her wish to possess a copy for her own use, he is later horrified to find that she has composed a response, as a public performance of his lyric segues into his beloved's own virelay. Her poem is an expression of delight at the lover's suffering, as the refrain argues, 'Car toute merancolie /Li affiert bien a porter' ['For it suits him well to bear every melancholy'] (429–34). Deborah McGrady has convincingly argued that Flos's anguish registers the poet's distress at an inability to control reader response, however, his pain is also a testament to the accuracy of her observations:[28]

---

[27]   See Jessica Rosenfeld, 'The Doubled Joys of *Troilus and Criseyde*', in Léglu and Milner (eds), *The Erotics of Consolation*, 44–7.

[28]   McGrady, *Controlling Readers*, 176–9.

Et quant penser le remort,
Par plaisance il s'i endort
Si longement
Qu'on feroit painne et tort,
Qui li torroit le resort
De pensement.
Car en pensant il s'oublie
Et deduit et esbanie (448–55)

[And when thought torments him, he slumbers with pleasure so long that one
would harm and wrong him, who relieved him of his remedy of contemplation.
For in thought he forgets himself, and delights and enjoys himself]

Flos reacts by threatening to compose a new poem, so clear that she will easily
understand 'Si c'est a faute ou s'est a voir /Que merencolie me touce' ['whether
it is false or it is true that melancholy affects me'] (532–3). Yet his aspiration
precisely neglects the truth recognised by his beloved, that the pain of love and
the contemplative remedies employed to control the affective response induce
delights of their own. Writing not only offers consolations for the pain of
unsatisfied longing, but the enjoyment of sublimation is its essence, as the imagery
of composition as a pleasurable bondage implies. The conception of poetry that
informs the lady's virelay is paralleled in Slavoj Žižek's observation that 'Poetry,
the specific poetic *jouissance*, emerges when *the very symbolic articulation of* [...]
Loss gives rise to a pleasure of its own'.[29]

It is only through his correspondence with Rose that Flos is able to acknowledge
the truth of this assertion, recognising the pleasures of the prison of love, and
articulating them most explicitly in the final letter of their exchange. The initial
expression of Flos's devotion to his lady, in an anonymous textual circulation,
recoils from the open avowal of affection that might have resulted in a more
substantial commitment to her, through the establishment of contractual bonds of
obligation. His actions contrast with those of Rose, whose admission that he is the
author of the letter his beloved received leads to his acceptance as her lover (III.
56–7, p. 69). Flos's response to Rose's first letter likewise exemplifies a form of
commitment that entails recognised bonds of duty analogous to physical bonds:

Rescripsi je moult liement,
Par bon et droit aliement,
Que d'or en avant voel tenir
A Rose, qui voelt devenir
Mon compagnon et mon secré (747–51)

[I replied very joyfully, out of a good and just obligation, that from now on I
wished to be attached to Rose, who wishes to become my companion and my
confidant]

---

[29] Žižek, *Plague of Fantasies*, his emphasis, 58.

This act of writing involves both joy and obligation, conditions whose similarity is underlined by the homonymity of *liement* and *aliement*, a rhyme that links pleasure with the contractual bond of loyalty between lord and subject, and evokes the physical act of binding.[30]

The conception of literal bondage as a state conducive to pleasure, and especially associated with writing, is also reflected in other aspects of the *Prison*'s treatment of the conditions of textual production and reception. Having described the enclosure of his first letter to Rose in a volume with a ballade, Flos explains:

> [...] je remés:
> Dedens mon hostel enfremés.
> Non que g'i soie trop enclose
> Mes pour l'amour dou joli clos
> [...]
> Volentiers je m'i esbatoie (792–95, 800)

> [I remained: shut up in my lodging, not because I was locked away there, but for love of the pleasant close...I amused myself there willingly]

In order to write, Flos confines himself to his quarters, yet his experience of incarceration is not distressing, but instead pleasurable and suffered of free will, and his solitude accords with the conditions thought most suitable for the exercise of memory involved in composition. The theme of enclosure as a corollary to writing reappears in the preface to the tale of Pynoteüs and Neptisphelé: 'j'entrai dedens mon estude, /Qui n'est ne villainne ne rude, /Mes belle pour estudiier' ['I went into my study, which is neither unattractive nor unpleasant, but good for working'] (1290–92). Commenting on this and other examples of the treatment of confinement within the *Prison*, Keith Busby draws attention to the recurrent emphasis on enclosure in descriptions of the physical form of the letters and poems, while reading them not only involves a withdrawal from society, but also enacts a liberation: 'Et puis si me tournai a part. /Des lettres le signet rompi /Et tout bellement les ouvri' ['Then I turned away. I broke the seal on the letters and opened them very carefully'] (915–17).[31] Detailed accounts of the ways in which the letters are tied serve a similar purpose, underscoring the material qualities of these documents and their bound state (2016–17, 3496–7). In effect, constraint or enclosure is presented as a necessary condition of writing and its uses.

The centrepiece of the correspondence bound up in the *Prison* itself, the narrative that Rose commissions from Flos, and the various responses it evokes, further illuminate the relationship between writing and imprisonment, in modelling a solution for Rose's problem, the government of the appetitive will. Flos's Ovidian tale focuses on the question of how to address the problem of frustrated desire by exploring the implications of death, as the irretrievable loss

---

[30] On *aliement*, see Fourrier's note to line 748, 181.

[31] Keith Busby, 'Froissart's Poetic Prison: Enclosure as Image and Structure in the Narrative Poetry', in Maddox and Sturm-Maddox (eds), 90–93, 100n18.

of the beloved object. Following the death of his beloved Neptisphelé, the poet Pynoteüs seeks consolation for the pain of grief. His affection is conceived as a memorial bond, analogous to physical constraint: as he exclaims, 'Comment vous poroi je oubliier /Ne nulle aultre a moy allier?' ['how could I forget you, or join myself to any other?'] (1462–3, echoed in lines 1604–5). Having satisfied a craving for vengeance by orchestrating the punishment of the lion responsible for her demise, Pynoteüs considers and rejects the idea of making an Orphean attempt to recover her from the underworld. Instead, he constructs an image of his lost love and implores Phoebus to bring it to life. His prayer granted, Pynoteüs is reunited with a Neptisphelé indistinguishable from the original: 'C'est m'amie ne plus ne mains' ['It is my love, no more, no less'] (1960).

The idea of an art that can overcome death, through the creation of a synthetic being capable of supplanting the human subject, not only in the affections of a lover, but also in the eyes of a father, suggests both the promise and the threat of human invention. It presages the hopes and fears of a post-industrial society contemplating the prospect of an immortality achieved by technological means, and a technology animate with a consciousness of its own, indistinguishable from the human. Froissart's narrative conceives of poetry as a form of making analogous to the construction of material forms and mechanisms, linking these modes of production through the figure of Pynoteüs, who is at once a consummate poet and a master of the plastic arts.[32] A passage that purports to identify the source of this tale presents a suggestive conjunction:

> [...] une glose
> Qui nous approeve et nous acorde,
> Si com Ovides le recorde,
> Les oeuvres de Pynoteüs,
> Qui par grant art et non par us
> Fist l'ymage parlans et vive,
> D'aige et de terre (1295–301)

> [a text that presents and attests, quite as Ovide records them, the works of Pynoteüs, he who through great artistry and in no common way, made a speaking and living image from water and earth]

As de Looze argues, the fusion of water and earth in the image parallels the combination of mythic elements in Flos's tale, while Pynoteüs's *oeuvres* may also be of a textual nature.[33] The avowal that Pynoteüs made his image 'par grant art et non par us' takes on an additional resonance in this context, since the idea of a mode of artistic production that does not follow established models suggests the

---

[32]   On the influence and development of this conception of poetry as invention in the Renaissance, see Sawday, *Engines of the Imagination*, 166–206.

[33]   De Looze, *Pseudo-Autobiography*, 121–3. On Froissart's intertextual practice, see also Claire Nouvet, 'Pour une économie de la dé-limitation: la *Prison amoureuse* de Jean Froissart', *Neophilologus*, 70 (1986): 341–56 (350).

conception of rhetorical invention as a refashioning of traditional source materials. Distinguishing poets from commentators by the degree of innovation with which they treat received materials, this model informs Flos's own construction of his artistic practice, in the claim that his tale is made 'de la plus nouvelle matere que j'aie trouvé entre les anchiiennes hystores' ['from the newest matter that I could find amongst the antique stories'] (VI. 7–8, p. 103).[34] In locating the artistry of Pynoteüs's design in his unconventional treatment of received material, Froissart maps a conception of artistic practice that serves to identify himself, and his literary analogues, as innovators – as poets.

As Jacqueline Cerquiglini-Toulet observes, Froissart's vocabulary underlines the function of the image of Neptisphelé as a textual object, forging links between the description of the making of the mould used to produce the artificial woman and the process of poetic composition. In both acts of production, the maker *ordonne* (arranges) and *taille* (cuts) his materials in accordance with the demands of the form (1719–23; 2200–201, 3008). Moreover, the shape of the mould, and its function as a container for a textual form, recalls the multiple vessels in which poems are enclosed within the *Prison*.[35] The image of the mould thus activates the bodily involvement of texts and their vessels, including the codex, as forms in which the products of human language achieve concrete expression, reifying the natural rhythms of speech, and obscuring the corporeal associations of lyric, in its relationship to song and its articulation of emotion.[36]

A consolation for loss and a form of text, the image of Neptisphelé suggests the role of the inventive faculty of memory, in supplying a likeness of the inaccessible object of desire that provides solace and enables the subject to function in society.[37] Froissart's adaptation of mythic elements in the tale envisages the practice of image making as the alternative to an Orphic journey to the underworld, doomed to failure and linked with a fall into vice.[38] The idea of a descent associated with an excess of sentiment and indulgence in unproductive modes of enjoyment is also at issue in the body of the *Prison*, in a passage which forges intertextual links with the Boethian tradition. Describing the experience of love, Flos argues:

---

[34]   On rhetorical invention as 'hermeneutical performance on a traditional textual source', see Copeland, *Rhetoric, Hermeneutics, and Translation*, 179.

[35]   Cerquiglini-Toulet, 'Fullness and Emptiness', 235.

[36]   On verse and the enclosure of living bodies, see Cerquiglini, *La Couleur de la mélancolie: La fréquentation des livres au XIVe siècle 1300–1415* (Paris: Haiter, 1993), 67; *Un Engin si soutil*, 194–5.

[37]   For valuable readings of Froissart's approach to memory and mnemonic consolation in other works, see Swift, '*Tamainte Consolation*'; Sarah Kay, '"Le moment de conclure": Initiation as Retrospection in Froissart's *Dits amoureux*', in Nicola F. McDonald and W.M. Ormrod (eds), *Rites of Passage: Cultures of Transition in the Fourteenth Century* (York: York Medieval Press, 2004), 153–71, and *The Place of Thought*, 123–49.

[38]   On Froissart's adaptation of the Orpheus myth, see Huot, *From Song to Book*, 312–13; and Douglas Kelly, 'Les inventions ovidiennes de Froissart: Reflexions intertextuelles comme imagination', *Littérature* 41 (1981): 82–92.

> [...] il n'est lettres ne consaus
> Ne avis ne science d'omme
> Qu valoir y puist une pomme,
> Fors seulement li aventure.
> Tout ensi comme on s'aventure
> En le mer ou on puet nagier,
> Ou on se met en grant dangier,
> Car entre le vie et le mort
> N'i a q'une asselle de bort
> Ensi en amours (624–33)

[...there is neither text nor counsel, wisdom nor human knowledge worth an apple in this case, excepting only fortune. Just as one ventures into the sea where one may sail, putting oneself into great danger there, for between life and death there is only a little plank of wood, so it is in love]

Recollecting his own reaction to disappointment in love, he describes how, on parting from his beloved, 'Merancolïeus et pensieus, /Contre terre clinans mes ieus' ['Melancholy and thoughtful, I cast my eyes to the ground'] (657–8). The figure of driftwood on the sea recalls the pervasive Boethian imagery of the mutable world as a perilous ocean, and it is also reminiscent of the discussion of idolatry offered in the book of Wisdom, contrasting the sure hope of safety felt by those who trust in God's ark, the covenant of faith, with the folly of those who call on wooden idols (Wisdom 14. 1–11). In association with Flos's downcast gaze, this passage evokes the Boethian metaphor of spiritual descent, where the casting of one's eyes to the ground marks the state of being in exile from oneself, in bondage to the material world. Through its adaptation in Machaut's *Confort d'ami*, discussed above, this metaphor had been recast in erotic terms, as the image of the effect of ungoverned libidinous desire on the judgement. Machaut links this figure with idolatry, since it entails an inability to escape from a focus on matter as a thing in itself, rather than a sign that the subject might use to achieve redemptive understanding.[39] The gesture of casting one's eyes earthward is repeated in Froissart's poetic corpus, as an expression of the lover's inner turmoil, and against the background of the Boethian tradition, it becomes a metaphor for those moments when desire exceeds control, producing a state of deadlock in which the subject is tormented by frustrated longing.[40]

Froissart adapts the Pygmalion legend in the tale of Pynoteüs, intermingling elements from various myths, in a narrative that evokes not only the story of Orpheus, but also that of Pyramus and Thisbe, amongst others.[41] In framing the creation of Pynoteüs's image as a response to loss, rather than a self-contained

---

[39]   See above and Cropp, 'The Medieval French Tradition', 255–65.

[40]   Jean Froissart, *L'Espinette amoureuse*, ed. Anthime Fourrier (Paris: Klincksieck, 1963), ll. 1195, 3355, 3795.

[41]   On Froissart's treatment of myth, see Huot, *From Song to Book*, 312–14 and Lechat, *Dire par fiction*, 281–93.

action, Froissart constructs the use of art as a conscious effort on the part of the wounded subject to heal itself: as Pynoteüs argues, 'Neptisphelé ne rarai mes, / Mes j'en ferai bien une tele' ['I shall never have Neptisphelé back, but I can surely make one such'] (1689–90). Pynoteüs's actions reflect the use of the faculty of memory, which issues in writing, in creating a mental image of the desired object that can effectively replace it. As an allegory of literary invention, the making of the second Neptisphelé suggests a link between the activities of human artificers and the creative act of ineffable God, as the construction of signs to be used, rather than enjoyed as things in themselves. The point is underlined in Pynoteüs' prayer to Phoebus:

> [...] la Terre en quoi tu oevres
> Et escrips lettres et signaus
> Generaus et especiaus
> [...]
> Tes merveilles innumerable
> Sont si grandes et si notables
> Que bouce ne le poroit dire
> Ne mains volume ne escrire
> (1889–91, 1908–11)

> [... the Earth over which you rule and wherein you write letters and signals both general and ... Your innumerable marvels are so great and notable that mouth cannot tell them, nor hands compile them in a book, nor write them]

Froissart's substitution of Phoebus for Venus as the deity who gives life to the image lends a Christian resonance to the function of the divine in investing the products of human art with meaning. Some medieval theologians identified the scientific properties of light as a particular manifestation of the nature of divinity in the material world, supplying a context in which Phoebus Apollo might function as an analogue for God, as in the opening of Dante's *Paradiso*.[42] Against this background, the role of Phoebus in the *Prison* suggests the conception of the moral significance of secular writing as a form of *auctoritas* derived from God, rather than the human author. As a sun-god, Phoebus perhaps also suggests the effect of a work's title: medieval commentators etymologised the term *titulus* to an analogy with Titan, since both have illuminating properties.[43] Froissart's tale underlines the sense that the proper use of signs entails a consciousness that their meaning is not intrinsic, and demands an appeal to the divine.

The figure of Phoebus Apollo also recalls another aspect of textual production, the relationship between patron and poet. As Sylvia Huot argues, the god offers an

---

[42]   Dante Alighieri, *The Divine Comedy of Dante Alighieri III: Paradiso*, trans. John D. Sinclair (Oxford: Oxford University Press, 1961) 1.13–27, and see Monica Rutledge, 'Dante, the Body and Light', *Dante Studies*, 113 (1995): 151–65.

[43]   On the interpretation of secular works and *auctoritas*, see Minnis, *Medieval Theory of Authorship*, and for the etymology of *titulus*, 19.

appropriate emblem for the authority of the patron, while his association with music and poetry links him to the poet. His laurel emblem recalls the metamorphosis of Daphne, the symbol of a desire that issues in literary invention rather than sexual congress, apposite to the clerical narrator.[44] The tale thus flatters the patron, indicating his inspirational role in commissioning the work, while it also suggests the practice of the writer. A laurel leaf is central to the ritual that brings the second Neptisphelé to life, whose effect suggests the quickening effect of inspiration upon a text, as Kevin Brownlee has observed; the leaf's mediating role additionally evokes the function of leaves of paper or parchment, as the materials that facilitate the process of book production. [45]

Framed as a response to the tale of Pynoteüs, Rose's dream operates as the first of a series of interlinked commentaries on Flos's work.[46] In thus presenting the allegorical materials that serve to locate the work in contemporary political society as literary criticism, Froissart requires the reader to focus on imprisonment as a subjective experience, rather than a historical fact. Flos's multiple gloss on the dream deepens this impression, as he interprets the referential elements of the dream as aspects of 'la vie amoureuse de vous et de vostre dame' ['the love life of you and your lady'] (IX. 53, p. 152). The prison itself is glossed as the lethargy to which Rose falls prey when disappointed in love (IX 62–7, p. 152). Yet the terms of the allegory suggest another interpretation: the image of Rose as a prisoner in the castle of Atemprance, consoled by Souvenir (Memory), who enables him to communicate with his lady, is an apt reflection of the subject who uses the faculty of memory to overcome the pain of misfortune and to moderate the appetitive will. Through the interplay of allegory and history, Wenceslas's experience of captivity is imaginatively recast as a Boethian education, through which he develops the ability to imprison himself through the pleasant exercise of discipline. This redemptive reading of imprisonment finds expression in the consolation Souvenir offers to Rose: 'Vous en vaurrés encore le mieus /De vo prison et de vo prise!' ['you will be accounted still more worthy for your imprisonment and capture!] (3284–5). Souvenir advises him to be 'D'entention ferme et estable' ['steadfast and steady of will'], and to remember that 'Li apris et chil a aprendre /Ne sont repris ne a reprendre' ['those who are learned and the one who is to learn are not blamed, nor are they to be reproached'] (3303; 3305–6). As the prison is recast as a place of instruction, the stigma of imprisonment dissipates, while the naming of Rose's cell as 'Amoureuse li bien celee' ['love, the well-concealed'] suggests the conception of a well-regulated affection as the means to self-government (3290).

---

44 Sylvia Huot, 'The Daisy and the Laurel: Myths of Desire and Creativity in the Poetry of Jean Froissart', *Yale French Studies* (special edition), *Contexts: Style and Values in Medieval Art and Literature* (1991): 240–251 (244–6).

45 Kevin Brownlee, 'Ovide et le Moi poétique "moderne" à la fin du Moyen Âge: Jean Froissart et Christine de Pizan', in Brigitte Cazelles and Charles Méla (eds.), *Modernité au moyen âge: Le défi du passé* (Geneva: Droz, 1990), 160–61.

46 On commentary within the *Prison*, see Douglas Kelly, 'Imitation, Metamorphosis, and Froissart's use of the exemplary *Modus tractandi*', in Maddox and Sturm-Maddox (eds), *Froissart Across the Genres,* 101–18.

The conception of love as an instrument of governance is still more powerfully expressed in the final gloss supplied by Flos, an interpretation of the myth of Phaeton, recounted in Pynoteüs's prayer. Emphasising the subjective experience of love, Flos interprets Phaeton's mother, Clymene, as 'l'imagination d'un amant la quele engender un desir et dou quel Amours est peres' ['a lover's imagination, which engenders a desire fathered by Amours'] (XII. 70–71, p. 172). Phaeton's catastrophic attempt to drive Phoebus' chariot is interpreted as the outcome of desire's government of the *vie amoureuse*. Desire is unable to keep to the path of Reason, even with the aid of bridle of Cognissance (knowledge): 'ensi que li amans fort enamourés […] pert souvent maniere, avis et contenance, et oublie au ferir et au cachier les chevaus de l'escorgie d'Atemprance, mes chemine tous jour savant, sans rieule et sans mesure' ['just as the lover who is deeply enamoured ... often loses his comportment and discretion, and is put out of countenance, forgetting to his and urge the horses on with the whip of moderation, but keeps driving on, without control or restraint'] (XII. 130–35, p. 174). The image of love as a chariot occurs in Andreas Capellanus, as Douglas Kelly has observed, yet it also evokes the Boethian image of divine love as the charioteer who holds the reins of the universe (2.m.8).[47] In both the *Consolation* and the myth of Phaeton, the absence of Love's guidance results in disaster. In Froissart's *Prison*, the function of Amours as charioteer suggests the role of a benevolent love that brings the appetitive will into accord with reason, as the means to maintain the equilibrium of the soul and avoid despair. However, in Flos's interpretations of both Rose's dream and the myth of Phaeton, the lover does not escape the prison of longing through his own self-discipline, but through the intervention of Francise (generosity, IX. 79–83, p. 153; XII. 139–50, p. 174). This emphasis on external influence complements the role of Phoebus in the tale of Pynoteüs, implying that the success of human efforts is ultimately dependent on their relation to the divine. The human subject, whose will is tainted by the Fall, can aspire to redeem appetite through self-government, but true liberation can only be achieved through the mercy of divine grace.

In realising and expanding a dream through the production of texts in an epistolary exchange between poet and patron, Froissart exposes the function of the vision as an image of literary composition within Machaut's *Fonteinne amoureuse*. The resemblance between these two texts is underlined by the duplication of the gift of a ruby ring as a love token given to the nobleman by the lady (*Prison* 3180–81; *Fonteinne* 2504–6, 2523–4). These echoes highlight the *Prison*'s didactic intent: in order to protect himself against the assaults of the appetitive will and overcome the peril of misfortune, the prince must take on the qualities of the poet. In Froissart's text, the figure of Wenceslas of Brabant is presented as a master of the mnemonic and inventive skills employed in the composition of poetry, and as an exemplary moral subject whose nobility constrains him to remain in love's prison in order to live. To him, 'est ceste prison jolie et amoureuse' ['this prison is pleasant and agreeable'] (XII. 29, p. 171). Through their shared effort of textual production, both poet and patron are imagined as the subjects of a Boethian redemption.

---

[47]   Kelly, *Medieval Imagination*, 167.

Chapter 5
Redeeming Memory:
Thomas Usk's *Testament of Love*

'Many men there ben that with eeres openly sprad so moche swalowen the delyciousnesse of jestes and of ryme by queynt knyttyng colours, that of the goodnesse or of the badnesse of the sentence take they lytel hede or els none'.[1] In the first line of *The Testament of Love*, Thomas Usk draws attention to a susceptibility to the pleasures of textual consumption that causes the reader to suspend moral judgement. Yet, Usk pleads that his own writing lacks this immersive property, since 'Sothely, dul wytte and a thoughtful soule so sore have myned and graffed in my spyrites that suche craft of endytyng wol not ben of myn acqueyntaunce' (45). Usk's ambiguous confession is prescient in identifying his character and personal experience as factors limiting the *Testament*'s capacity to engage the reader: the autobiographical qualities of Usk's prose narrative evoke his notorious involvement in the factional politics of Ricardian London, his defection from the party of his former master, John Northampton, and his decision to testify against him on charges of treason in 1384.[2] Himself executed for treason at the hands of the Merciless Parliament in 1388, Usk anticipates the suspicions of an audience unwilling to withhold judgement.

In its modern form, the hypercritical tendency to elide the distinction between Usk's life and work is typified by W.W. Skeat's assessment of the *Testament*: 'there is much about the piece that is vague, shifty, and unsatisfactory. He is too full of excuses, and too plausible; in a word, too selfish'.[3] A similar fusion of literature and life is reflected in persistent attempts to position Usk as Chaucer's unsuccessful counterpart: as Thomas Prendergast observes, critical insistence upon Usk's aesthetic, political and personal failings facilitates the retrospective construction of Chaucer as a writer whose poetic skill is an index of his political acumen.[4] For Paul Strohm, Chaucer exhibits a 'more successful attitude toward

---

[1]   Thomas Usk, *Testament of Love*, ed. Gary W. Shawver (Toronto: University of Toronto Press, 2002), 45. Subsequent quotations are from this edition.

[2]   Useful detailed accounts of Usk's life include Paul Strohm, 'Politics and Poetics: Usk and Chaucer in the 1380s', in Lee Patterson (ed.), *Literary Practice and Social Change in Britain, 1380–1550* (Berkeley: University of California Press, 1990), 83–112; and the introduction to Shawver's edition, 7–23.

[3]   W.W. Skeat, *The Complete Works of Chaucer: Chaucerian and Other Pieces*, vol. 7 (Oxford: Clarendon, 1897), xxv.

[4]   On this critical tendency, see Thomas A. Prendergast, 'Chaucer's Doppelgänger: Thomas Usk and the Reformation of Chaucer', in Thomas A. Prendergast and Barbara Kline (eds), *Rewriting Chaucer: Culture, Authority, and the Idea of the Authentic Text, 1400–1602* (Columbus: Ohio State University Press, 1999), 258–69.

both the politics and the poetics of faction', while 'Usk's highly self-interested and precipitate personal choices seem consistent with his attempts to bend literary form to personal purposes of immediate advancement'.[5] Yet, recent work illuminating the ideological landscape of fourteenth-century London undermines the assumption that participation in the factionalist world of contemporary politics was prohibitively dangerous for the bureaucrats of the 1380s. Marion Turner's analysis of Usk's professional connections indicates that such variations in political allegiance were not uncommon, while Clementine Oliver has examined the active production and circulation of political pamphlets by bureaucrats like Thomas Fovent.[6] The drive to produce a moral evaluation of Usk and his narrative risks the misrepresentation of both the text and contemporary political culture. As Isabel Davis argues, 'critical distaste at the self-interest with which language is deployed in the *Testament* is disingenuous about the nature of writing in general and life writing in particular, which is always, surely, put to subjective use'.[7] Rather than seeking to vindicate or censure Usk's actions, this chapter explores the *Testament* as a textual engagement with *The Consolation of Philosophy* in its enlarged role as a model for conceptualising experience. Within the *Testament*, self-construction coincides with the formulation of an ideology of public service, as Usk recasts personal history in Boethian terms.

In imagining disarming rhetoric as a craft that 'wol not ben of myn acqueyntaunce', Usk anticipates the autobiographical content of the *Testament*, in which he presents himself as a marginalised subject, alienated from society by his disloyalty to his former associates. Historically, this act of betrayal was itself bound up with the practice of writing: Usk entered Northampton's service in his capacity as a scribe, and his defection is embodied in the documentary form of his testimony, the *appellum* he composed in 1384. In place of the customary oral deposition, Usk supplied written evidence, invoking the genre of the approver's appeal to produce a text that recognises his own, compromised status, as a witness who is himself complicit in the treasonous plot he denounces. As Paul Strohm argues, the absence of evidence to suggest that Usk was formally charged with any crime at this juncture indicates a creative use of the concept of appellancy, which typically enabled felons to mitigate their punishment through confession and the provision of testimony contributing to the conviction of their accomplices. Usk's testimony employs the approver's appeal as a form that 'converts complicity into a source of authority if not a virtue in its own right'.[8] The *appellum* emphasises a

---

5   Strohm, 'Politics and Poetics', 112.

6   Clementine Oliver, *Parliament and Political Pamphleteering in Fourteenth-Century England* (Woodbridge: York Medieval Press, 2010), incorporating a revised version of 'A Political Pamphleteer in Late Medieval England: Thomas Fovent, Geoffrey Chaucer, Thomas Usk, and the Merciless Parliament of 1388', *New Medieval Literatures* 6 (2003): 167–98; Marion Turner, 'Usk and the Goldsmiths', *New Medieval Literatures* 9 (2008): 139–77.

7   Isabel Davis, *Writing Masculinity in the Later Middle Ages* (Cambridge: Cambridge University Press, 2006), 39.

8   Paul Strohm, *Hochon's Arrow: The Social Imagination of Fourteenth-Century Texts* (Princeton: Princeton University Press, 1992), 148; on Usk's 'Appeal', see 145–60.

culpability given even greater prominence when Usk delivered his accusations in person at Northampton's arraignment in Reading, 18 August 1384: according to the Westminster chronicler, Usk prefaced each article with the words 'Ego, T. H., proditor'.[9]

The strategic attempt to transform weakness into a source of authority also characterises the *Testament*. Usk's admission that he lacks the skill that might facilitate the seduction of the reader gives way to the claim that the deficient text has redeeming qualities of its own: 'for rude wordes and boystous percen the herte of the herer to the inrest poynte and planten there the sentence of thynges so that with lytel helpe it is able to spring' (45). Usk's partial apology recalls the enduring suspicion of fiction as a form of falsehood, and his aesthetic choices resonate with the increasing cultural tendency to conceive prose as the most appropriate medium for veridical discourse. In consequence, as Michael Hanrahan argues, the *Testament*'s relationship to *The Consolation of Philosophy* positions Usk's deliberate production of a text that lacks the seductive properties of rhyme as counterpart to Philosophy's banishment of the strumpet muses of poetry from Boethius's company.[10] Yet, if Usk dissociates his work from the most intoxicating effects of poetry, his figurative language nevertheless insistently frames the reading of prose in terms of erotic seduction: in piercing the heart, 'rude wordes' resemble Cupid's arrows. Rather than representing a tactical oversight that undermines Usk's project of self-vindication, as Hanrahan claims, the seductions of the *Testament* instead serve to acknowledge the affective character of embodied experience, and its implications for pedagogical practice.[11]

In representing the transmission of knowledge as a forcible blow that penetrates the heart of the hearer, Usk evokes the metaphoric role of the heart as the seat of memory. The material character of Usk's image underlines the conception of sensory perception and memory as physiological processes, whose operation entails a form of inscription: the 'sentence' implanted in the heart of the hearer recalls the perennial model of memory as writing surface, as a book or set of wax tablets.[12] At once associated with physical violence and intense emotion, the image of the wounded heart recognises information as being inextricably intertwined with the material forms in which it is instantiated, in a mutually transformative relation. As a corporeal object, whose surface must be broken in order to plant a verbal message there, the heart recalls the animal skins pierced and marked in medieval writing praxis. In connecting inscription with the breaching of bodily

Usk's testimony is published as 'The Appeal of Thomas Usk against John Northampton', in R.W. Chambers and Marjorie Daunt (eds), *A Book of London English 1384–1425* (Oxford: Clarendon Press, 1967), 22–31.

[9]   'I, Thomas Usk, traitor', *The Westminster Chronicle, 1381–1394*, ed. and trans. L.C. Hector and B.F. Harvey (Oxford: Clarendon Press, 1982) 92–3.

[10]   Michael Hanrahan, 'The Seduction of *The Testament of Love*', *Literature and History* 7.1 (1998): 1–15 (4, 13n12).

[11]   Hanrahan, 'The Seduction'.

[12]   On medieval conceptions of memory, see Carruthers, *The Book of Memory*, especially 24–5, 139–40.

boundaries, the transfixed heart also resonates with more familiar representations of Christ's body as a charter penned in blood.[13] Like these images, the wounded heart emphasises the part affect has to play in recollection: it acknowledges the relationship between strong emotions and the things we remember, in the involuntary sentiments stirred up by human experience, and as a tool consciously employed by practitioners of the arts of memory to stimulate reminiscence. Usk's use of this image suggests that, in common with Thomas Aquinas, he conceives learning as a process that necessarily involves the senses, where 'simple and spiritual ideas' must be 'tied [...] to bodily images', because 'human knowledge has more mastery over objects of sense'.[14] For both, concentration is not a purely mental phenomenon, but an affective and sensual one.[15]

Usk's sense of the tangibility of information is also articulated in his attention to the materiality of the book; as the editors of Usk's prologue remark, he is 'hauntingly aware of the embodiedness of textual production'.[16] Within the prologue, the juxtaposition of 'rude wordes' and 'semelych' rhetorical colours gives way to a contrast drawn between literal practices of illumination: 'Some men there ben that peynten with colours ryche, and some with vers, as with red ynke, and some with coles and chalke' (45). As Ardis Butterfield observes, the association of verse with red ink reflects scribal conventions adopted to represent poetry in manuscript copies of vernacular texts and sermons produced in England and France.[17] Usk's consciousness of the material qualities of the text, and their impact upon reception, is also witnessed by the acrostic embedded within the *Testament*. Formed from the initial letters of each chapter, the acrostic identifies the work as a petition: MARGARETE OF VIRTW HAVE MERCI ON THIN USK.[18] This acrostic phrase is doubly obscured within the only surviving version of the text, published by William Thynne 144 years after Usk's death: the misattribution suggested by the *Testament*'s publication in *The Workes of Geffray Chaucer* was apparently compounded by the misconstruction of several chapter divisions and the disordering of some quires.[19] Despite its problems, however, Thynne's text nevertheless incorporates ornaments, in the form of woodblock initials, indicating structural divisions within the text, and facilitating the retrieval of the acrostic.

---

[13] Carruthers, *The Craft of Thought*, 100–103; Emily Steiner, *Documentary Culture and the Making of Medieval English Literature* (Cambridge: Cambridge University Press, 2003), 18.

[14] Thomas Aquinas, *Summa Theologiæ*, 2a2æ. 49. I, 63.

[15] Carruthers, *The Book of Memory*, 216–17.

[16] Headnote to '*The Testament of Love*: Prologue (Extract),' in Jocelyn Wogan-Browne et al. (eds), *The Idea of the Vernacular: An Anthology of Middle English Literary Theory, 1280–1520* (Exeter: University of Exeter Press, 1999), 29.

[17] Ardis Butterfield, *The Familiar Enemy: Chaucer, Language and Nation in the Hundred Years War* (Cambridge: Cambridge University Press, 2003) 338n97.

[18] On the acrostic, see Henry Bradley, 'Thomas Usk and the "Testament of Love"', *Englische Studien* 23 (1897): 437–8; for a slightly different rendering, see Shawver, 4–5.

[19] *The Workes of Geffray Chaucer newly printed with dyuers workes whiche were neuer in print before*, ed. William Thynne (London: Thomas Godfray 1532), STC 5068.

In her astute reconstructive account of Thynne's lost exemplar, Anne Middleton infers that, in this respect, the printer's choices reflect the decorative program of his manuscript source, and its role in signing the *ordinatio* of the *Testament*.[20] Usk's acrostic suggests an acute scribal awareness of the value of bibliographical codes, shaping the material components of the text to enlarge and reinforce its meaning.

In this context, the close proximity of Usk's insistence that his writing lacks the seductive potency of rhyme to his eroticised image of the impact of prose does not subvert his argument in the way that Hanrahan claims. Instead, it serves as an acknowledgement that, for embodied subjects, sensory experience is a precondition of knowledge. Usk's prologue offers a further indication of the extent to which bodily apprehension is regarded as being fundamental to cognition, and of its role in shaping the language used to discuss thought. An expression of anxiety about the risks associated with bodily perviousness, of what might be swallowed by 'eeres openly sprad' as the senses are seduced by pleasurable sensation, Usk's opening sentence taps into a rich vein of associations between reading and eating. Surviving in the term rumination, a metaphor suggested by the movement of the mouth in early reading practice, the idea of eating the book is conceptually linked with memory in medieval tradition.[21] The metaphoric identification of memory and digestion presents the remediation of texts from the page to the mind as a process that entails material change, altering both subjects and their textual objects. Since memory was conventionally identified as the basis of ethical character, the materiality of these conceptions suggests the key role of the senses in medieval epistemology and morality.

If embodied interactions with the material world are conceived as being highly significant for human learning, however, they are not unproblematic. Usk's sense of the position of human subjects in relation to their environment is indicated by his extensive use of *De Concordia* in the third book of the *Testament*, appropriating Anselm's treatise on the compatibility of divine foreknowledge, predestination, grace and free will to frame his own narrative.[22] Anselm argues that human subjects deprived themselves of their original justice or rectitude of will at the Fall; unable to regain this uprightness of will except through grace, they nevertheless retained the will to happiness.[23] Translating Anselm, Usk defines happiness or 'blysse' as a

---

[20] Anne Middleton, 'Thomas Usk's "Perdurable Letters": The *Testament of Love* From Script to Print', *Studies in Bibliography* 51 (1998): 63–116 (72–4).

[21] Carruthers, *The Book of Memory*, 53, 205–11.

[22] George Sanderlin demonstrates Usk's use of approximately 45 percent of Anselm's treatise, while R. Allen Shoaf estimates that 'this 45% amounts to slightly more than the same percentage of *TL* 3'. Thomas Usk, *The Testament of Love*, ed. R. Allen Shoaf (Kalamazoo: Medieval Institute Publications, 1998), 431; George Sanderlin, 'Usk's *Testament of Love* and St. Anselm', *Speculum* 17 (1942): 69–73.

[23] Anselm of Canterbury, *De Concordia* (The Compatibility of God's Foreknowledge, Predestination, and Grace with Human Freedom), trans. Thomas Bermingham, *The Major Works*, ed. Brian Davies and G. R. Evans (Oxford: Oxford University Press, 1998), 3.7, 3.12, 3.13.

state in which nothing is lacking, 'suffysaunce of covenable comodytees without any maner nede' (3.8, 184).[24] Within the *Testament*, modelled upon the *Consolation*, this definition strongly evokes the Boethian identification of sufficiency as the end instinctively pursued by human subjects. Although 'evenliche purposed to the good folk and to the badde', however, this sovereign good can only be achieved by those whose desire is correctly oriented: 'the gode folk seken it by naturel office of vertus, and the schrewes enforcen hem to getin it by diverse coveytise of erthly thinges, whiche that nys noon naturel office to gete thilke same soverein good'.[25] Usk frames Anselm's analysis of the problem in erotic terms: 'thus for [mankind] weyved rightfulnesse, lost hath he his blysse, but fayle of his desyre in his owne comodyte may he not, and were comodytes to his reasonable nature […] may he not have, to false lustes, whiche been bestyal appetytes, he is turned'.[26] Will is 'not maked yvel, but unrightful, by absence of rightfulnesse': desire is no longer intuitively directed towards the good, but nor is it inherently evil (3.8, 188).

In this respect, my reading of Usk's treatment of Anselm differs from that of Sanderlin, who finds that the most distinctive feature of Usk's translation is also its most confusing: the application of Anselm's theological arguments to the interlocutor's love for Margaret, through the substitution of 'love' for Anselm's *rectitudo*. For Sanderlin, rendering 'recta voluntas' as 'lovinge wil' confounds the end of the will, rectitude, with a particular act of the will, love: 'it makes little sense to talk about how the will attains or strives after the *act* of love when, as St Augustine says, in its essence the will *is* love. Love is not an *end* of the will'.[27] Yet Sanderlin's analysis in itself points towards an alternative interpretation of Usk's argument, which links the Boethian conception of the subject's frustrated desire for the sovereign good with theological traditions articulated in Anselm, that identify carnal appetites, the lust of the flesh against the spirit, as the consequence of original sin.[28] Thomas Aquinas's formulation illustrates the logic of this argument: the loss of original justice at the Fall, as the will is turned away from God, effects the 'disorder of the other powers of the soul […] chiefly noticeable in an unruled turning to goods that pass away, which disorder can be designated by the term "concupiscence"'. As he argues, 'the disorder of concupiscence is attributed to concupiscence in as much as this is a primal passion, containing in a sense all other passions of the soul'.[29] Rather than referring to an act of the will, in substituting *love* for *rectitude*, Usk defines the *telos* of the will in terms of a distinction between love and concupiscence: the essence of an upright will is desire directed towards the true good, rather than false objects.

The association of love and correctly oriented desire is born out in Usk's gloss on Margaret, which identifies her as an appropriate symbolic object for an upright

---

[24]   Anselm, *De Concordia*, 3.13.
[25]   Geoffrey Chaucer, *Boece*, in Larry D. Benson (gen. ed.), *The Riverside Chaucer*, 4.pr.2.
[26]   Anselm, *De Concordia*, 3.13.
[27]   Sanderlin, 'Usk's *Testament*', 70.
[28]   Examples available to Usk through *De Concordia* include 3.7, 3.12.
[29]   Trans. in Thomas Aquinas, *Summa Theologiæ*, vol. 26, 1a2æ. 82, 3, 39.

will: 'Margarite a woman betokeneth grace, lernyng, or wisdom of God, or els holy church' (3.9, 196). Usk's use of Anselm thus functions to identify the text's autobiographical narrative as an account of the restoration of uprightness within a particular subject. Yet, Usk follows Anselm in emphasising that rectitude of will should be attributed to grace: 'neyther might I without grace toforn-goyng, and afterwarde-folowyng, thilke grace get ne kepe, and lese shal I it never, but if fre wyl it make' (3.8,180; *De Concordia* 3.4). Only grace enables the interlocutor to orientate his desire towards the good, achieving a state of grace that can only be lost of his own free will.

The reparation of the will, as a process entailing the provisional restoration of the ability to distinguish the sovereign good from 'false lustes', is also central to the narrative arc traced within *The Consolation of Philosophy*. Usk's substitution of Love for Philosophy as the advisory figure at the heart of his allegorical vision adapts Boethius along principles like those applied to Anselm, distinguishing love as the source of a knowledge which enables a reformation of the self. The *Testament* also evokes the *Consolation* in its use of autobiographical material to explore and recast a particular experience of political disgrace and imprisonment as an example with universal value. Inviting the reader to identify his own past experience with that of the interlocutor, Usk underlines the extent to which his position is emblematic of the human condition, and in doing so, he transforms his culpability into a source of authority. Like Boethius, Usk characterises his past error as the effect of a misdirected will, through his use of Anselm and through the analogy Love offers for the experience of the interlocutor and 'al other that amysse have erred', adapted from Proverbs 7 (2.14, 123). Love argues that the 'scholer, lernynge of my lore, in sechyng of my blysse', who finds himself afflicted by the 'derknesse of many doutes' is like an innocent who meets a woman 'as a strumpet arayed' on a dark night, and is seduced. Because 'he ne wote in what waye he is in', he 'may lightly ben begyled' by 'love fayned, not clothed of my lyvery, but unleful lustye habyte'. The woman's seductive invitation, 'Come and be we dronken of our swete pappes', is glossed as the 'fayre honyed wordes' of 'heretykes and missemenynge people' (2.14, 124). As several critics have noted, the analogy serves in part as self-justification for Usk's involvement with Northampton's party.[30] Usk identifies his error, not as disloyalty to his former masters, but as having been seduced by rhetoric to support their cause. Usk's analogy functions to inscribe this experience as an illustration of human susceptibility to sensual pleasures, the effect of an inability to differentiate between the 'blysse' of Love and concupiscence.

The association of darkness and sensual intoxication in Usk's passage, in the context of a text modelled upon the *Consolation*, also recalls Boethius' analogy for the human position: 'men the corage alwey reherceth and seketh the sovereyne

---

[30] See, for example, Davis, *Writing Masculinity*, 66; Andrew Galloway, 'Private Selves and the Intellectual Marketplace in Late Fourteenth-Century England: The Case of the Two Usks', *New Literary History* 28.2 (1997): 291–318 (297); Ramona Bressie, 'The Date of Thomas Usk's "Testament of Love"', *Modern Philology* 26.1 (1928): 17–29 (25).

good, al be it so that it be with a dyrkyd memorie; but he not by whiche path, ryght as a dronke man not nat by which path he may retourne hom to his hous' (3.pr.2). Like Usk's formulation of Proverbs 7, Boethius' analogy reflects a conception of human subjects as endowed with an innate desire to seek out the satisfactions of the sovereign good, although their ability to determine its source has been damaged.

In both the *Consolation* and the *Testament*, the interlocutors' dejection is presented as symptom of spiritual impairment, of their difficulty in recognising the sovereign good. Their shared condition of imprisonment bears a similar interpretation, at once marking a physical location and a metaphysical state. The traditional identification of Boethius as prisoner is paralleled in the captivity of Usk's protagonist, perhaps a more literal representation of Usk's situation than has sometimes been allowed. As a result of his involvement with Northampton, Usk was imprisoned at least twice, once in 1384, for a period of approximately six weeks, and for some two months prior to his execution on 4 March 1388. An entry in the issue rolls of the exchequer suggests that Usk was also in custody between December 1384 and June 1385, on charges relating to the making of the *appellum*.[31] Yet, whether or not the *Testament* was composed during this, or Usk's final period of imprisonment, Usk's text emphasises incarceration as ontological condition.[32] The 'derke' and 'contrarious prison' forms part of a spiritual topography: 'in this pynynge pytte with wo I lygge ystocked, with chaynes lynked of care and of tene. It is so hye from thens I lye and the commune erth, there ne is cable in no lande maked that myght stretche to me to drawe me into blysse; ne steyers to stey on is none' (1.1.48–89). Like Boethius, Usk's protagonist also conceives his state as a subjective form of banishment, pleading 'my wytte is exiled' (1.1.49). In these analogies, coercive discipline offers a metaphor for the punishment of a guilt both ontological and ordinary.

Usk's error is presented as the effect of a characteristically human fallibility, the mark of a common punishment, and a fault itself deserving of punishment. The penalty exacted is not simply retributive, however: it has a pedagogical purpose. Love underlines the point in her interpretation of human suffering: 'with the more sorowe that a thynge is getten, the more he hath joye the ilke thyng afterwardes to kepe, as it fareth by chyldren in schole that for lernynge arne beaten, whan their lesson they foryetten. Commenly after a good disciplynyng with a yerde, they kepe right wel doctryne of their schole' (2.11, 117). Usk's explanation reflects a contemporary pedagogical ideology that constructs violence 'as a veritable

---

[31]   Exchequer, Issue Rolls, P.R.O., E 403/508, m. 17, excerpted in Ramona Bressie, 'The Date', citing E403/508, m. 6, and published in Shawver, 19.

[32]   Shawver and Bressie argue for composition between December 1384 and June 1385. Paul Strohm favours 1385–1386, arguing that the treatment of imprisonment is figurative, rather than literal, 'Politics and Poetics', 88. Stephen Medcalf hypothesises two phases of composition, the first prior to Usk's appointment as under-sheriff of Middlesex, the second during his final imprisonment, 'The World and Heart of Thomas Usk', in A.J. Minnis, Charlotte C. Morse and Thorlac Turville-Petre (eds), *Essays on Ricardian Literature in Honour of J.A. Burrow* (Oxford: Clarendon, 1997), 232.

mnemonic principle': as Robert Mills observes, corporal punishment is imagined not only as a bodily discipline, but as a means of inscribing knowledge in the mind.[33] The presence of this tradition within the *Testament* endorses the conception of learning as a process that entails bodily affect, indicating the materiality of memory. Love's analogy is offered to assuage the interlocutor's present suffering, and its effect is to construct Usk's own experience of political misfortune as a mark of divine authority's care for his spiritual education. In its emphasis on the instructive value of adversity, Usk's point corresponds to Philosophy's analysis of Boethius's misfortune: 'thilke blynde goddesse Fortune [...] that yit covereth and wympleth hir to other folk, hath schewyd hir every del to the' (2.pr.1). Love's argument not only applies to the interlocutor's particular misfortune, however, but describes an inescapable part of the human condition: 'there is no man on lyve that maye come to a precious thyng longe coveyted, but he somtyme suffre teneful diseases' (2.1, 117). In this respect, Usk's image of flagellation finds a parallel in Anselm's *De Concordia*, where the scourge functions as a metaphor for the penalty of original sin that remains with the living despite their reconciliation with Christ through baptism, at once as a deserved punishment, and an opportunity for the acquisition of merit through faith and hope (*De Concordia*, 3. 9). Here too, punishment is both a mark of fault, and a means to improvement.

Usk's interlocutor acknowledges the double guilt of personal error and original sin. Guilt and redemption are at once particular and universal problems, whose relationship is clarified as Usk identifies the *Testament* as the microcosmic reflection of Christian temporality. The book's tripartite form is modelled on 'this worlde in thre tymes [...] devyded':

> the first is cleped de[vi]acion, that is to say, goyng out of trewe way; and al that tho dyeden, in hel were thy punisshed, for a mans synn, tyl grace and mercy fette hem thence [...]The seconde tyme lasteth from the commyng of merciable grace untyl the ende of transytorie tyme, in whiche is shewed the true way in fordoynge of the badde; and that is ycleped tyme of grace. And that thynge is not yeven by deserte of yeldynge one benefyte for another, but onely through goodnesse of the Yever of grace in thilke tyme. Who-so can wel understande is shapen to be saved in souled blysse. The thirde tyme shal gyn whan transytorie thynges of worldes han made their ende, and that shal been in joye, glorie, and rest, both body and soule, that wel han deserved in the tyme of grace. (3.1, 126)

Usk argues that his 'leude boke in thre maters accordaunt to tho tymes, lyghtly by a good inseer, may been understode':

> in the firste, erroure of myssegoynge is shewed, with sorowful pyne, punysshed [that] is cryed after mercy. In the seconde, is grace in good waye proved, whiche

---

[33]   Robert Mills, *Suspended Animation: Pain, Pleasure and Punishment in Medieval Culture* (London: Reaktion, 2005), 154–5. Mills's analysis is influenced by Jody Enders, *The Medieval Theatre of Cruelty: Rhetoric, Memory, Violence* (Ithaca, NY: Cornell University Press, 1999), 129–40.

is faylinge, without deserte, thylke first mysse amendynge in correction of tho erroures [in] even waye to bringe, with comforte of welfare into amendement wexynge. And in the thirde, joye and blysse graunted to hym that wel canne deserve it, and hath savour of understandynge in the tyme of grace. (3.1, 126–7)[34]

The structure and content of Usk's narrative are presented as a picture in little of the error and redemption of humankind. Yet, an uneasy relationship between desert and grace exists within this passage, and this is perhaps not entirely attributable to textual corruption. Emphasis on the orthodox argument that grace is a matter of God's goodness, 'not yeven by deserte', stands in tension with the claim that those who achieve bliss 'wel han deserved'.

Usk's conception of the relationship between human effort and salvation is also at stake in the treatment of Margaret, described both as a woman, and as her lapidary namesake, the margarite 'perle' once 'closed in a muskle with a blewe shell' (2.12, 118). Margaret's function as an emblem of 'grace [...] or wisdom of God' is indicated in the intertextual character of the interlocutor's complaint, which associates her with the parable of the pearl of great price (3.9, 196; Matt. 13.45–6). The interlocutor presents his situation as a counterpoint to that of the merchant of the parable: while the merchant sells all that he has to purchase the precious pearl, he protests, 'my moeble is insuffysaunt to countervayle the price of this jewel, or els to make theschange' (1.3, 58). Medieval exegetical tradition typically identifies the pearl of the parable with salvation, made possible through the renunciation of earthly goods.[35] Usk's formulation at once reflects the sense that human sacrifice cannot merit divine reward, and a particular anxiety about his own social position, as the interlocutor continues, 'no wight is worthy such perles to weare, but kynges or princes, or els their peres' (1.3, 58).

At this stage, the interlocutor's wits are clouded by sorrow, so his analysis is not fully endorsed by the text, but Usk's own position is clarified by the teachings attributed to Love, the centre of moral authority within the *Testament*. In the third book, Love answers the interlocutor's enquiry as to the nature of the reward he is to receive for his 'longe travayle': 'retrybucion of thy good wylles to have of the Margaryte perle, it beareth not the name of mede, but onely of good grace, and that cometh not of thy deserte, but of thy Margarytes goodnesse and vertue alone' (3.7, 176). Love's discourse draws on Anselm's *De Concordia* to establish that the interlocutor's efforts 'of wyl, of love, and of reson' are 'nothyng else but yeldyng of thy dette in quitynge of thy grace, which she the lent whan ye first mette' (176). Employing the analogy of a gift of clothing, which in Anselm is associated with God's gift of uprightness to a subject he has already endowed with free choice, Love explains: 'thou that were naked of love, and of thyselfe non have mightest, it is not to put to thyne owne persone, sythen thy love came throwe thy Margaryte

---

[34]   Shawver's text: '[v]aylinge', emended here to reflect Thynne. There is no editorial consensus on the emendation of this problematic word.

[35]   D.W. Robertson, Jr., 'The Pearl as a Symbol', *Modern Language Notes* 65 (1950): 155–61 (159).

perle. *Ergo* she was yever of the love althoughe thou it use, and there lent she the grace thy servyce to begynne'.[36] In this context, Margaret appears as the origin of goodness, while the interlocutor only has the use of it, and so cannot claim desert as a result of his labour: 'Al the thoughtes, besy doynges, and plesaunce in thy might and in thy wordes that thou canste devyse ben but right lytel in quitynge of thy dette [...] So al these maters kyndely drawen homewarde to this Margaryte perle, for from thence were they borowed' (176). In this respect, Margaret's function is analogous to that of the Boethian conception of the sovereign good, as the essence of God, the happiness which is 'the sovereyn fyn and the cause of alle the thinges that ben to reqiren', the true object of desire, and the universal point of origin (*Boece* 3.pr.10).[37]

Although Usk's argument emphasises the divine origins of goodness, and the impossibility of deserving grace, the text nevertheless suggests a degree of optimism in its approach to the mystery of salvation. Usk's interlocutor argues, 'if I, by my good wyl, deserve this Margarit perle and am nat thereto compelled and have free choice to do what me lyketh, she is than holden, as me thynketh to rewarde thentent of my god wyl'. Love responds, 'Goddes forbode els [...] Free wyle of good hert after-mede deserveth' (3.2, 133). In conjunction with Love's insistence that the recompense the interlocutor is to receive from Margaret is not the settling of a debt, but the effect of grace, this suggests a position comparable with *via moderna* theology. Theologians such as Robert Holcot understood justification as a matter of covenant between God and man: through mercy, God undertakes to offer grace to the subject who does what is in him (*facere quod in se est*). Although human works are insufficient in themselves to merit salvation, if subjects make the best use of their abilities, God will not fail to extend grace.[38] The claim that Margaret is 'holden' to reward Usk's good will reflects a similar, covenantal understanding of justification. Yet, in allowing a role, however limited, for human action in bringing about salvation, the *Testament* maps out a significant area of ambiguity at the intersection between the material and the spiritual.

The ambivalence within Usk's treatment of grace is appropriate to matters of faith, which coexists with, and is dependent upon the uncertainty of divine

---

[36] Anselm, *De Concordia*, 3.5.

[37] Geoffrey Chaucer, *Boece*, in Larry D. Benson (gen. ed.), *The Riverside Chaucer*, 3rd edn (Oxford: Oxford University Press, 1988), 397–469. Chaucer's *Boece* is cited as a contemporary English translation on which Usk drew in writing the *Testament*, although there is some debate as to which other versions he used. Virginia Bording Jellech argues for Usk's use of Jean de Meun's translation of the *Consolation*, 'The Testament of Love by Thomas Usk: A New Edition,' D. Phil. Diss., St. Louis: Washington University, 1970), 53–70. For analysis of Usk's use of the *Consolation*, see Stephen Medcalf, 'Transposition: Thomas Usk's *Testament of Love*', in Ellis (ed.), *The Medieval Translator*, 181–95; Shawver's edition, 29; and Siennicki, 'No Harbour', 100–112 and Appendix A.

[38] On Holcot and *via moderna* theology, see Heiko A. Oberman, *The Harvest of Medieval Theology: Gabriel Biel and Late-Medieval Nominalism* (Cambridge, MA.: Harvard University Press, 1963), 235–48; A.J. Minnis, 'Looking for a Sign: The Quest for Nominalism in Chaucer and Langland', in Minnis, Morse and Turville-Petre (eds), *Essays on Ricardian Literature*, 142–78.

mysteries that transcend the grasp of reason. Usk underlines this point in his conclusion, offering up a prayer 'that every man parfytly mowe knowe throwe what intencion of herte this treatyse have I drawe' (3.9, 196). His final gloss on the nature of Margaret is prefaced with an important comparison: 'Howe was it that syghtful Manna in deserte to chyldren of Israel was spirytuel meate; bodily also it was, for mennes bodies it norisshe[d]. And yet never-the-later, Christ it signyfyed'. Usk's argument emphasises the possibility that spiritual largesse may coincide with material sustenance, while nevertheless insisting upon the primacy of the spiritual within this mysterious process of transubstantiation: 'If breed thorowe vertue is made holy flesshe, what is [it] that our God saythe? It is the spyrite that yeveth lyfe; the flesshe of nothyng it profyteth. Flesshe is flesshly understandynge; flessh without grace and love naught is worth. The letter sleeth; the spyrit yeveth lyfelych understandyng' (196). As a clarification of authorial intention, the comparison functions to suggest that any material benefit Usk might derive from writing the *Testament* is a mark of divine favour, while insisting that such benefits are significant only insofar as they contribute to his spiritual health. Usk's comparison of his own state with that of the Israelites in exile articulates the sense that aspects of human sociality, including the political community, point towards the perfect concord of the divine order.

The obscure interrelation of divine and worldly favour underwrites the numerous interpretations that seek to identify Margaret with patronage, whether as the transmuted object of a desire for material advantage, or as the symbol of a particular benefactor. Usk's treatment of Margaret is not always consistent with his final identification of her as a transcendent object, an ambiguity illustrated by Love's proposition that Margaret will suffer divine sanctions if she does not take pity on her lover, or in the interlocutor's anxiety that his 'false fame' will come to Margaret's ears, 'so shal I ben hyndred withouten any measure of truth' (1.9, 76; 1.6, 68). Proposed identities for Usk's Margaret include Richard II, Queen Anne, and Margaret Berkeley, yet the particularity of any historical referent is arguably of lesser significance than the effect of Margaret's indeterminacy, in signalling a relationship between terrestrial politics and the kingdom of heaven.[39] The charges of self-interest levelled against Usk, in critical arguments that identify the *Testament*'s involvement in contemporary factional politics as being incompatible with the text's overtly devotional purposes, neglect the extent to which Usk engages with the problematic consequences of an embodied subject's

---

[39]   On Margaret as Richard II, see Joanna Summers, *Late-Medieval Prison Writing*, 49–59; Barbara Lorraine Siennicki, 'No Harbour for the "Shippe of Traveyle": A Study of Thomas Usk's *Testament of Love*', unpublished D. Phil. Thesis (Ontario: Queen's University, 1984); for Queen Anne, see Bressie, 'The Date'. Alice Spencer argues for a reconciliation of these readings as being compatible with an endorsement of 'absolutist royal authority', *Dialogues of Love and Government: A Study of the Erotic Dialogue Form in some Texts from the Courtly Love Tradition* (Newcastle: Cambridge Scholars Publishing, 2007), 107. For Margaret Berkeley, see Lucy Lewis, 'The Identity of Margaret in Thomas Usk's *Testament of Love*', *Medium Aevum* 68 (1999): 63–72.

desire to pursue the sovereign good, and the practical and material ways in which that desire finds expression.[40]

Usk presents the writing of his text as an ethical act that will contribute to the satisfaction of rational beings' 'appetyte to their perfection', whose 'most soverayne and fynal' form is 'in knowyng of a sothe, withouten any entent disceyvable, and in love of one very God that is inchaungeable' (46). For Usk, the principal means of coming to know and love God 'is the consyderacion of thynges made by the creatour, wherthrough, be thylke thynges that ben made understonding here to our wyttes, arne the unsene privytees of God made to us sightful and knowyng in our contemplacion and understondyng' (46). His analysis emphasises the particular value of perceptible, material forms as a stimulus to human cognition, the role of the senses in conceiving an ineffable God. Usk's autobiographical narrative will also serve to make information visible: 'for every man therby may, as by a perpetual myrrour, sene the vyces or vertues of other, in whiche thyng lightly may be conceyved to eschewe peryls and necessaryes to catche after' (45–6). As a book about love 'and the pryme causes of sterynge in that doynge', Usk's *Testament* is associated with the work of philosophers like Aristotle, who 'with a lyvely studye, many noble thynges ryght precious and worthy to memory writen, and, by a great swetande travayle, to us leften *Of Causes [of] the Propertyes in Natures of Thynges*' (46). In writing books that illuminate the properties of creation, these philosophers secure their own inscription within another volume, the book of life, amongst the saved: 'the names of hem in the boke of perpetual memory, in vertue and peace, arn wryten; and in the contrarye, that is to sayne, in Stixe, the foule pytte of helle, arn thilke pressed that suche goodnesse hated' (46; cf. Revelation 20:12, 20:15, 21:27). Usk's prologue reflects the hope that his *Testament of Love* might be the agent of his own perfection, as well as that of his audience.

The audacity of Usk's spiritual ambition is immediately acknowledged and diminished, however, with the introduction of an elaborate modesty topos, adapted from Ranulph Higden's *Polychronicon*.[41] Like Hidgen, Usk anticipates the derisive laughter of the reader confronted with his attempt to address such elevated subject matter in the wake of the *auctores*, comparing his own efforts to the boast of 'a dwarfe, or els halfe a man', that 'he wyl rende out the swerde of Hercules handes' (46–7).[42] The impossibility of the task is further exaggerated in the *Testament*, as Usk caricatures himself not only as an absurd challenger to Hercules, but to other historic figures:

---

[40] For example, Summers, *Late-Medieval Prison Writing*, concludes, 'He was not writing to save his soul, but to save his career and win release' (59). See also Strohm, 'Politics and Poetics', and Marion Turner, *Chaucerian Conflict: Languages of Antagonism in Late-Fourteenth Century London* (Oxford: Oxford University Press, 2007), 93–126.

[41] Bressie, 'The Date', demonstrates Usk's use of the Latin text, while Shawver argues that this was supplemented by the use of John Trevisa's translation, 213–14, 34.

[42] Ranulph Higden, *Polychronicon Ranulphi Higden monachi Cestrensis; Together with the English Translations of John Trevisa and of an Unknown Writer of the Fifteenth Century*, ed. Churchill Babington, vol. 1 (London: Longman, 1865), 1.1.8, 11, 13.

and, over that, he had power of strengthe to pul up the spere that Alisander
the noble might never wagge; and that passyng al thynge, to ben mayster of
Fraunce by myght, there-as the noble, gracyous Edwarde the thyrde, for al his
great prowesse in victories, ne myght al yet conquere. (47)

Usk evokes the anxieties attached to the project of shaping an English vernacular
eloquence, a work of cultural appropriation conceived in militaristic and
territorial terms and, as Ardis Butterfield argues, 'he is intensely aware of his
temerity in writing on love in a language other than French'.[43] Yet, the imagery
of preposterous martial acts of aggression stands in contrast to the central trope
within both versions of this passage, the gleaner, derived from the Book of Ruth.
As Ellen Martin observes, the Biblical narrative in which Ruth obtains permission
from her kinsman, Boaz, to come late to the field and gather remnants from the
harvest, came to serve as a conventional justification for the latter-day practice of
biblical exegesis, carried out in the shadow of earlier commentary. In adapting
this figure to validate contemporary writing praxis, Higden provided a model for
Chaucer's use of the topos in defence of vernacular composition on the potentially
tired poetic subject of love, in the prologue to *The Legend of Good Women*.[44] Usk's
complex appropriation of this trope contributes to the justification of writing not
only as an aesthetic practice, but as a profoundly ethical activity.

The status of Ruth as a stranger, a marginalised figure whose transgressive
behaviour is rewarded with an extraordinary act of kindness, is emphasised in
both Higden and Usk, as the biblical allusion is paired with another, the episode
of the Canaanite woman who begs Jesus to heal her daughter (Matthew 15: 22–8).
Initially refused, because she is not an Israelite, the Canaanite woman disputes
Jesus's claim that to assist her would be to give the bread of children to dogs; she
argues that pups are allowed to eat crumbs from their masters' table. Her plea is
granted as a tribute to her faith, and the episode is often cited alongside Ruth.[45]
Within the *Testament*, the significance of these allusions is underlined as Usk
supplements them with a further citation not present in Higden, and not commonly
associated with Ruth. Usk argues

> Certes, I wote wel, ther shal be made more scorne and jape of me, that I, so
> unworthely clothed altogyder in a cloudy cloude of unconnynge, wyl putten
> me in prees to speke of love, or else of the causes in that matter, sythen al the
> grettest clerkes han had ynough to don, and (as who sayth) gathered up clene
> toforne hem, and with theyr sharpe sythes of connyng al mowen and made therof
> great rekes and noble, ful of al plentyes, to fede me and many another. […]
> And, althoughe these noble repers, as good workmen and worthy theyr hyer,
> han al drawe and bounde up in the sheves and made many shockes, yet have
> I ensample to gader the smale crommes, and fullyn my walet of tho that fallen

---

[43]   Butterfield, *The Familiar Enemy*, 339.

[44]   Ellen E. Martin, 'Chaucer's Ruth: An Exegetical Poetic in the Prologue to the
Legend of Good Women', *Exemplaria* 3.2 (1991): 467–90.

[45]   Martin, 'Chaucer's Ruth', 467–8.

from the borde amonge the smale houndes, notwithstandynge the travayle of the almoygner, that hath drawe up in the cloth al the remyssayles, as trenchours, and the relyef to bere to the almesse. Yet also have I leve of the noble husbande Boece, although I be a straunger of connynge, to come after his doctryne, and these great workmen, and glene my handfuls of the shedynge after theyr handes. And if me fayle ought of my ful, to encrease my porcyon with that I shal drawe by privytyes out of the schoke. A slye servaunt in his owne helpe is often moche commended. (46–7)

In offering the 'slye servaunt' as a model for his own actions, Usk associates himself with the parable of the unjust steward (Luke 16.1–8). Threatened with dismissal for wasting his master's wealth, the steward calls in his employer's debts at discounted rates, so that the grateful debtors will welcome him into their houses. His master praises his wisdom, and medieval commentators typically resolve the difficulty posed by this apparent commendation of sharp practice by glossing the steward as the human subject, who has failed in God's service, but can still amend the fault.[46] The common thread linking these biblical narratives is the extension of grace to those who are not only without entitlement to relief, but are themselves culpable.

In combining these three episodes, Usk highlights the shared inheritance of ontological guilt that characterises the human condition, and the particular transgression of individual subjects. Exegesis of Ruth encompasses a tradition identifying Boaz as a type of Christ: his benevolence to Ruth, a gentile and a stranger, lacking rights under the law, prefigures Jesus's merciful treatment of an inherently sinful humanity, who can never merit grace.[47] In this context, Boaz's redemption of Ruth by marriage functions as counterpart to the exegetical tradition associated with the Song of Songs, in conceiving the union of Christ and the soul in terms of a sacramental union between male and female. At the literal level, Ruth's conventional status as one of the four sinful women in the genealogy of Christ allows her a practical role in laying the groundwork for the incarnation. For Hugh of St Cher, her eponymous function emphasises the extent of divine grace.[48] In common with the episode of the unjust steward and the Canaanite woman, Ruth's story stages the acceptance of an outcast into the Christian community, a process of incorporation that finds a complement in the shared consumption of food, in which Ruth participates, and which Christ and the Canaanite woman imagine. Yet, as Ellen Martin argues, the structure of the Canaanite woman's metaphor indicates that incorporation does not necessarily dissolve distinctions between centre and margin: like the whelps at the table, her status is liminal.[49]

---

[46] On the medieval interpretations of this parable, see Stephen L. Wailes, *Medieval Allegories of Jesus' Parables* (Berkeley: University of California Press, 1987), 245–53.

[47] This strand of interpretation is well represented in the anthology of Lesley Smith, ed. and trans., *Medieval Exegesis in Translation: Commentaries on the Book of Ruth* (Kalamazoo: Medieval Institute Publications, 1996).

[48] 'Postills on Ruth', trans. Smith, in *Medieval Exegesis*, 41.

[49] Martin, 'Chaucer's Ruth', 468.

The citation of these biblical exempla within Usk's autobiographical narrative resonates beyond the conventional apologia for the belated activity of vernacular composition, to suggest a more personal justification for the attempt to redeem himself, both from the guilt of original sin, and from his own past faults. In calling attention to scriptural figures who breach the boundaries of acceptable behaviour in order to secure material advantage for themselves, and whose transgression is itself the means by which they find grace, Usk offers a powerful rationale for the production of the *Testament*. His exempla reflect an acknowledgement of the guilt of his own error, in serving Northampton's cause, and simultaneously assert his right to aspire to material and spiritual preferment. Their function within an apologia for writing suggests that composition will serve as the medium of Usk's amelioration, echoing the connection between textual production and salvation established in his earlier allusion to the 'lyvely studye' of philosophers.

Usk's adaptation of Higden's modesty topos also tenders a playful hint as to the form of his own engagement with the textual inheritance of the *auctores* in adopting a modified spelling of Boaz, given in the various Latin and English versions of *Polychronicon* edited by Churchill Babington as 'Booz'. As Anne Middleton argues, Usk's acknowledgement of his debt to 'the noble husbande Boece' suggests a punning allusion to the *Testament*'s major literary model, the *Consolation*.[50] Usk imagines himself at once as a gleaner, gathering material from the *auctores*, and from Boethius in particular, and also as producer of a text that represents his own 'aventures' (46). Rather than being mutually exclusive, compilation and the expression of personal experience are conceived as complementary activities, an association that prefigures the role of commonplace books in the production of autobiographical writing in early modern England. As Adam Smyth argues, practices of commonplacing undermine individualistic conceptions of subjectivity, as they 'reveal the degree to which a compiler's identity might be constructed through a process of alignment with other figures, narratives, and events; through a pursuit of parallels; through an interest in sameness, not difference'.[51] Usk's *Testament* exemplifies both material and mental processes of gathering, evoking the memorial praxis by which textual fragments are collected in the storehouse of memory as the means to build up one's own ethical character, and to construct new texts.[52] Usk's use of the *Consolation* functions to suggest the sense that his experience repeats that of Boethius, enlarging the meaning of the Boethian text as he reformulates his own identity for his readers.

The *Testament* emphasises the relationship between selfhood and material practices of writing, in imagining the interlocutor's transformation as a process of inscription, where memory becomes a form of palimpsest. Usk's first chapter opens with the interlocutor's sorrowful avowal, 'Trewly, I leve, in myn herte is writte, of perdurable letters, al the entencyons of lamentacion that nowe ben ynempned' (1.1, 48). After Love's departure, the nature of this internal writing has changed:

---

[50]   Middleton, 'Thomas Usk', 96.
[51]   Smyth, *Autobiography in Early Modern England*, 5–6.
[52]   On the ethical function of memory, see Carruthers, *The Book of Memory*.

> I founde of perdurable letters wonderly there graven [...] Certes, none age ne other thynge in erthe maye the leest syllable of this in no poynte deface, but clerely as the sonne in myne understandynge soule they shynen. This maye never out of my mynde (3.8, 178)

Love's teaching is imprinted within the interlocutor's mind, marking the resolution of an essentially cognitive problem, an affliction of memory. In his initial sorrow, the interlocutor pleads that 'Remembraunce of love lythe so sore under my brest, that other thought cometh not in my mynde' (1.1, 49). This surfeit of memory entails both pain and pleasure: 'My great joye it is to have in meditacion the bounties, the vertues, the nobley in you printed; sorowe and hel comen at ones to suppose that I be veyned' (1.1, 49). The expression of an intense, if insufficiently controlled, meditative faculty, the interlocutor's passion imaginatively lends bodily form to auditory matter:

> Trewly, me thynketh that the sowne of my lamentacious wepyng is right nowe flowe into your presence, and there cryeth after mercy and grace, to which thing, me semeth, the lyst none answere to yeve; by with a deynoous chere ye commaunden it to avoyde (1.1, 50)

The capacity to create vivid mental scenes, and to transpose aural materials into visual images, is one of the core skills employed in medieval memory training, while writing itself was sometimes conceived as a mnemonic practice whose effect is to associate ideas with tangible signs.[53]

The *Testament*'s relationship to the *Consolation* reinforces its function as a text concerned with the exercise of memory as an ethical activity, and its role in rhetorical invention. If the vision at the heart of the *Consolation* lends itself to interpretation as the product of memory work, performed under the classic mnemonic conditions of solitude, and the stimulus of emotional anxiety, so too does the experience described within the *Testament*.[54] The opening of Usk's book, with a plea for divine mercy that gives way to a state of compunction, has drawn comparisons to the mystic writings of Richard Rolle and Julian of Norwich: as Barbara Siennicki argues, the interlocutor's emotions suggest a type of fear not unlike the 'reverent drede' that Julian of Norwich identifies as a mindset pleasing to God.[55] A ceaseless movement of recollection produces a heightened mental state: 'Rehersynge these thynges and many other, without tyme or moment of rest, me semed, for anguysshe of disease, that altogyder I was ravyisshed [...] And sodainly, a maner of drede light in me al at ones' (1.2, 51). Yet, this dread is 'noght such feare as folke have of an enemy'; instead it originates in 'goodly subjection', as 'aungels ben aferde of our savyour in heven', 'lovers in presence

---

[53] Carruthers, *The Book of Memory*, 10, 34–6, 139–40, 279–80.

[54] On this interpretation of the *Consolation*, see Carruthers, *The Craft of Thought*, 173–6.

[55] Siennicki, 'No Harbour', 140; Julian of Norwich, *A Revelation of Love*, ed. Marion Glasscoe (Exeter: University of Exeter Press, 1976), 89.

of their loves, and subjects aforne their soveraynes' (1.2, 51). In positioning the interlocutor's vision as the consequence of a state of *compunctio cordis* that yields to rapture, Usk evokes the idea of the mnemonic trance in the form most familiar to a medieval audience, as it appears in devotional writing.[56] Rather than contradicting the prologue, with its emphasis on composition as a process of gleaning fragments from the field harvested by the *auctores*, Usk's narrative acknowledges the function of the monastic vision genre in representing mnemonic invention as the basis of textual production, as new matter is generated through meditative rumination on the contents of the storehouse of memory.[57]

In this respect, the *Testament* is framed at once as a mnemonic vision whose genesis resembles that of the *Consolation*, and as the product of meditation on the *Consolation* itself. Usk's technique entails the reformulation of narrative elements, as the *Testament* traces a sequence of events that repeats and revises those of the *Consolation* in substituting a vision of Philosophy for a vision of Love, as well as the citation and adaptation of the rhetorical fabric of the text. The figure of Love emerges as a composite, generated by the interlocutor as he seeks to console himself, in meditating on the contents of the *Consolation*. Her diagnosis of his problem as a form of amnesia both signals the *Testament*'s particular concern with memory, and identifies Usk's book as the product of the mnemonic faculty of rhetorical invention, since her words themselves are a form of citation: 'hast so mykel eeten of the potages of foryefulnesse and dronken so of ignorance, that the olde soukyng whiche thou haddest of me arne amaystred and lorn fro al maner of knowyng?' (1.4, 59; cf. *Boece* 1.pr.2). The *Testament* represents the mental process of gathering, through which the mnemonist collects textual matter from the places of memory, and functions as a literal instance of the embodied practices of book production to which these forms of memory work contribute. Usk's writing entails the accumulation of textual fragments, incorporated into a new whole; it shares features with the making of commonplace books and, in conceiving textual production in terms of the physical movement and arrangement of objects in space, it evokes the metaphorical relationship between building, rhetoric and exegesis attested by writers such as Hugh of St Victor and Geoffrey of Vinsauf.[58]

Usk's use of citation functions to situate his text, and the experience it depicts, in relation to other figures and narratives familiar to a contemporary audience. Described by Skeat as 'the most barefaced and deliberate plagiarism', Usk's appropriation of textual materials is more properly understood as a creative practice in line with medieval attitudes to rhetorical invention, where transposition alters both the quotation and its new context.[59] Although direct citations from Boethius

---

[56]   See references to 'fear and meditation' indexed in Carruthers, *The Craft of Thought*.

[57]   Carruthers, *The Craft of Thought*, 179–83.

[58]   Hugh of St Victor, *Didascalicon*, ed. C.H. Buttimer (Washington: Catholic University Press, 1939), VI. 4, 120.6–8, and see Carruthers, *The Craft of Thought*, 16–24; Geoffrey of Vinsauf, *Poetria Nova*, in ed. Edmond Faral, *Les Arts poétiques du XIIe et du XIIIe siècle: recherches et documents sur la technique littéraire du moyen âge*, (Paris: Champion, 1962) I.43–7.

[59]   Skeat, *Chaucerian and Other Pieces*, 7.xxv.

are far fewer than Skeat supposed, to the extent that there is some doubt as to which versions of the *Consolation* Usk used, in those instances where material is borrowed almost verbatim, the effect is innovative, as analysis of the most autobiographical section of the *Testament* demonstrates.[60]

In describing a past experience that invites identification with Usk's own personal history, the interlocutor rationalises the betrayal of his former allies as the expression of loyalty to a value whose preservation would supersede even closer ties: 'al shulde I therthrough enpeche myn owne fere, if he were gylty and to do misdede assentaunt' (1.6, 66). Usk's emphasis is consistent with the Christian renunciation of familial ties for Jesus' sake (Matt. 19.29). The interlocutor identifies his error, not as political inconstancy, but as a failure to recognise the intention hidden beneath a seductive surface: 'thilke thynges ben my drawers in and exitours to tho maters werne so paynted and coloured, that (at the *prime face*) me semed them noble and glorious to al the people' (1.6, 65). His analysis closely resembles that offered in Usk's *Appellum*, where Northampton's party are accused of concealing their 'fals & wykked menyng [...] vnder colour of wordes of comun profit' (*Appellum*, 29). Coming to consciousness of his mistake, the interlocutor 'declared certayne poyntes in this wyse', presenting a list of charges that reflect the contents of the *Appellum* (1.6, 66). Yet, the relationship between the *Appellum* and this section of the *Testament* is complicated by Usk's interpolation of lines from Chaucer's *Boece*, as the reported speech of his unnamed demagogues: '"The governements," quod they, "of your cyte lefte in the handes of torcencious cytezyns, shal bringe in pestylence and distruction to you good men. And, therefore, let us have the comune admynistracion to abate suche yvels"' (1.6, 66–7). As Shawver argues, this cross fertilisation illustrates Usk's characteristic location of personal experience 'in a literary and philosophical context [...] he was less concerned with chronicling events than with conveying his sense of their full significance' (17). Usk's borrowed words are taken from a summary of Philosophy's teaching:

> Thou seidest eek by the mouth of the same Plato that it was a necessarie cause wise men to taken and desire the governance of comune thynges, for that the governementz of cites, ilefte in the handes of felonous turentours citezeens, ne shulde noght bryngen in pestilence and destruccioun to good folk (*Boece* 1.pr.4)

The intertextual relationship between these two passages indicates the concealment of malevolence under a veneer of words associated with the philosophical imperative to work for common profit. Its effect is at once to mitigate Usk's error, and to give substance to his allusions to the deceptive seductions of rhetoric. Usk represents the recognition of this fault as an experience of conversion, identifying an irreproachable precedent for altered faith in Christian doctrine:

> ye remembre wel, that in moste laude and praysyng of certayne sayntes in holy churche, is to rehersen their convercion from badde into good; and that is so

---

60   For analysis of Usk's use of the *Consolation*, see Medcalf; Shawver's edition, 29; and Siennicki, 'No Harbour', 100–112 and Appendix A.

rehersed, as by a perpetual myrrour of remembraunce in worshyppyng of tho
sayntes, and good ensample to other misdoers in amendment (1.6, 65)

In this context, change is a moral imperative, rather than a fault.[61] The interlocutor
recognises his error 'by counsayle of myne inwytte', producing a compunction of
heart manifested in tears and revelation, as his situation is 'shewed so openly, that
had I ben blynde, with mynde hondes, al the circumstaunce I might wel have feled'
(1.6, 65). This haptic sense of circumstance recognises the interpenetration of the
material and the spiritual, marking the role of the body in mapping the relation
between self and world. Comparison of the interlocutor's actions with those of
the mysterious 'Romayne Zedeoreys', who joined Hannibal 'ayenst his kynde
nacioun', before returning 'to his olde alyes', perhaps serves a similar purpose,
in tracing the ways in which the divine manifests itself in the material world (1.6,
65).[62] Insofar as the success of the Roman Empire was conceived as an expression
of divine providence, establishing a political unity that contributed to the formation
of Christendom, Usk's example points towards a significant concordance between
human politics and the divine order.[63]

Usk's allusions to other texts also foster a vivid sense of the intersection
between spiritual and physical terrain. The closing lines of the prologue position
the *Testament* as a journey, 'whan I pilgrymaged out of my kyth in wynter'
(47). Potentially referring to Usk's own departure from London in late 1384,
the interlocutor's journey takes on an allegorical cast.[64] Menaced by beasts, he
takes refuge on the 'shype of traveyle', crewed by Sight, Lust, Thought, and Will,
and is driven 'by mokel duresse of wethers and of stormes' to the isle where he
meets Love, and glimpses the Margaret pearl (1.3.56). Beginning as he 'walked
thynkynge alone a wonder great whyle' the interlocutor's voyage is a contemplative
journey whose details strongly resemble the allegorical vision of the Peasant's
Revolt that appears in Book I of John Gower's *Vox Clamantis* (1.3, 56).[65] Summers
and Strohm argue that Usk's adaptation functions to underline the conservatism
of his new position, casting Northampton and his supporters as incendiaries to
be condemned like the rebels of 1381. Each reads the ship as representation of
Usk's political and legal difficulties, the island refuge as the security of his new
commitment to the royalist party.[66] Yet, the terms of the allegory prioritise the

---

[61]   Rather than being an 'odd declaration', as Turner argues, the allusion is consistent
with the theological perspective Usk adopts in his treatment of his own experience,
Chaucerian Conflict, 112. Conversion is also evoked as a model at 1.8, 71; 3.2, 130.

[62]   On Zedeoreys, see Shoaf's edition, 330, and Shawver, 232.

[63]   On the Roman Empire and divine providence, see Ernst Breisach, *Historiography:
Ancient, Medieval, and Modern*. 3rd edn (Chicago: University of Chicago Press, 2007),
86–8.

[64]   Exchequer, Issue Rolls, P.R.O., E 403/508, m. 17 implies such a departure, see
Shawver, 20.

[65]   For detailed analysis of the correspondences, see Joanna Summers, 'Gower's *Vox
Clamantis* and Usk's *Testament of Love*', *Medium Ævum* 68.1 (1999): 55–62, and *Late-
Medieval Prison Writing*, 31–6.

[66]   Strohm, 'Politics and Poetics', 102; Summers, *Late-Medieval Prison Writing*, 32.

psychological dimension of experience: as Summers recognises, both Usk and Gower connect the endangered ship with the state of mental turmoil.[67] The image of life as a perilous sea-voyage is common to the *Consolation* and scripture, emphasising the threat existence in a mutable world poses to the spiritual health of the subject. Against this background, the image of the ship implies that the risk incurred is not that of worldly failure, but rather that a reversal of fortune might upset the equilibrium of the subject. In this context, the interlocutor's passage to the safety of the island suggests the achievement of a more secure mental state. Moreover, in identifying the interlocutor with Gower's narrator, as a figure moved to cry out against the abuses he has witnessed in contemporary society, Usk invites his readers to recognise the *Testament* as a project inspired by the desire to work for the common good, in exposing dangers to the stability of the social order.

The sense of a reciprocal relation between material and physical activity is most strongly articulated in Usk's use of metaphorical conceptions of building that intersect with the Pauline trope of edification. Emphasising a Christian duty to construct a godly self, and to contribute to the edification of the community and its members, the Pauline metaphor nourished an abundant tradition of medieval allegory.[68] Usk's formulation of the architectural metaphor is coloured by its development in the *Consolation*, as an analogy for the dangers involved in founding happiness on transient objects, vulnerable to fortune. Philosophy advises the interlocutor to avoid mountains, exposed to the wind, unstable sand and the dangerous sea, instead building a house on the rock (2.m.4). Recalling the imagistic function of the ocean as an emblem of mutability elsewhere in the *Consolation*, the figure is also reminiscent of the parable of the wise and foolish builders that concludes the Sermon on the Mount: the wise builder is the hearer who founds his actions upon the rock of Christ's teaching (Matt. 7.24–7). Allegories of edification, of internal acts of building that construct the ethical self, are also central to the conception of memory training, finding articulation in architectural models of artificial memory. Usk invokes these reciprocal traditions in elaborating his own architectural metaphor.

Love identifies those who 'in their rychesse supposed suffysance have folowed' as deficient builders on sand and gravel. As the sea ebbs, it 'pulleth ayen under wawe' all these works, except where 'good pyles of noble governaunce in love, in wel-meanynge maner, ben sadly grounded, to which holde thilke gravel as for a whyle, that ayen lightly mowe not it turne' (2.5, 95–96). A recurrent image within the *Testament*, this variant form of the trope of edification identifies the secure building with a foundation that is not laid directly upon rock, but stabilised by piles (see 1.5, 63; 2.1, 81; 2.7, 101; 2.8, 106; 2.14, 125). An accurate reflection

---

[67] Summers, *Late-Medieval Prison Writing*, 33; Eric W. Stockton, ed. and trans., *The Major Latin Works of John Gower: The Voice of One Crying and the Tripartite Chronicle* (Seattle: University of Washington Press, 1962), 91.

[68] David Cowling identifies I Thess. 5.11 and I Cor. 3.9–10; 3.16–18; 6.19–20 as particular models for vernacular allegory, *Building the Text: Architecture as Metaphor in Late Medieval and Early Modern France* (Oxford: Clarendon, 1998), and see especially 55–60.

of building methods still adopted to deal with unsatisfactory ground, Usk's image is also an apt expression of the problem of constructing an ethical self without immediate access to divine truth. Established by an embodied subject in a mutable world, the foundation of virtue is not absolute; it suggests the provisional security of faith, rather than certain knowledge.

In its emphasis on a secure foundation, Usk's architectural imagery is complemented by another traditional model for memory incorporated within the *Testament*, the tree.[69] Offered as an analogy for the relationship between the bliss of grace, free will and love, the tree is also presented as a pattern for the establishment of virtue as a habit of mind, preserved in memory.[70] Advising the interlocutor on how best to cultivate the tree whose fruit is grace, Love tells him that he 'must set thy werke on grounde syker and good [...] set thy purpose there virtue foloweth, and not to loke after the bodily goodes' (3.5, 162). The interlocutor frames his difficulty with this task in terms suggestive of the common mnemonic problem of emotional distraction:

> my wyl may ben turned by f[erdn]es, and disease of menace, and thretnyng in lesynge of my lyfe and of my lymmes [...] also it mote ofte ben out of thought, for no remembraunce may holde one thing contynuelly in herte, be it never so lusty desyred (3.5, 162)

Unlike 'Sottes and fooles', who 'lette lightly out of mynde the good that men teacheth hem', the interlocutor's desire is to fix his will on one object (3.7, 175). The identification of the stable foundation with 'noble governaunce in love' complements the *Testament*'s use of elements drawn from Boethius and Anselm, indicating that the goal of Love's teaching is a reorientation of will towards the good.

The allegories of physical development Usk uses to represent this object are supplemented by another image of the formation of a material structure associated with fastening, the knot. Like the piled foundation, the knot is an apposite image of self-discipline, conceived as an internal prosthesis, consistent with John Sutton's observation that 'highly socialised and morally charged quests for mastery of the self by the self', for civilisation, often 'require a kind of self-oppression, in which control of the brain involves the assimilation of symbolic props and pivots'.[71] In Usk's analogy, knot and foundation interact: if the 'knotte is false; whan the see ebbeth and withdraweth the gravel that such rychesse voydeth, thilke knotte wol unknytte' (2.5, 96). Functioning as an emblem of the sovereign good, and of 'God,

---

[69]   On the tree as mnemonic structure, see Carruthers, *The Book of Memory*, 259, 329, 333; Kay, *The Place of Thought*, 19–41.

[70]   On the tree and its possible relationship to *Piers Plowman*, see notes to Shawver and Shoaf, and Lucy Lewis, 'Langland's Tree of Charity and Usk's Wexing Tree', *Notes and Queries*, 42 (1995): 429–33.

[71]   John Sutton, 'Porous Memory and the Cognitive Life of Things', in Darren Tofts, Annemarie Jonson, and Alessio Cavallaro (eds), *Prefiguring Cyberculture: An Intellectual History*, (Cambridge, MA: MIT Press, 2002), 137.

knotte of al goodnesse', the image of the knot suggests a consolidating impulse enacted within the self and beyond its boundaries (2.13, 121). It is associated with the institution of marriage, conceived as an ideal: 'none age, none overtournynge tyme, but hyt herto had no tyme ne power to chaunge the weddyng, ne the knotte to unbynde of two hertes thorowe one assent in my presence togyther accorden to enduren tyle dethe hem departe' (1.9, 76). As Isabel Davis argues, Usk's analysis of marriage represents 'an accurate and strict interpretation of canon legal theory', in emphasising intellectual assent as the basis of union.[72] Consummation is not essential, 'for consente of two hertes alone maketh the fastenynge of the knotte' (1.9, 76). In this respect, marriage offers a model instance of how the upright will, a love oriented towards the sovereign good, can feed into human sociality.

In associating the union of marriage formed by consent with the transcendent unity of the divine, Usk concurs with the Augustinian sense that the marital bond is 'an expression of the primal and enduring nature of men and women as ineradicably social beings'. Rather than marking a postlapsarian degeneration, 'the present concord of a husband and a wife pointed forward to the final unity of the City of God'.[73] As an ideal, consensual marriage offered a model for other forms of social institution: as Heather Richardson Hayton argues, Usk's treatment of love reflects the contemporary function of conjugal affection in political discourse, as an analogy for good governance. Marriage offered a consensual model of hierarchical authority, in which the dominance of the husband parallels that of the sovereign within an aristocracy.[74] The conception of properly regulated love as a force underpinning social harmony is consistent with the Boethian image of chaste marriage, true friendship, and political cohesion, as bonds held together through the influence of divine love (2.m.8).

In this context, Usk's emphasis on the erotic does not signal a withdrawal from politics into the realms of private affection, but instead develops a political philosophy.[75] Within the *Testament*, Usk traces the sense in which the proper expression and regulation of love for a particular object can become a means of contributing to the production of a society whose unity and justice, however precarious and imperfect those states might be, point towards the unanimity of the divine Jerusalem. Primarily represented in terms of the interlocutor's desire for Margaret, the dynamic between particular affection and divine love is also articulated in his relationship to 'the cytie of London, that is to me so dere and

---

[72] Davis, *Writing Masculinity*, 69.

[73] Brown, *The Body and Society*, 403.

[74] Heather Richardson Hayton, '"Many privy thinges wimpled and folde": Governance and mutual obligation in Usk's *Testament of Love*', *Studies in Philology* 96.1 (1999): 22–41.

[75] In contrast, see Hanrahan, 'The Seduction', and David R. Carlson, 'Chaucer's Boethius and Thomas Usk's *Testament of Love:* Politics and Love in the Chaucerian Tradition,' in R.A. Taylor et al. (eds), *The Centre and its Compass: Studies in Medieval Literature in Honor of Professor John Leyerle*, (Kalamazoo: Western Michigan University, 1993), 29–70. For a reading illustrating the consistency of a political reading of Usk's *Testament* with Boethius's *Consolation*, see Jennifer Arch, 'The Boethian *Testament of Love*', *Studies in Philology*, 105.4 (2008): 448–62.

swete, in whiche I was forthe growen'. As the interlocutor explains, 'more kyndely love have I to that place than to any other in erthe, as every kyndely creature hath ful appetyte to that place of his kyndly engendrure and to wylne reste and peace in that stede to abyde' (1.6, 66). Usk justifies his disloyalty to his former allies on the grounds that 'peace that most in comunaltie shulde be desyred was in poynte to be broken and adnulled' (1.6, 66). Yet, his argument conceives the keeping of the peace not in terms of expediency, but as a form of *imitatio Christi* that reiterates and fulfils the terms of the covenant between God and humanity:

> For knowe thynge it is, al men that desyren to comen to the perfyte peace everlastyng, must the peace by God commended bothe mayntayne and kepe. This peace by angels voyce was confyrmed, our God entrynge in this worlde. This as for his Testament, he left to al his frendes, whanne he retourned to the place from whence he came. This his Apostel amonesteth to holden, without whiche man perfytely may have none insyght. Also this God, by his comyng, made not peace alone betwene hevenly and erthly bodyes, but also amonge us on erthe; so he peace confyrmed that in one heed of love one body we shulde performe. (1.6, 66)

Informed by the Pauline conception of the Christian community as a body with Christ as its head, Usk's conception of social harmony identifies the desire for the maintenance of peace inspired by a particular love of London as the basis of actions that prefigure the unity of the City of God.[76] In identifying the keeping of the peace as a prerequisite for 'insyght', Usk establishes a link between political stability and the mental equilibrium associated with rectitude of will. The idea that divine love drives the impulse towards harmonious social cohesion also recalls Love's earlier expression of the incarnation in terms of contemporary legal practice: 'maked I not a lovedaye bytwene God and mankynde, and chese an mayde to be nompere, to put the quarel at ende?' (1.2, 53). If the reputation of the loveday as an occasion for the amicable resolution of quarrels had suffered in the late fourteenth century, here it evidently typifies the Christian principle of reconciliation.[77] On its own terms, Usk's *Testament* is itself a contribution to the maintenance of concord, illustrating the principle that divine loyalties supersede human bonds, and reiterating the terms of a covenant that depends upon the social enactment of religious beliefs for a contemporary audience.

Usk's ideology of social responsibility has been defined by Anne Middleton as 'common love', an ideal that exists in 'symmetry and contrast with that singular passion which expresses itself in literature in the inward self-cultivation sometimes called "courtly love" [...] it issues in acts of social amelioration rather

---

[76]   See Jacques Le Goff, 'Head or Heart? The Political Use of Body Metaphors in the Middle Ages', trans. Patricia Ranum, in Michel Feher (ed.), *Fragments for a History of the Body*, vol. 3 (New York: Zone, 1989), 13–56.

[77]   On lovedays, see Josephine Waters Bennett, 'The Medieval Loveday', *Speculum* 33.3 (1958): 351–70; John Webster Spargo, 'Chaucer's Love-Days', *Speculum* 15.1 (1940): 36–56.

than in the refinement of inwardness'.[78] Yet, rather than representing a formulation distinct from erotic love, Usk's social eros reflects the ethical management of desire, its direction towards its proper object. As such, it is appropriate that Usk underlines the implications of this process in the redirection of elements from one of his most prominent textual sources, Chaucer's *Troilus and Criseyde*. Marion Turner develops a detailed analysis of Usk's treatment of this material, arguing that Usk attempts to displace Chaucer 'by endeavouring to imbue his words with greater moral "seriousness"', in transferring Pandarus's words to Love's mouth.[79] Rather than an attempt to 'pull the wool over the reader's eyes, by maintaining that Love's words have a purely spiritual connotation', however, Usk's appropriation of Pandarus's weasel words invites the audience to recollect the contents of Chaucer's work.[80] The palpable tension between the immorality of the original application of Pandarus's phrases and their appearance in the mouth of Usk's authority illustrates the sense that the redirection of the appetitive will towards its real, transcendent object always involves effort, reflecting the disjunction between spiritual and material realms. Similarly, Usk's recognition that the exercise of power is susceptible to the perils of corruption, articulated in Love's attack on the excesses of Nero, Herod, and King John, should not necessarily be regarded as sitting 'uncomfortably with Love's comments on the sacred nature of sovereignty' (2.6, 98).[81] Instead, Usk's juxtaposition of the image of an idealised order with fearful acknowledgement of the constant danger of debasement acknowledges that the perfection anticipated in human sociality cannot be realised in this world, but is the property of the New Jerusalem. Usk's treatment of sovereignty anticipates the Lacanian point that madness characterises not only the beggar who believes himself to be a king, but also the king who believes himself to be so.[82] The ideal is not fully habitable by embodied subjects.

Love concludes her advice to the interlocutor by taking root in his heart, with the words 'Here I wol onbyde […] for ever, and never wol I gon hence. And I wol kepe the from medlynge, while me lyste here onbyde. Thyne entermetyng maners into stedfastnesse shullen be changed' (3.8, 178). Playing on the association of

---

[78]   Anne Middleton, 'The Idea of Public Poetry in the Reign of Richard II', *Speculum* 53.1 (1978): 94–114 (96).

[79]   Marion Turner, *Chaucerian Conflict*, 98, and '"Certaynly His Noble Sayenges Can I Not Amende": Thomas Usk and *Troilus and Criseyde*', *Chaucer Review* 37 (2002): 26–39.

[80]   Turner, *Chaucerian Conflict*, 99. Usk's audience has been identified with the 'textworkers and bibliophiles' familiar with Chaucer's work by May Newman Hallmundson, 'The Community of Law and Letters: Some Notes on Thomas Usk's Audience,' *Viator* 9 (1978): 357–65, whose findings are confirmed and expanded by Middleton, 'Thomas Usk', 68; and Kathryn Kerby-Fulton and Steven Justice, 'Langlandian Reading Circles and the Civil Service in London and Dublin, 1380–1427,' *New Medieval Literatures* 1 (1997): 59–83.

[81]   Turner, *Chaucerian Conflict*, 125.

[82]   Slavoj Žižek, *The Ticklish Subject: The Absent Centre of Political Ontology* (London: Verso, 2008), 327.

memory and heart, Usk's *Testament* presents a powerful image of the completion of a visionary process of self-development that leaves its subject endowed with the internal stability that characterises the subject able to work towards the establishment of a social justice that prefigures the divine. Whether or not Usk's book ever reached the hands of a political patron, the ideology of public service it presents would offer both a compelling argument for his final elevation, as under-sheriff of Middlesex, in autumn 1387, and for his violent execution at the hands of the interests whose motives he had implicitly questioned. In identifying himself with the example of Boethius, and as a master of those techniques of mnemonic self-consolation Boethius employed, Usk appropriates examples characteristic of aristocratic self-fashioning. If his approach is touched with presumption, however, the acrostic puzzle embedded in his work invites a communal endorsement of the transformation to which the *Testament* aspires.

In acknowledging and resolving the puzzle of Usk's acrostic plea, 'MARGARETE OF VIRTW HAVE MERCI ON THIN USK', the reader recognises Usk, and the validity of the version of his experience inscribed within the *Testament*. As the ambiguity of the interlocutor's status is dispelled, the reader performs a work of reauthorship that lends a particular significance to the interlocutor's final prayer:

> I desyre not onely a good reader, but also I coveyte and pray a good booke amender, in correction of wordes and of sentence. And onely this mede I coveyte for my travayle, that every inseer and herer of this leude fantasye, devoute horisons and prayers to God the great juge yelden, and prayen for me in that wyse that in his dome my synnes mowe ben released and foryeven. He that prayeth for other, for himselfe travayleth. Also I praye that every man parfytly mowe knowe thorowe what intencion of herte this treatyse have I drawe. (3.9, 196)

Here both book and life are offered up as texts to be amended, and the reader's willingness to conceive Usk's works as the products of benevolent intention foreshadows the act of the deity whom he prays will at last write his name in 'the boke of perpetual memory'. The remaking of his material book anticipates the transmutation of the self, in his own perfection at the Day of Judgement. If Usk's prayer expresses a desire for temporal mercy, for a forgiveness signified by the reader's own prayer, it is as the sign and symbol of the divine redemption only his God can convey.

Chapter 6
Textual Authority and the Making of a Model Prince: James I of Scotland and *The Kingis Quair*

In common with the texts by Machaut, Froissart and Usk examined in previous chapters, *The Kingis Quair* presents a significant conjunction between the authority of Boethius's *Consolation of Philosophy* and the narration of a history at once personal and political. Attributed to James I of Scotland in the only surviving manuscript, Bodleian Library MS Arch. Selden. B.24, the *Quair* is conceived as a first-person meditation on the king's experience as a prisoner in a foreign land. The unnamed narrator's account of his capture at sea and subsequent imprisonment, 'Nere by the space of yeris twise nyne', closely corresponds to events in James's own early life: taken by pirates as he sailed for France in 1406, he remained a hostage in England until 1424, when he returned to Scotland as king (173).[1] Allusions within the poem locate the narrator's capture in March, consistent with James's seizure on 22 March 1406, and the evidence of the manuscript implies that the *Quair*'s earliest known scribes and readers recognised the affinity between poetry and history, in making the identification explicit.[2]

Although the manuscript is a relatively late witness, its close association with the Sinclair family represents a plausible channel for the transmission of a text at least approved, if not produced, by James Stewart.[3] The authorship of the

---

[1]   John Norton-Smith (ed.), *James I of Scotland: The Kingis Quair* (Oxford: Clarendon), all subsequent references are to this edition, cited by line number. On James's capture, see Michael Brown, *James I*, rev. edn (East Linton: Tuckwell, 2000), 17; for a more detailed biography, see E.W.M. Balfour-Melville, *James I, King of Scots, 1406–1437* (London: Methuen, 1936).

[2]   A scribal colophon appearing on 211r and a later inscription on 191v identify James as author, Julia Boffey and A.S.G. Edwards, *The Works of Geoffrey Chaucer and the Kingis Quair: A Facsimile of Bodleian Library, Oxford, MS Arch. Selden. B. 24* (Cambridge: Brewer, 1997). On the role of astronomical allusions in lines 134–47 dating the capture described within the poem, see Matthew P. McDiarmid (ed.), *The Kingis Quair of James Stewart* (London: Heinemann, 1973), 40.

[3]   A *terminus ad quem* is provided by the inclusion of the arms Henry, Lord Sinclair assumed after 26 January 1489. On William Sinclair's long association with James I, see Boffey and Edwards's introduction to the facsimile, 10–11. Elsewhere, Boffey argues persuasively that the Selden manuscript may have served the interests of familial piety, 'Bodleian Library MS Arch. Selden. B. 24 and the Definitions of the "Household Book"', in A.S.G. Edwards, Vincent Gillespie and Ralph Hanna (eds), *The English Medieval Book: Studies in Memory of Jeremy Griffiths* (London: British Library, 2000), 125–34. More

Quair is the subject of a longstanding controversy, now lapsed into silence, as a question thought to have 'diverted criticism from its main task of elucidation',[4] yet the attempt to separate critical analysis and attribution is symptomatic of a methodology ill-equipped to address the *Quair*'s autobiographical narrative. In restricting the definition of authorship to the manufacture of a written text, such critics neglect the extent to which James's authorial function is constructed within the *Quair*. The identification of the historical James as basis for the *Quair*'s protagonist and narrator is undisputed, and a more nuanced model of authorship facilitates recognition of the dialogic interaction of literature, experience and textual production staged within the poem. Of particular relevance here is the authorial role Harold Love terms 'declarative authorship', distinguishing the individual or individuals credited with the composition of a text.[5] Even where the declarative author has no further connection with the work, as in cases of mistaken attribution, this function impacts upon its meaning in influencing readers' responses. Within the *Quair*, the function of declarative authorship is imbricated in the text, as James's personal history shapes the form and content of the poem.

The concept of declarative authorship serves to establish the minimum contribution James makes to the *Quair*. Attribution studies are currently unable to determine responsibility for the composition of the poem, a function Love terms executive authorship, since techniques such as stylometry depend upon the survival of other samples for comparison. Analysis of the areal linguistic features present in the poem has also proven inconclusive as neither the character of James's speech after his long captivity in England, nor the degree of scribal intervention in the surviving text, can be conclusively ascertained.[6] Although the question is incapable of definitive resolution, the principle of parsimony would suggest that

---

recently, Sally Mapstone has suggested that the main scribe of the Selden MS may himself have been a member of the Sinclair family, Alexander Sinclair, 'Introduction: Older Scots and the Fifteenth Century', in Sally Mapstone (ed.), *Older Scots Literature* (Edinburgh: Birlinn, 2005), 5–6.

4   Derek Pearsall, 'The English Chaucerians', in D.S. Brewer (ed.), *Chaucer and Chaucerians: Critical Studies in Middle English Literature* (London: Nelson, 1966), 226–7. For a useful summary of the authorship controversy, see Alessandra Petrina, *The Kingis Quair of James I of Scotland* (Padova: Unipress, 1997), 53–9, and commentary in Elizabeth Elliott, 'The Open Sentence: Memory, Identity and Translation in the *Kingis Quair*', in Sarah Carpenter and Sarah M. Dunnigan (eds), *'Joyous Sweit Imaginatioun'*: *Essays on Scottish Literature in Honour of R. D. S. Jack*, SCROLL (Amsterdam and New York: Rodopi, 2007), 23–39.

5   Harold Love, *Attributing Authorship: An Introduction* (Cambridge: Cambridge University Press, 2002), 44–6.

6   On the distinctive linguistic features of the MS, see Julia Boffey and A.S.G. Edwards, 'Bodleian MS Arch. Selden. B. 24 and the "Scotticization" of Middle English Verse', in Prendergast and Kline (eds), *Rewriting Chaucer*, 166–85, and C.D. Jeffrey, 'Anglo-Scots Poetry and the *Kingis Quair*', in Jean-Jacques Blanchot and Claude Graf (eds), *Actes du 2e colloque de langue et de littérature écossaises (Moyen Âge et Renaissance)*, Université de Strasbourg 5–11 Juillet 1978 (Strasbourg: Université de Strasbourg, 1979), 198–206.

James is both executive and declarative author of the *Quair*.[7] Yet, even if the issue of executive authorship is regarded as intractable, the effect of James's inscription within the poem as author and subject cannot be neglected: arguments like those of Vincent Carretta and Clair F. James, who read the *Quair* as an ironic meditation on erotic love, are flawed because they do not attempt any serious discussion of why James I should appear as the target of such satire.[8] Acknowledging James's function as a presence invoked and constructed within the *Quair*, this chapter explores the reciprocal relationship between king and poem, and the *Quair*'s role in shaping the personal history of James I as literary artefact.

The opening of the *Quair* stages the reading of *The Consolation of Philosophy*, an experience presented as the stimulus for the narrator's own composition. Waking alone, the narrator hopes to 'borowe a slepe' in reading, but instead finds himself absorbed (30). His situation as a solitary reader, working late at night, coincides with conditions recognised as being especially conducive to the practice of the arts of memory. Indeed, from its inception, the *Quair* raises expectations that reading will give way to dreaming, in accordance with the conventional function of the literary dream vision as shorthand for the role of inventive meditation on authoritative textual sources in generating new compositions.[9] The substitution of writing for dreaming renders the process of textual composition explicit, articulating a relationship that enacts a creative reformulation of an authoritative source. This adaptation of a conventional acknowledgement of influence clarifies the effect of the poet's presentation of his debt to Boethius, in the stanzas describing the narrator's encounter with the text. Rather than seeking to valorise his vernacular composition by emphasising its role as an exegetical supplement to Boethius's Latin authority, the narrator freely admits that he is ill equipped to carry out the work of commentary, and differentiates the object of his own writing:

> With mony a noble resoun (as him likit)
> Enditing in his fair[e] Latyne tong,
> So full of fruyte and rethorikly pykit,
> Quhich to declare my scole is ouer yong.
> Therfore I lat him pas, and in my tong
> Procede I will agayn to my sentence
> Of my mater, and leue all incidence. (43–9)

If 'sentence' or meaning of the narrator's subject matter is distinguished from exposition, however, his writing is nevertheless authorised by Boethius's

---

[7]   It is worth noting that the original challenge to James's authorship levelled by Brown was partially based on the misapprehension that James's capture took place in February 1406, J.T.T. Brown, *Authorship of The Kingis Quair: A New Criticism* (Glasgow: MacLehose, 1896), 48–60.

[8]   Vincent Carretta, 'The *Kingis Quair* and the *Consolation of Philosophy*', *Studies in Scottish Literature* 16 (1981): 14–28; Clair F. James, '*The Kingis Quair*: The Plight of the Courtly Lover', in David Chamberlain (ed.), *New Readings of Late Medieval Love Poems* (Lanham: University Press of America, 1993): 95–118.

[9]   Carruthers, *The Craft of Thought*, 171–20.

Consolation. Reading the text provokes reflection on 'how that eche estate, /As Fortune lykith, thame will [ay] translate', and finally on his own 'fortune and vre', inspiring his composition (55–6, 65).

Although writing displaces dreaming within the *Quair*, 'fantasye' still plays a part in the poetic process as it is represented in the text, in the narrator's experience of the Matins bell: 'suich a fantasye /Fell me to mind that ay me thought the bell /Said to me "tell on, man, quhat thee befell"' (75–7). His response astutely indicates the ambiguous powers of imagination, its potential as an instrument of creative invention, and its capacity to delude:

> This is myn awin ymagynacioun,
> It is no lyf that spekis vnto me,
> It is a bell–or that impressioun
> Of my thoght causith this illusioun
> That dooth me think so nycely in this wise. (79–84)

The bell's voice bears interpretation as a mental construct, an illustration of the creative role of the imagination in generating vivid images of the kind employed in memory work, either to process received textual matter or to create new work. Indicating the narrator's proficiency in the arts of memory, the fantasy of the bell also offers a justification for writing about personal experience. In this respect, it complements the role of Boethius in authorising the production of the *Quair*. As Dante argues, the solipsistic act of writing about the self is permissible only 'in cases of necessity', to vindicate oneself in the absence of any other advocate, or 'when by speaking of oneself very great benefit comes to another by way of instruction'. For Dante, Boethius serves as an example of the former kind, since 'since no one else rose to his defence, he sought under the pretext of finding consolation, to defend himself against the everlasting disgrace of his exile by showing that it had been unjust'.[10]

In identifying the experience of reading the *Consolation* as the catalyst for his composition, however, the narrator of the *Quair* associates the Boethian text with the didactic property of life writing, establishing a valuable precedent for his own work. The *Quair*'s evocation of mnemonic practices of invention is in sympathy with the conception of the *Consolation* as depicting a process of therapeutic meditation that entails the exercise of the faculty of memory, whose influence is traced throughout this study.[11] In this context, Boethius becomes an instructive instance of the value of such meditation in reconciling oneself to adversity, to be emulated by those suffering the effects of misfortune as a practice that facilitates moral action. The therapeutic aspect of the *Consolation* is emphasised in the *Quair*'s description of Boethius as

---

[10]   Dante Alighieri, *The Banquet*, Book 1, Chapter 2, 17.

[11]   See also Letizia A. Panizza, 'Stoic Psychotherapy in the Middle Ages and Renaissance: Petrarch's *De Remediis*', in Léglu and Milner (eds), *The Erotics of Consolation*, 117–39, and Carruthers, *The Craft of Thought*, 171–220.

> [...] this noble man,
> That in himself the full recouer wan
> Of his infortune, pouert and distresse,
> And in tham set his verray sekernesse. (32–5)

In positioning Boethius as the inspiration for a parallel act of self-writing, the narrator of the *Quair* plants the idea that his own life history will offer a similarly instructive example.

The fantasy of the bell further serves to validate the narrator's vernacular and personal writing project in positioning it as an act of Christian worship, an impression reinforced by the narrator's making of a cross with his pen to begin his book, an act whose material performance is reflected in the penned cross drawn by the scribe at this point in the manuscript copy (91). A convention most prominent in manuals for teaching the alphabet to children, the making of the cross underlines the poem's relationship to devotional practice, suggesting the thematic relevance of the psalms commonly incorporated in Matins observances to the subjects addressed within the *Quair*.[12] Psalm 24, as Matthew McDiarmid argues, shares the *Quair*'s concern with the frailty of youth;[13] such intertextual relations represent an appeal to the poem's readers, tapping into a common memory of the familiar content of the Matins service, a device that further emphasises the role of the remembrance of texts within the *Quair*.

It is possible that those other texts remembered within the *Quair* include the poetry of Machaut and Froissart examined elsewhere in this study, as the prestige and influence of French is articulated within the multilingual literatures and cultures of Scotland and England.[14] Like these texts, and like *The Testament* of Thomas

---

[12]   See Walter W. Skeat (ed.), *The Kingis Quair: Together with A Ballad of Good Counsel: by King James I. of Scotland* 2nd edn Scottish Text Society, n.s. 1 (Edinburgh: Blackwood, 1911), 61.

[13]   See notes to McDiarmid, *The Kingis Quair*, 119, and Michael D. Cherniss, *Boethian Apocalypse: Studies in Middle English Vision Poetry* (Norman, OK: Pilgrim, 1986), 196.

[14]   For an analysis of parallels between the *Quair* and its French analogues, see William Calin, 'The *dit amoureux* and the Makars: an Essay on *The Kingis Quair* and *The Testament of Cresseid*', *Florilegium* 25 (2008): 217–50, and Elliott, 'The Counsele of Philosophy: The *Kingis Quair* and the Medieval Reception History of the *Consolation of Philosophy* in Vernacular Literature', PhD Diss., University of Edinburgh, 2006. Notable recent studies emphasising the prestige of French include Butterfield, *The Familiar Enemy*; for a comprehensive overview of the French presence in English literature, see William Calin, *The French Tradition and the Literature of Medieval England* (Toronto: University of Toronto Press, 1994). Calin's forthcoming study, *The French Tradition and the Literature of Medieval and Early Modern Scotland* will provide similar coverage of Scottish writing, superseding the pioneering early work of Janet M. Smith, *The French Background of Middle Scots Literature* (Edinburgh: Oliver and Boyd, 1934). This influence is also addressed in Calin's 'The *dit amoureux*, Alain Chartier, and the *Belle Dame sans mercy* Cycle in Scotland: John Rolland's *The Court of Venus*', in Emma Cayley and Ashby Kinch (eds), *Chartier in Europe* (Cambridge: Brewer, 2008), 149–64; and 'The French Presence in Medieval Scotland: Le roi René and *King Hart*', *Florilegium* 24 (2007): 11–20.

Usk, the *Quair* brings Boethius, politics, and arts of memory into a significant conjunction. The autobiographical elements so prominently incorporated within the *Quair* render James's identity and experience as an imprisoned king present within the narrative while, in describing Boethius as 'noble senatore' and 'worthy lord', rather than classifying him as a philosopher, the poet suggests a particular concern with his involvement in politics, and the risks that office entails (18, 22).[15] This political emphasis at once reflects the personal context of the narrator's engagement with the *Consolation*, as a text that evokes specific memories, and resonates with the wider reception of Boethius's narrative as being especially relevant to those active in public life.

The convergence of themes is reiterated in the image of 'the schip that sailith stereles', introduced as a symbol of unripe youth, 'of wit wayke and vnstable /To fortune both and to infortune hable' (101, 95–6). Both ship and youth 'wantis that suld gyde all thy viage'(105), and the image of the imperilled vessel concurrently recalls its biblical function, in representing the situation of the human soul in a mutable world, and its particular role within the *Consolation*, as the text inspiring this reflection. The Boethian interlocutor's sorrow and confusion stem from forgetfulness of the helmsman who controls the vicissitudes of fortune, the supreme Good, a lack to be remedied through Philosophy's teaching (1.pr.6; 3.pr.12). Within the *Quair*, vulnerability to fortune is similarly linked with deficient knowledge: 'The rypenesse of resoun lak[it] I /To gouerne with my will, so lyte I couth' (108–9). Both the politicised reception of the *Consolation* and the *Quair*'s representation of the experience of a king suggest a further dimension to the maritime image, through its currency within writing on governance: as Mapstone argues, its appearance within the *Quair* implies a particular desire to establish James's fitness to rule the kingdom of Scotland, a land without a king since the death of Robert III in 1406, on hearing news of his son's capture.[16] Perhaps reflecting the influence of Gower and Hoccleve, for whom the unquiet sea functioned as an image of political insecurity, the *Quair*'s inflection of the ship image links the capacity for self-government stemming from the acquisition of reason with aptitude for political governance.[17]

---

[15]   Maury McCrillis III, 'Narrative Subjectivity and Narrative Distancing in James I of Scotland's *Kingis Quair*,' in G. Caie et al. (eds), *The European Sun: Proceedings of the Seventh International Conference on Medieval and Renaissance Scottish Language and Literature* (East Linton: Tuckwell, 2001), 208.

[16]   Sally Mapstone, 'Kingship and the *Kingis Quair*', in Helen Cooper and Sally Mapstone (eds), *The Long Fifteenth Century: Essays for Douglas Gray* (Oxford: Clarendon, 1997), 55–6.

[17]   On the *Quair*'s relationship to these authors, see Joanna Martin, 'The Translations of Fortune: James I's *Kingis Quair* and the Rereading of Lancastrian Poetry', in Nicola Royan (ed.), *Langage Cleir Illumynate: Scottish Poetry from Barbour to Drummond, 1375–1630* (Amsterdam: Rodopi, 2007), 43–60; and commentary in her *Kingship and Love in Scottish Poetry, 1424–1540* (Aldershot: Ashgate, 2008), 19–31. On the relationship between self-government and political governance in Gower, see also Porter, 'Gower's Ethical Microcosm'.

The political applications of the maritime image remain in force as the narrator gives another twist to the figure, connecting it with his experience in writing:

> The rokkis clepe I the prolixitee
> Of doubilnesse that doith my wittis pall:
> The lak of wynd is the deficultee
> In enditing of this lytill trety small:
> The bote I clepe the mater hole of all:
> My with, vnto the saile that now I wynd
> To seke conning, though I bot lytill fynd. (120–26)

Playing on the traditional association of this trope with poetry, the narrator's vivid expression of anxiety is not simply a modesty topos, but signals a difficulty in translating the subjects of his meditation into literary material.[18] A problem anticipated in the narrator's allusion to 'ink and paper spent /To lyte effect', his struggle, and the terms in which it is expressed, imply that the writing of the poem is itself bound up in the process of learning how to govern both oneself and others within a mutable world (87–8).[19] The convergence of poetics, ethics and politics in the ship metaphor in this respect foreshadows the association of writing and governance in the poem's penultimate stanza: in an echo of the *Quair*'s first line, 'Hich in the hevynnis figure circulere', the celestial sphere is identified as a visible reflection of the influence of 'hevyn quhare powar is commytt /Of gouirnance', the space of God's obscure prophetic writing (1372, 1367–8). Signalling an affinity between divine, political and literary authority, the association of writing and governance is in sympathy with medieval rhetorical theory, which regarded the linguistic order as an expression of the political order, since language facilitates civilisation, while grammatical features such as gender and verbal government mirror aspects of human society.[20] Within the Boethian tradition, such correlations between rhetoric and politics inform the emphasis on the role of poet as source of a knowledge relevant to practices of rule, in texts such as the *Prison amoureuse* and *Confort d'ami*. Against this background, the opening of the *Quair*, with its emphasis on the stylistic qualities of Boethius's 'metir suete', 'rethorikly pykit', gains new meaning (23, 45). In a context where rhetorical skill is entwined with ethical character, an equation fundamental to medieval conceptions of the arts of memory, this ability forms a vital part of a writer's authority; the difficulties that beset the narrator of the *Quair* as he begins to write are therefore such as to problematise his whole didactic enterprise.

The nature of the narrator's problem is further defined in his invocation of the poetic Muses, appealing first to Calliope for the 'wynd suld blowe /Me to the port,

---

[18]   On writing and the ship metaphor, see Ernst Robert Curtius, *European Literature and the Latin Middle Ages*, trans. Willard R. Trask (London: Routledge, 1953), 129.

[19]   On the metaphor's function in linking the themes of writing and statecraft, see Lois A. Ebin, 'Boethius, Chaucer and *The Kingis Quair*', *Philological Quarterly* 53 (1974): 321–41 (338–9).

[20]   Vance, *Mervelous Signals*, 256–63.

quhar gynneth all my game', to remove his difficulty in 'enditing of this lytill trety small' (117–18, 123). In hope 'To seke conning', he offers a plea:

> At my begynning first I clepe and call
> To you, Cleo, and to yow, Polymye,
> With Thesiphone, goddis and sistris all,
> In nowmer nine, as bokis specifye:
> In this processe my wilsum wittis gye,
> And with your bryght lanternis wele conuoye
> My pen, to write my turment and my ioye. (127–33)[21]

The context and ordering of his supplication is consistent with the influence of the Fulgentian tradition of mythography that identifies the Muses with stages in the acquisition of knowledge.[22] Describing a process whose conclusion is associated with the ability to articulate what has been learnt, Fulgentius's scheme shares common features with accounts of the art of memory, appropriate to the Muses' status as daughters of Mnemosyne. For example, Melpomene is identified with focused meditation, Erato with the searching out of likenesses to assist memory.[23] The narrator's appeal to Calliope, the final Muse in the Fulgentian scheme, is apposite to the moment when he begins to write, giving expression to the fruit of his search for knowledge, in the concluding stage of the process he is setting out to describe. Clio, identified with the desire for learning stirred by the hope to survive in the memory of posterity, and Polyhymnia, associated with capacious memory, are also pertinent to his poetic enterprise.[24]

---

[21]   As McDiarmid argues, the inclusion of the Fury Tisiphone does not indicate the poet's ignorance of her place in classical mythology, but follows the practice of Chaucer and Lydgate, whose *Temple of Glas* makes a clear distinction between Muses and Furies, *The Kingis Quair*, 120.

[22]   Phillipa Hardman, 'Chaucer's Muses and His "Art Poetical",' *Review of English Studies*. n.s. 37 (1986): 478–94.

[23]   Fulgentius, *Mitologiarum Libri Tres, Opera*, ed. R. Helm (Leipzig: Teubner, 1898), 1.15, 25–7.

[24]   It is interesting to note that at least one variation on the Fulgentian scheme identifies Calliope as head of the Muses, as the Muse of poetry and emblem of the ability to articulate knowledge, in Coluccio Salutati's *De laboribus Herculis*. A copy of this work (now Vatican, BAV MS Urb. Lat. 694) was present in Duke Humfrey's library, potentially accessible to James during his imprisonment. See Concetta Carestia Greenfield, *Humanist and Scholastic Poetics, 1250–1500* (Toronto: Associated University Presses, 1981), 138. On the composition of Duke Humfrey's library, see Alfonso Sammut, *Unfredo duca di Gloucester e gli umanisti italiani* (Padova: Antenore, 1980), Alessandra Petrina, *Cultural Politics in Fifteenth-Century England: The Case of Humfrey, Duke of Gloucester* (Leiden: Brill, 2004); and articles by David Rundle: 'On the Difference between Virtue and Weiss: Humanist Texts in England during the Fifteenth Century,' in D.E.S. Dunn (ed.), *Courts, Counties, and the Capital in the Later Middle Ages* (New York: St. Martins Press, 1996), 181–203; 'Humanism before the Tudors: On Nobility and the reception of *Studia Humanistas* in Fifteenth-Century England', in J. Woolfson (ed.), *Reassessing Tudor Humanism* (Basingstoke: Palgrave Macmillan, 2002), 22–42; 'Habits of Manuscript

The invocation of the Muses within the *Quair* reflects the humanist rehabilitation of classical tradition, yet the emphasis on Boethius' *Consolation* within the poem's opening also recalls Philosophy's condemnation of the Muses, an instance of the repudiation of idolatry typical of the early Christian era, when paganism remained an active force.[25] Rather than dispelling the humanist associations the Muses had accrued, however, the Boethian echo introduces an ambiguous note, a reminder that the pleasures of art can deceive, as well as instruct.[26] The narrator's prayer for guidance for his 'wilsum wittis' reflects the consequences of such aesthetic seduction, suggesting the problem of *curiositas* or mental wandering that inhibits the action of memory (131).

The analepsis that follows emphasises the subjective dimension of the narrator's confinement 'in strayte ward and in strong prisoun', the scene of his incarceration coinciding with the introspective turn in his thoughts in his punning claim, 'in ward full oft I wold bewaille' (169, 176). Imprisonment is experienced as cause for reflection on its potential moral causes, as he questions 'quhat haue I gilt to faille /My fredome in this warld and my plesance?' (179–80). In contrast with the 'suffisance' of others, his own lack of autonomy is perceived as a disturbance in the natural order that must be rationalised: 'The bird, the best, the fisch eke in the see, /They lyve in fredome, euerich in his kynd. /And I a man, and lakkith libertee' (180, 183–5). This emphasis on his present state of insufficiency takes up the earlier claim that 'nature gave me suffisance in youth', although he lacked 'The rypenesse of resoun [...] To gouerne with my will' (107, 108, 109). The apparent poverty of his internal resources marks a disparity between the narrator's younger self and his own description of Boethius:

> Fortune the bak him turnyt, and therfore
> He makith ioye and confort that he quit is
> Of thir vnsekir warldis appetitis.
> And so, aworth he takith his penance,
> And of his vertew maid it suffisance (38–42)

In these contexts, the recurrence of the term 'suffisance' recalls the function of *sufficientia* in the Latin *Consolation*, as a state unmarked by the indigence of need that participates in the divine, object of the search for the supreme Good, and the related role of its French and English equivalents within the Boethian tradition.[27]

Collecting: The Dispersals of the Library of Humfrey, Duke of Gloucester,' in James Raven (ed.), *Lost Libraries: The Destruction of Great Book Collections since Antiquity* (London: Palgrave Macmillan, 2004), 106–23.

[25] See Paul Beekman Taylor and Sophie Bordier, 'Chaucer and the Latin Muses', *Traditio* 47 (1992): 215–32 (231–2).

[26] For an argument that the invocation has an ironic function, see William Quinn, 'Memory and the Matrix of Unity in *The Kingis Quair*.' *Chaucer Review* 15 (1981): 332–55.

[27] On *sufficientia*, see Asbell, 'The Philosophical Background', 3–16. Cooper's concordance to Boethius lists five instances of *sufficientia*, and eleven of its cognates, all in book 3, Lane Cooper, *A Concordance of Boethius: The Five Theological Tractates*

Within the *Quair*, its use signals a shared concern with the Boethian subject of self-sufficiency and the potential for its attainment.

The response to this problem framed within the poem evokes the action of Chaucer's *Knight's Tale*, and distinguishes itself from it, as the narrator falls in love with a woman glimpsed from his prison window. For Palamon and Arcite, love represents a travesty of Boethian wisdom: rather than liberating them from bondage to fortune, it increases their subjection, ultimately causing Arcite's death.[28] Yet, the *Quair* differs in its Christian context, and in the genesis of the love it describes: rather than being an entirely spontaneous response to the sight of the woman, it follows the narrator's deliberations on love, conceived as a lord 'of so noble myght and kynde, /Lufing his folk' (254–5). Reflecting a movement from introversion to a desire for social involvement, as Julia Boffey argues, the narrator's desire to serve this lord also marks a transition from a frustrated and impossible longing for untrammelled freedom to the free acceptance of a higher authority.[29] Following the narrator's prayer that Love's 'blisfull grace benigne' might 'hable me vnto his seruice digne', the woman's appearance signals the formation of a homosocial bond (270–71). Consonant with the political function of erotic discourse in contemporary society, the presentation of love within the *Quair* strongly resembles the *Prison amoureuse*, with its opening declaration of loyalty to 'Amours, mon signeur et mon mestre' (*Prison* 27).

The experience of love the poem describes acts as a stimulus to the faculties associated with mnemonic praxis, as the 'suete sicht' of the woman's 'ymage' simultaneously produces a sensation of spiritual flight and of bondage to a particular object: 'my spirit was so light /Me thought I flawe for ioye without arest, /So were my wittis boundin all to fest' (424, 425–7). A form of devotion identified with prayer, the narrator's meditative response issues in the composition of a 'ditee' interpolated within the narrative, reflecting the association of memory work with both piety and literary composition (429): [30]

> Quhen sall your merci rew vpon your man
> Quhois seruice is yit vncouth vnto yow?
> Sen quhen ye go, there is noght ellis than!
> Bot hert, quhere as the body many not throu,

---

and the Consolation of Philosophy (Cambridge, MA.: Medieval Academy of America, 1928). Although statistics are lacking, Chaucer's *Boece* offers one illustration, with the concordance listing seventeen occurrences of variant forms of *suffisance*, alongside other cognates, John S.P. Tatlock, *A Concordance to the Complete Works of Geoffrey Chaucer and to the Romaunt of the Rose* (Washington: Carnegie, 1927). *Souffissance* is also highlighted within the *Remede de Fortune*, 463, 1046, 1146, 1621, 2009, 2488, 2747, 2777, 2790, 2890, 3348.

[28]   Kolve, *Chaucer*, 90–2, Ebin, 'Boethius, Chaucer', 324.

[29]   Julia Boffey, 'Chaucerian Prisoners: The Context of *The Kingis Quair*', in Julia Boffey and Janet Cowen (eds), *Chaucer and Fifteenth-Century Poetry* (London: King's College, 1991), 97.

[30]   See Carruthers, *The Craft of Thought*.

Folow thy hevin: quho suld be glad bot thou
That suich a gyde to folow has vndertake?
Were it throu hell, the way thou noght forsake! (435–41)

The emphasis on 'hert' as a means by which the narrator might follow his heaven recalls the metaphorical role of the heart as seat of memory, and the remedial properties attributed to the mnemonic capacity for visualisation as a means to overcome the pain of absence. Yet, the narrator's rhetorical question suggests the dark underside of affectivity: the sensual response might shade into enjoyment, rather than use of the sign to a moral end. Desire might render the subject bestial, a possibility acknowledged in the narrator's whim to change places with the 'lytill hound' that plays at his beloved's feet (368). The disparate possibilities of affection are intimated as the narrator questions how 'deth and lyf – bothe tueyne – /Sall bothe atonis in a creature /Togidder duell', identifying the woman as a figure 'That me may gyde to turment and to ioye' (474–6, 497).

Absence elicits a further response consistent with the practice of the mnemonic arts: the beloved's departure from the garden prompts an excess of passionate sorrow that lasts until evening, when

Ourset so sorow had bothe hert and mynd,
That to the cold[e] stone my hede on wrye
I laid, and lent amaisit verily,
Half sleping and half suoun in suich a wise;
And quhat I met I will you now deuise. (505–11)

Positioning emotional distress as precursor to a trance state, the poet evokes the characteristic use of emotion as stimulus to recollection, while isolation and a nocturnal setting suggest the absence of potential sensory distractions that facilitates memory work.

The topography of the dream that follows also evokes some of the most familiar techniques adopted to assist with the creation of mental spaces and structures, and the organisation of information within them. Opening with an ascent 'fro spere to spere [...] vnto the circle clere /Of Signifer' accords with the use of celestial objects in arts of memory (526, 528–9): astronomy was employed as a source of schemes for data storage and inventive meditation, with the Zodiac enjoying particular recognition as the basis of the system associated with the classical authority on memory, Metrodorus of Scepsis.[31] The dream's celestial setting also recalls the opening line of the *Quair*, and its cyclical echo in the poem's penultimate verse, 'Heigh in the hevynnis figure circulere', as the text itself assumes a form whose associations with mnemonic praxis befit its didactic and memorial content (1, cf. 1372).

---

[31] On astronomical memory schemes, see Mary Carruthers and Jan M. Ziolkowski (eds), *The Medieval Craft of Memory: An Anthology of Texts and Pictures* (Philadelphia: University of Pennsylvania Press, 2002) 15–16. On Metrodorus, see Yates, *The Art of Memory*, 38–9, 53

Temporally located prior to the narrator's reading of the *Consolation*, the dream described within the *Quair* is presented as a visionary experience that parallels Boethius's own encounter with Philosophy, and its content also resonates with Boethian tradition. The vision turns upon the narrator's successive encounters with Venus, Minerva and Fortune, a conjunction of goddesses that, as critics such as Louise Olga Fradenburg argue, recalls the Judgement of Paris.[32] Several of the texts examined within this study incorporate notable references to the Judgement, or narrative episodes recounting or reimagining the myth, an activity that finds a precedent in Boethian translation and commentary.[33] Although Boethius does not allude to the Judgement of Paris within the *Consolation* itself, the myth became associated with the text through the authority of one of the most important and widely circulated commentaries, William of Conches's early twelfth-century *Glosae super Boethium*. William of Conches uses the myth of the Judgement in expounding the significance of the punishment of Ixion, briefly mentioned in 3 m. 12 of the *Consolation*.[34] The influence of his commentary, and the extent to which the myth of the Judgement subsequently became identified with the *Consolation*, are illustrated by the case of a fourteenth-century Picard verse translation surviving in two manuscripts. Within this translation, the Judgement is presented as an integral part of the *Consolation*, one of several narratives interpolated by the anonymous translator.[35] In the context of the broad tradition of Boethian commentary, translation and adaptation that informs *The Kingis Quair*, the Judgement of Paris thus emerges as a familiar motif.

The presence of Fortune, rather than Juno, within the poem, is consistent with medieval conceptions of classical mythology: medieval versions of the Judgement perpetuate the traditional identification of Juno as goddess of riches and kingdoms, temporal goods offered to Paris as an inducement to decide in her favour. Juno's association with goods typically conceived as the gifts of Fortune marks a point of intersection between these allegorical figures that finds explicit acknowledgement in a medieval redaction of the Judgement within the influential fourteenth-century French poem, the *Echecs amoureux*. Of the two known

---

[32] Louise Olga Fradenburg, *City, Marriage, Tournament: Arts of Rule in Late Medieval Scotland* (Madison: University of Wisconsin Press, 1991), 113, 131–3; and see also Lucy Catherine Lewis, 'British Boethianism 1380–1436, PhD. Diss., University of London, 2000, 260–2.

[33] On the Judgement in Machaut and Froissart, see Ehrhart, *The Judgment*, 130–141 (*Fonteinne*), 192–3 (*Confort*), and on another prominent episode incorporated in Froissart's *Espinette amoureuse* (1369), see 141–51.

[34] Gvillelmi de Conchis, *Glosae svper Boetivm*, ed. L. Nauta (Turnhout: Brepols, 1999) 211. For an analysis of William of Conches's treatment of the Judgement and its impact on this translation, see Ehrhart, *The Judgment*, 79–82. For a concise overview of his commentary and its influence, see Lodi Nauta, 'The *Consolation*: the Latin commentary tradition, 800–1700', in John Marenbon (ed.), *The Cambridge Companion to Boethius* (Cambridge: Cambridge University Press, 2009), 259–63.

[35] The version of the Judgement surviving in MS B.N. fr. 576, fols. 51^v–52^v, is printed in Dwyer, *Boethian Fictions*, 103–8; Atkinson, 'A Fourteenth-Century Picard'.

manuscript copies of the poem, the most complete, containing the Judgement, was severely damaged during World War II; however, a nineteenth-century synopsis prepared by Ernst Sieper evidences the description of Fortune as the blind goddess who distributes temporal goods on Juno's behalf.[36] In his treatise on free will, *De fato et fortuna* (*c*. 1396–1398), the humanist scholar Coluccio Salutati links the goddesses even more closely, citing the Judgement of Paris in claiming that Juno and Fortune are indubitably one and the same, as interchangeable terms poets use to denote the divine government of realms and worldly wealth.[37] The logic underpinning the association of Juno and Fortune in these French and Italian texts is evident, obviating the need to presuppose knowledge of a particular version of the Judgement on the part of the *Quair*-poet. Yet, it is worth noting that Salutati's treatise, at least, was potentially accessible to James I of Scotland: a manuscript of Salutati's work, including *De fato et fortuna*, is known to have been in England during the time of his captivity, and is later recorded in the ownership of Humfrey, Duke of Gloucester.[38]

In more general terms, evidence of the association of Juno and Fortune indicates the currency of a conceptual link between the two, and thus offers support for the identification of the Judgement as an influence on the *Quair*. Yet the *Quair* itself seems to frustrate the parallel between poem and myth: while the Judgement turns upon the rivalry of the three goddesses, the deities of the *Quair* collaborate with one another to help the narrator. In her discussion, Fradenburg concludes that the Judgement 'is not fully present in the *Quair* precisely for this reason'.[39] Closer examination of the mythographic tradition suggests that such concord is not necessarily at odds with the influence of the Judgement, however, and provides valuable support for Fradenburg's claim that 'the *Quair* shares with other love allegories that treat the Judgment of Paris more fully a concern with the reparation of the will, with the perils as well as the opportunities of those critical moments in which desire awakens.'[40]

Originating with Fulgentius, the most familiar interpretation of the Judgement in the Middle Ages reads the myth as an allegory of the human subject's exercise of free will, at liberty to choose between the active life, represented by Juno; the contemplative life of Pallas; or the voluptuous life, signified by Venus. The

---

[36]   Dresden, Sächsische Landesbibliothek Oc 66 (D), ff. 1–54 summarised in Ernst Sieper, *Les Echecs amoureux: Eine altfranzösische Nachahmung des Rosenromans und ihre englische Übertragung* (Weimar: Felber, 1898) f. 6b, discussed in Ehrhart, *The Judgment*, 154–5.

[37]   Coluccio Salutati, *De fato et fortuna*, ed. Concetta Bianca (Florence: Olschki, 1985), 144–5.

[38]   Now Manchester, Chetham's Library, MS Mun. A. 3.131 (27929). I am indebted to R.J. Lyall for the identification of the reference to the Judgement within *De fato et fortuna* as a potential influence on the *Quair*, and of this manuscript as a possible source. On the MS, see Sammut, *Unfredo duca di Gloucester*, 111–12.

[39]   Fradenburg, *City*, 133.

[40]   Fradenburg, *City*, 133.

highly influential vernacular moralisation of the *Metamorphoses* presented in the *Ovide moralisé* (*c.* 1316–1325) allegorises the Judgement in explicitly Christian terms, identifying the apple of Discord with the forbidden fruit of Eden, in an interpretation that reflects the Augustinian conception of the Fall as an event that marks a rupture between body and spirit, originating in the will's perverse rebellion against divine authority. After the Fall, the will is tainted, divided against itself; in consequence, individual subjects and human society are troubled by the proliferation of self-destructive appetites whose regulation requires the exercise of coercive discipline.[41] As Ehrhart argues, in the *Ovide moralisé*, the Judgement comes to represent 'not the fall of Adam and Eve but the fall of Everyman, the individual re-enactment of our first parents' sin': the choice of Paris symbolises the misdirected will of the subject who ignores reason to pursue contingent goods, in place of the ultimate good which alone can provide the satisfaction he desires.[42] The function of Venus within this allegorical interpretation reflects the continuing influence of a persistent tendency to identify sexuality as emblem of the antagonism inherent within the will.[43]

Pierre Bersuire's widely disseminated *Ovidius moralizatus* (*c.* 1340), adds a further interpretation, identifying the goddesses of the Judgement with the faculties of the soul: Pallas with *ratio* or reason, Juno with *memoria*, and Venus with the will (*voluntas*). The apple is glossed as the human heart, which folly offers up to appetite, in defiance of memory and reason. As Ehrhart argues, Bersuire's allegory most probably reflects an adaptation of the Augustinian conception of the intellectual soul, which images the Trinity in its tripartite nature, comprising memory, intelligence, and will.[44] In the later Paris redaction of the *Ovidius moralizatus* (*c.* 1342), this allegorical reading is located against the background of salvation history:

in homine qui dicitur minor indus tres dee id est tres anime potentie primo fueresse[n]t concordes et quia spiritualis rationi obediebat nulla erat discordia inter partes. Homo cum deo concors erat et inter se talis erat concordia quod nequaquam caro spiritum repugnabat. Denique dea vel deus discordie id est dyabolus vel cum superbia vel concupiscentia pomum vetitum sibi pericat [...] ideo pacem et concordiam enervauit et regum anime dissipavit.

[in man, who is called India Minor, the three goddesses, or three powers of the soul, were first in agreement, and because the spirit obeyed reason there was no discord among the parts. Man was in harmony with God, and between them there was such concord that not at all did the flesh oppose the spirit. Finally the goddess or god of discord, that is, the devil, with pride or concupiscence, threw

---

[41]   Augustine, *The City of God*, 14.23, 623–5; Brown, *The Body and Society*, 404–5.

[42]   Ehrhart, *Judgment*, 92.

[43]   Brown, 'Bodies and Minds', 481.

[44]   Ehrhart, *Judgment*, 99; Augustine, *De Trinitate, Opera*, part 16,1, ed. W.J. Mountain, Corpus Christianorum, Series Latina (Turnhout: Brepols, 1968) 10.11.18, 330.

him the forbidden apple; he weakened peace and concord and destroyed the rule
[...] of the soul.][45]

The divine rivalry of the Judgement becomes an image of spiritual discord within
the individual soul: the effect of original sin upon the psyche is the disturbance of
the concord that once sustained the rule of reason.

Although the original state of concord cannot be fully regained in a postlapsarian
world, the didactic purpose of Bersuire's allegory endorses the idea that the proper
exercise of reason might moderate the effects of the Fall, restoring order within
the soul. Against the background of Bersuire's interpretation, the image of the
goddesses of the Judgement working in harmony would function as an allegory
of the well-regulated soul, whose powers exist in a state of concord recalling the
prelapsarian condition. Bersuire's interpretation of the Judgement thus supplies
a context in which the absence of rivalry amongst the goddesses of the *Quair*
acquires new significance, underlining the poem's concern with the reparation
of the appetitive will. Bersuire's text was also potentially accessible to James I
of Scotland, with a copy of the *Ovidius moralizatus* later recorded amongst the
manuscripts donated to the University of Oxford by Duke Humfrey in 1444.[46]

As Sally Mapstone observes, the genre of advice to princes literature to which
the *Quair* is affiliated commonly uses devices such as allegory in order to imply
that 'the prime advisory context was the king's own mental realm, and that in this
sense the regulatory principles of self-government came essentially from within
himself.'[47] Taking the form of a dream vision, the narrator locates his divine
encounters in a space that is potentially internal, opening up the possibility that he
is describing a journey through imagined territories, the places of his mind. Against
this background, the three goddesses of the *Quair* may be understood as attributes
of the narrator himself, as the three powers of the soul. Read as an allegory of
the well-ordered soul, in which the appetitive will has been subordinated to the
powers of reason and memory, the dream vision serves to identify the narrator as
an example of the spiritual concord produced by successful self-government.

The goddesses at the heart of the narrator's dream are consistent with the
methodological emphasis on the generation and manipulation of versatile mental
images, capable of sustaining complex meanings, within the arts of memory.
Pagan gods were good to think with, the pantheon providing a ready source of
figures capable of signifying abstract concepts, already imbricated in a network of
cultural associations and narratives.[48] The particular use that might be made of the
pagan gods in the construction of a memory system is most clearly illustrated with
reference to a later example, the memory theatre built by Giulio Camillo in the
sixteenth century. Envisioned as a model of the human mind, Camillo's theatre was

---

[45]   MS Paris, B.N. Lat. 16787, f. 58r, published and translated in Ehrhart, *Judgment*,
100, 257n87.

[46]   Sammut, *Unfredo duca di Gloucester*, 83.

[47]   Sally Mapstone, 'Kingship and the *Kingis Quair*', 60.

[48]   See Minnis, 'Medieval Imagination and Memory', 262.

designed as a system able to encompass the totality of knowledge; it was a tangible version of the organisation of memory on spatial principles. Within Camillo's memory system, the pagan gods function explicitly as headings or locations for the storage and retrieval of information. In this setting, Venus is used as a heading for storing matter relating to appetite and the government of human affections by the will.[49] The function and organisation of Camillo's material memory theatre illuminates the mnemonic principles that shape the *Quair*, where Venus fulfils a similar purpose, her court operating as a mental heading or memory place.

In the context of a dream suggestive of a mnemonic state, Venus's palace recalls the architectural backgrounds that are a recurrent feature of artificial memory systems. With its diverse inhabitants, the court represents a gathering of exempla embodying particular experiences and conceptions of love, and its encyclopaedic function as a memory palace is indicated in a significant omission:

> [...] present in that place
> Me thoght I sawe of euery nacioun
> Loueris that endit thair lyfis space
> In Iovis seruice, mony a mylioun.
> Of quhois chancis maid is mencioun
> In diuerse bukis (quho thame list to se),
> And therfore here thair namys lat I be. (540–46)

Rather than supplying a catalogue of lovers, the narrator identifies the missing information as data that also exists in other archives, in the shared spaces of cultural memory. In this respect, the narrator's vision suggests the exercise of memory, as he reviews his knowledge of love in order to resolve his present amatory problem.

If pagan gods have a recognised value for mnemonic practice, the particular association of Venus, Minerva and Fortune wihtin a dream that functions as an allegory of mind carries a significance of its own. The interpretation of the Judgement of Paris that finds expression in Bersuire's *Ovidius moralizatus* identifies the goddesses with the powers of the soul, yet, in replacing the Augustinian term *intelligentia* with *ratio*, Bersuire perpetuates a common confusion between the faculties of the intellectual and animal soul.[50] Medieval faculty psychology locates the powers of the sensible soul within the brain, and the operation of these internal senses illuminates the adaptation of the Judgement of Paris enacted in the *Quair*.

In his translation of Bartholomaeus Anglicus's *De proprietatibus rerum*, John Trevisa offers an influential formulation of the threefold model of the brain as it was theorised in medieval faculty psychology:

> The innere witte is departed aþre by þre regiouns of þe brayn, for in þe brayn beþ þre smalle celles. Þe formest hatte *ymaginatiua*, þerin þingis þat þe vttir witte apprehendiþ withoute beþ i-ordeyned and iput togedres withinne [...]Þe

---

[49]   Yates, *Art of Memory*, 77, 135–74.

[50]   On this confusion, see Kathryn L. Lynch, *The High Medieval Dream Vision: Poetry, Philosophy, and Literary Form* (Stanford: Stanford University Press, 1988), 95.

middil chambre hatte *logica* þerin þe vertu estimatiue is maister. Þe þridde and
þe laste is *memoratiua*, þe vertu of mynde. Þat vertu holdiþ and kepiþ in þe
tresour þingis þat beþ apprehendid and iknowe by þe ymaginatif and *racio.*[51]

As Trevisa explains, the faculties located in the anterior, middle, and posterior
ventricles work in concert:

what þe vertu ymaginatif shapiþ and ymagineþ he sendiþ hit to the doom of
resoun. What resoun fongiþ of þe ymaginatiue, resoun demeþ hit as a iuge and
sendiþ hit to the vertu of mynde. þe vertu of mynde fongiþ what is [demed in]
vndirstondinge and kepeþ it and saueþ it stedefastliche forto he bringe it forþ in
acte and in dede.[52]

The first of these faculties, *ymaginatiua*, also known as *phantasia*, is associated
with the assimilation of information derived from the senses, in the form of images
or phantasms; it also facilitates the combination of data to generate unfamiliar
forms. Conceived as the foundation of insight and knowledge, imagination was
also regarded as being perilous because it responds to corporeal matter, but differs
from it in substance, a disjunction that holds potential for error.[53] In the middle
cell, the faculty whose various names include *logica, ratio* and estimative virtue
assesses the phantasms produced by imagination, judging their *intentiones*, or
capacity to benefit or harm the spirit. Conflation of the powers associated with
the intellectual and sensible soul obscured the distinction between this faculty and
the *ratio intellectiva*, the power of judgement facilitating spiritual progress. As a
result, reason was often conceived as a power of discrimination that transcends the
physical, serving a divine purpose.[54] The posterior chamber houses *memorativa*,
the faculty that preserves the judgements of reason until they are to be realised in
action, and this cell was sometimes also considered to be responsible for motion.[55]

In conventional representations of the Judgement of Paris, the three goddesses
are gathered in the same location, while the deities of the *Quair* occupy separate
places, although they collaborate with one another. The ordering and distribution
of the goddesses within the poem supports the hypothesis that the dream offers
a specific illustration of mental activity as it was understood in medieval faculty
psychology, tracing the process of apprehension. As a reaction to the experience
of falling in love with a woman glimpsed from his prison window, the dream
is a direct response to the stimulation of the senses, and the narrator's spiritual
migration to the sphere of Venus operates as a counterpart to the transmission of
impressions derived from the senses to the imagination as images.

---

[51]   Bartholomaeus Anglicus, *On the Properties of Things: John Trevisa's Translation of
Bartholomaeus Anglicus' De proprietatibus rerum*, ed. M.C. Seymour et al. 3 vols (Oxford:
Clarendon, 1975–1988) 1: 98, V.A. Kolve, *Chaucer and the Imagery of Narrative: The
First Five Canterbury Tales* (London: Arnold, 1984), 22–3.

[52]   Bartolomaeus Anglicus, *On the Properties of Things*, 1: 107.

[53]   Lynch, *The High Medieval Dream Vision*, 31–3.

[54]   Lynch, *The High Medieval Dream Vision*, 30–32.

[55]   Kolve, *Chaucer and the Imagery of Narrative*, 22.

Through her traditional association with the flesh, Venus is a suitable figure for imagination, with its dependency on sensory data. As an emblem of desire or will, which can guide the soul towards its true object, in the supreme good, or lead it into error, Venus captures the multivalent nature of imagination, at once an aid to learning and a potential source of harm. Admitting that she alone cannot determine the narrator's fate, Venus sends the narrator to Minerva, an action that corresponds to the function of imagination in transmitting phantasms to the seat of reason.

The correlation between Minerva and the faculty of *ratio* is underscored by the nature of her response to the narrator's request for aid: rather than offering the instruction that might be expected of the goddess of wisdom, Minerva's primary concern is the evaluation of the narrator's affection. Of 168 lines of dialogue, the greater part is devoted to her enquiry and the narrator's response to it, while the instruction she offers as remedy occupies only a quarter of the total.[56] Minerva's questioning itself has an advisory function, however, emphasising a Christian conception of edification that coheres with Boethian tradition in framing a concern with moral stability as the establishment of a secure foundation. Directing the narrator to 'on him traist and call /That corner-stone and ground is of the wall / That failis nought', Minerva observes

> For, lo, the werk that first is foundit sure
> May better bere a pace and hyar be
> Than othir-wise, and langer sall endure
> Be monyfald, this may thy resoun see,
> And stronger to defend aduersitee.
> Ground thy werk therfore vpon the stone,
> And thy desire sall forthward with the gone.
> (907–9, 911–17)

Minerva's architectural imagery is informed by the scriptural traditions whose influence is discussed by David Cowling, and by the Boethian and biblical figure of the house built on rock as metaphor for the spiritual edification that secures the subject from misfortune (2.m.4, Matt. 7.24–7).[57] In emphasising the necessity of a secure foundation, Minerva's advice resembles that offered by Usk's Love, a correspondence that underlines the texts' shared Boethian inheritance.[58]

Minerva's concern is not the expulsion of desire, but its appropriate expression: '"Desire", quod sche, "I nyl it noght deny /So thou it ground and set in Cristin wise"' (988–9). Her examination of the narrator establishes a significant context for the remedial advice she subsequently offers, culminating in the claim that

---

[56] Of lines 88–1052, 124 deal with Minerva's enquiry (884–1008), with 43 remaining (1009–52).

[57] Cowling, *Building the Text.*

[58] Usk, *The Testament of Love* 1.5, 63; 2.1, 81; 2.7, 101; 2.8, 106; 2.14, 125, and see above, Chapter 5. The *Quair*'s formulation of the metaphor is distinct from Usk's more technical image of the piled foundation, however, suggesting that its use is independent of the earlier text.

Fortune is most and strangest euermore
Quhare leste foreknawing or intelligence
Is in the man; and, sone, of wit or lore
Sen thou art wayke and feble, lo, therfore,
The more thou art in dangere and commune
With hir that clerkis clepen so Fortune. (1038–43)

Minerva's counsel has been characterised as 'less Boethian than Machiavellian', yet her use of the edification metaphor implies that her advice pertains to the moral wisdom or prudence conceived as a protection against the risk of pain associated with attachment to material goods, subject to loss.[59] Cultivation of a spiritual wisdom mindful of the nature of the supreme good holds out the possibility of an escape from subjection to the vicissitudes of fortune. Minerva's role in judging the tendency of the narrator's affections corresponds to the function assigned to *ratio* within the animal soul, which determines whether or not phantasms will harm the soul. In her particular concern with Christian orthodoxy, Minerva also evokes the *ratio intellectiva*, as a power of discrimination that facilitates spiritual development. Insofar as she represents an aspect of the narrator's psychology, her harmonious relationship with Venus takes on a significance emphasised in her injunction: 'gif thou will be wele fortunyt /Lat wisedom ay [vn] to thy will be iunyt' (930–31). The moral health and eternal fate of the subject are conceived as being dependent upon the subordination of the appetitive will to the rule of reason.

Minerva concludes her advice by directing the narrator to Fortune, whose terrestrial location offers an appropriate reflection of her association with worldly mutability, and of the anatomical position assigned to *memorativa* within contemporary models of brain function. The vivid finale of the narrator's vision serves as an illustration of the characteristic methods of the art of memory, in presenting a striking visual image conventionally used to fix the Boethian lesson of Fortune's instability in the minds of medieval audiences. Fortune's argument underlines the moral function of this visual prompt: 'For the nature of it is euermore, /After ane hicht, to vale and geue a fall' (1200–201). A concise demonstration of the techniques used to treasure up ideas and arguments in the storehouse of memory, the meeting with Fortune also indicates the success of the learning process the narrator has undergone. Climbing on Fortune's wheel in full awareness of her mutability, the narrator testifies to his own ability to act despite the threat of worldly loss that forms an inexorable part of mortal existence. According to the narrator, Fortune assists him not through direct intervention in his material circumstances; instead, she acts 'To quikin treuly day by day my lore /To my larges that I am cumin agayn' (1265–6). The insistence upon the increase of knowledge as a means to liberty is consistent with Minerva's advice, with its emphasis on wisdom's role in releasing the subject from bondage to fortune, and is especially apt if the goddesses are understood to form part of an allegory of apprehension. Insofar as the narrator's own progress within the dream traces the

---

[59] A.C. Spearing,'Dreams in the *Kingis Quair* and the Duke's Book', in Mary-Jo Arn (ed.), *Charles d'Orléans in England (1415–1440)* (Cambridge: Brewer, 2000), 130.

operation of the inward wit, Fortune's role in setting him in motion further reflects the role of *memorativa* in translating the judgements of reason into action.

A significant precedent for this interpretation of the *Quair*'s central allegory is associated with the reception history of the *Consolation*: the twelfth-century commentary on the *Aeneid* attributed to Bernardus Silvestris maintains that Aeneas's education follows a pattern similar to that traced within the consolation, and the commentator interprets the *Aeneid* as a journey through the faculties of mind.[60] Within the commentary, the interpretation of the sixth book of the *Aeneid* provides the nearest parallel to the reading I propose for the *Quair*, in associating the underworld with the cellular model of the brain.

Atque fornice: this is the vault of the human brain. *Portas*: the three chambers. We come to heavenly contemplation through these (as was said before) by exercising wit, reason, and memory [...] *Hec ubi:* at the gates, since Aeneas and the Sibyl are presently in the cells of memory [...] *Foribus propinquant*: 'they approach the gates' when with wit they discover something, with reason they discern it and they commit it to memory. *Occupat:* Aeneas occupies the entrance (*aditum*) when he exercises wit [...] since committing to memory follows discovery by wit, Aeneas places the branch (*ramum*) – philosophy – across the threshold (*adverso limine*), the rear chamber.[61]

As the commentator conceives it, the *Aeneid* here describes the process by which Aeneas commits philosophy to memory, housed in the posterior chamber of the brain. In doing so, he opens the way to Elysium, where he will encounter his father, and this aspect of his journey is interpreted as the spiritual exercise which will prepares the subject for a more metaphysical encounter, with the creator.[62]

The idea of the text as an allegorical journey through the mechanisms of apprehension is endorsed by the conception of the body and its faculties, not as a prison for the soul, but as instruments enabling humanity to bridge the gap between the material world, where the soul is in exile, and the divine realm which is its proper home. As Katherine Lynch argues, according to the logic of this conception, '[p]roper subordination of mental faculties in the hierarchy would ultimately stimulate the proper functioning of the will and promote the total harmony of the individual'.[63]

If, as I have argued, the adaptation of the Judgement of Paris enacted within the *Quair* is to be interpreted as an allegory of mind, the absence of the myth's characteristic rivalry suggests that the discord amongst the powers of the soul associated with the Fall has been overcome. Bearing witness to the harmonious function of a mind whose state recalls the equilibrium enjoyed by prelapsarian humanity, the allegory serves to identify the *Quair*'s narrator as a man capable

---

[60]   Lynch, *The High Medieval Dream Vision*, 62–3, 215n55.

[61]   Earl G. Schreiber, *Commentary on the First Six Books of Virgil's Aeneid*, trans. Thomas E. Maresca (Lincoln: University of Nebraska Press, 1979), 106–7.

[62]   See Lynch, *The High Medieval Dream Vision*, 63, and Paul Vincent Rockwell, *Rewriting Resemblance in Medieval French Romance* (London: Garland, 1995), 142–5.

[63]   Lynch, *The High Medieval Dream Vision*, 29.

of governing his mental faculties. As a vision whose form and context evokes mnemonic praxis, the dream also suggests the narrator's ability to use the arts of memory to address problems at once emotional and political. The narrator's initial response to the dream is an increased anxiety at the fantastic quality of his experience, however, and regret 'That nan othir thingis bot dremes had, / Nor sekernes, my spirit with to glad' (1217–18). Responsibility for his transition from painful uncertainty to assurance is ultimately located with the divine, as the narrator's prayer for 'more takenyng' to establish the heavenly origins of his dream is answered in the appearance of a turtledove bearing a flowering branch inscribed with a message of comfort in golden letters. Material proof of the truth of his vision, like its counterparts in the *Remede de Fortune* and *Fonteinne amoureuse*, this sign attests to the manifestation of the divine within the world, pointing towards the possibility that justice can be enacted within the individual subject and the social order.[64]

Within a poem that invites the identification of its narrator's experience with that of James I of Scotland, the effect of this allegorical vision is to present its subject as a model prince who possesses the skills of a philosopher, for whom the experience of captivity becomes a conduit for divine grace, and the prison scene of the mental enfranchisement produced by knowledge of the supreme good as the true object of desire. In positioning erotic desire for the woman glimpsed from the narrator's prison window as the direct stimulus for the narrator's visionary experience, moreover, the poem gestures towards the instrumental role of Joan Beaufort in facilitating James's return to Scotland. James's marriage to a noblewoman of royal descent emerged as a condition of his liberation at an early stage in the negotiations between Scotland and England and, from July 1423, the senior members of the Beaufort dynasty, Thomas, Duke of Exeter, and Henry, Bishop of Winchester, pursued an alliance between James and their niece Joan, granddaughter of John of Gaunt, finalised in February 1424.[65] The historical dimension of the *Quair* renders Joan's fictive counterpart the motive cause of a liberation at once physical and spiritual, a narrative flattering not only to James, but to Joan and her powerful relations.

With the completion of the *Quair*, the figure of the poet-narrator reaches the end point of a learning process that necessarily concludes with composition, articulating the object of the lesson for the benefit of a new audience. In doing so, the poem fulfils the promise of its own evocation of the art of memory, as a discipline traditionally associated with literary invention and the perfection of ethical character. If texts such as the *Fonteinne amoureuse* suggest the value of the poetic arts to the prince, in underlining his own role in the composition of the work in which he appears, the narrator of the *Quair* emphasises the authorial responsibility that remained implicit in Boethius, presenting James Stewart as the exemplary figure who perfects the roles of poet and politician by uniting them in his own person.

---

[64]   *Remede de Fortune*, 2094–6, 4055–98; *Fonteinne amoureuse* 2504–6, 2523–4. Fuog notes the relevance of the *Fonteinne*, '*The Kingis Quair* as Boethian Revision', 148.

[65]   Michael Brown, *James I*, 24–6.

Conclusion

'You have to begin to lose your memory, if only in bits and pieces, to realize that memory is what makes our lives [...] Our memory is our coherence, our reason, our feeling, even our action. Without it, we are nothing'.[1] Luis Buñuel's words mark a point of intersection between his own sense of identity and medieval conceptions of memory as the foundation of character. This book has sought to trace how medieval practices of memory function to mediate the coherence of selves, in considering how and why texts addressing personal experiences of exile and imprisonment might assume the forms of Boethian narrative. Conceiving both texts and selves as the products of interlinked processes of gathering and composition, mnemonic praxis recognises that literary form is implicated in the construction of social forms, in its possession of what Jameson calls 'Utopian power as the symbolic affirmation of a specific historical and class form of collective unity'.[2] In claiming community with Boethius, the writers and texts examined within this study create a common place. Constructing a homology in which Latin author and contemporary subject coincide, they enlarge the meaning of the *Consolation* in adding to a communal store of interpretations, forming a gathering that cumulatively foreshadows the plenitude of an inaccessible universal. An activity founded upon a rhetorical conception of ethics, as Mary Carruthers argues, it has social implications:[3] on the one hand, it imagines the possibility of inhabiting perfection, returning home from worldly exile to a transcendent place, becoming whole and unmarked by need. On the other, the very act of imagining such a place, in the construction of similitudes that seek to define the universal through accumulation, marks the gap that separates us from the ideal, as it multiplies difference and signals disunity.

Despite this antagonism, however, these rhetorical acts nevertheless affirm community in legitimating and perpetuating particular social structures. The desire for unity with the divine recognises the conditions of its own impossibility: its fulfilment would necessarily entail a radical self-abnegation, effacing local attachments and the particularity of embodied experience to merge into oneness.[4] In negotiating the problem posed by the inescapable desire for completeness, these writers also trace the contours of individual existence, as the fantasy of transcendence contributes to the production of practical strategies, facilitating agency within a mutable world. Seeking to translate the Boethian lesson into the familiar terms that sustain memory, making it literally part of themselves, they generate versions that incorporate the distinctive features of their own experience.

---

[1] Luis Buñuel, *My Last Breath*, trans. Abigail Israel (London: Vintage, 1994), 4–5.

[2] Fredric Jameson, *The Political Unconscious: Narrative as a Socially Symbolic Act* (London: Routledge, 1981), 281–2.

[3] Carruthers, *The Book of Memory*, 225.

[4] My sense of this problem is indebted to Miller, *Philosophical Chaucer*, 111–51.

Most evident in the engagement with particular lives and recent events, this is also manifested in the conceptual associations these works reproduce: participating in a longstanding tradition that identifies the *Consolation* as a resource with a particular value for the aristocracy, they conceive virtue as a standard of behaviour especially appropriate to the nobility, whose integrity sustains the social order in its extant form.

The texts I explore reflect a dynamic by which particular and local attachments become a foundation for universalism through the experience of loss, whether permanent or temporary. The pain of loss threatens the stability of the subject, but it also opens up an opportunity to recognise the sense in which selfhood is founded upon lack. Through the experience of loss, and especially the loss of liberty, or of a homeland, subjects become aware that the things they lost never truly belonged to them (or they could not have been lost), and that they were themselves always in exile. The sense of loss that triggers this experience is typically, although usually not exclusively, associated with the barrier imprisonment or exile poses to the satisfaction of erotic desire. A further reflection of the contextual nature of the conceptual associations embedded within such texts, this aspect of late-medieval Boethian narrative is indicative of the cultural value love had acquired in public discourse, as an aspirational practice that signals an ability to master the unruly appetitive will.

In this context, the Boethian recognition that sufficiency is the true object of desire is seen as a prophylactic against longing for contingent goods, for wealth, money, fame, power or pleasure, which cannot provide the satisfaction which would lead to a cessation of desire. This is precisely the knowledge that enables subjects to control their response to misfortune and to the itch of desire; in the Boethian tradition explored within this study, it is positioned as an understanding instilled and put into practice through the exercise of memory. Memory training is conceived as a form of mental prosthesis, an internalised practice of self-discipline that allows for the imaginative contemplation of an inaccessible object, removed from the potential harms of fortune. As a means to subdue and control desire, the discipline of memory has a universal value, mediating the desire for internal unity, and contributing to social harmony as a curb for the appetites that disrupt human relations. At the same time, however, it is recognised as a discipline of particular importance for the nobility, whose involvement in politics exposed them to the vicissitudes of fortune, and whose choices, as the case of Jean de Berry illustrates, impact upon the fate of the populace.

Insofar as the Boethian discipline of memory I trace within this study is associated with political activity and practices of government, it affirms a Utopian ideal of collective unity, provisionally restoring the harmony between will and reason whose loss marked the fall, and producing versions of human society that more effectively mirror the kingdom of heaven, conceived as the true homeland of human subjects. As a practice which entails the internal construction of systems which establish and sustain the place of reason, this form of mnemonic discipline prefigures the intersection between mechanics and philosophy in Renaissance intellectual culture, as analysed by Jessica Wolfe. In particular, Wolfe draws attention to the influence of a form of 'Lipsian neo-Stoicism that regards machinery as a symbol of right reason and as therapy for the Stoic sage', articulated in the belief that mechanics are applicable 'to Stoic values such as resistance to adversity and mitigating the deleterious effects of the passions'.[5] The politicised practices of artificial memory manifested in the Boethian tradition, and their stabilising effects, offer a precedent for such neo-Stoical developments.

In drawing attention to the role of Boethius's *Consolation* in mediating the representation of experiences of exile and imprisonment in the Middle Ages, this book has traced the ways in which a desire for unity and sameness contributes to practices of self-construction. Imagining the prospect of a perfect community and contributing to social cohesion, the Boethian tradition simultaneously attends to the particularity of embodied existence, and promotes practices of life writing.

---

[5]   Jessica Wolfe, *Humanism, Machinery, and Renaissance*, 18–19.

Works Cited

Adorno, Theodor W., *Prisms*, trans. Samuel and Shierry Weber (Cambridge, MA: MIT, 1981).

Aers, David, 'A Whisper in the Ear of Early Modernists; or, Reflections on Literary Critics Writing the 'History of the Subject,' in David Aers (ed.), *Culture and History, 1350–1660: Essays on English Communities, Identities and Writing* (Detroit: Wayne State University Press, 1992), 177–202.

Agamben, Giorgio, *The Coming Community*, trans. Michael Hardt (Minneapolis: University of Minnesota Press, 1993).

———, *Stanzas: Word and Phantasm in Western Culture*, trans. Ronald L. Martinez (Minneapolis: University of Minnesota Press, 1993)

Anselm of Canterbury, *De Concordia* (The Compatibility of God's Foreknowledge, Predestination, and Grace with Human Freedom), trans. Thomas Bermingham, *The Major Works*, ed. Brian Davies and G. R. Evans (Oxford: Oxford University Press, 1998).

Aquinas, Thomas, *Summa Theologiæ*, Thomas Gilby (ed.), vol. 36 (Cambridge: Cambridge University Press, 2006).

Arch, Jennifer, 'The Boethian *Testament of Love*', *Studies in Philology*, 105.4 (2008): 448–62.

Aristotle, *Nicomachean Ethics*, trans. W.D. Ross, in Jonathan Barnes (ed.), *The Complete Works of Aristotle*, 2 vols (Princeton: Princeton University Press, 1984).

Asbell, William J., Jr., 'The Philosophical Background of *Sufficientia* in Boethius's *Consolation*, Book 3', in Noel Harold Kaylor, Jr., and Philip Edward Phillips (eds), *New Directions in Boethian Studies* (Kalamazoo: Medieval Institute Publications, 2007), 3–16.

Astell, Ann W., *Job, Boethius, and Epic Truth* (Ithaca: Cornell University Press, 1994).

———, 'Visualizing Boethius's *Consolation* as Romance', in Noel Harold Kaylor, Jr. and Philip Edward Phillips (eds), *New Directions in Boethian Studies* (Kalamazoo: Medieval Institute Publications, 2007), 111–24.

Atkinson, J. Keith, 'A Fourteenth-Century Picard Translation-Commentary of the "Consolatio Philosophiae"', in Minnis (ed.), *The Medieval Boethius*, 32–62.

Atkinson, J. Keith, and Béatrice Atherton, 'Les Manuscrits du *Roman de Fortune et de Félicité*', *Revue d'Histoire des Textes*, 22 (1992): 169–251.

Atkinson, J.K., and A.M. Babbi (eds), *L''Orphée' de Boèce au Moyen Âge: Traductions françaises et commentaries latins (XIIe-XVe siècles)* (Verona: Fiorini, 2000).

Attwood, Catherine, *Dynamic Dichotomy: The Poetic 'I' in Fourteenth and Fifteenth-Century French Lyric Poetry* (Amsterdam: Rodopi, 1998).

Augustine, *Confessions*, trans. William Watts. 2 vols (London: Heinemann, 1912).
————, *De Trinitate, Opera*, part 16,1, ed. W.J. Mountain, Corpus Christianorum, Series Latina (Turnhout: Brepols, 1968).
————, *De Doctrina Christiana*, ed. and trans. R.P.H. Green (Oxford: Clarendon, 1995).
————, *The City of God against the Pagans*, ed. and trans. R.W. Dyson (Cambridge: Cambridge University Press, 1998).
Autrand, Françoise, *Jean de Berry* (Paris: Fayard, 2000).
Badel, Pierre-Yves, *Le 'Roman de la Rose' au XIV siècle: Étude de la reception de l'œuvre* (Geneva: Droz, 1980).
Balfour-Melville, E.W.M., *James I, King of Scots, 1406–1437* (London: Methuen, 1936).
Bartholomaeus Anglicus, *On the Properties of Things: John Trevisa's Translation of Bartholomaeus Anglicus' De proprietatibus rerum*, ed. M.C. Seymour et al. 3 vols (Oxford: Clarendon, 1975–1988).
Bennett, Josephine Waters, 'The Medieval Loveday', *Speculum* 33.3 (1958): 351–70.
Bennett, Philip E., '*Ut pictura memoria*: Froissart's Quest for Lost Time', *Zeitschrift für französische Sprache und Literatur* 120.3 (2010): 229–44.
Bétemps, Isabelle. *L'Imaginaire dans l'œuvre de Guillaume de Machaut* (Paris: Champion, 1998).
Bétemps, Isabelle, et al., (eds), La Consolation de la Philosophie *de Boèce: dans une traduction attribuée à Jean de Meun: d'après le manuscrit Leber 817 de la Bibliothèque Municipale de Rouen* ([Mont-Saint-Aignan: Publications de l'Université de Rouen, 2004).
Bieler, Ludwig (ed.), *Anicii Manlii Severini Boethii* Philosophiae Consolatio, CCL 94 (Turnhout: Brepols, 1957).
Blumenfeld-Kosinski, *Renate, Reading Myth: Classical Mythology and Its Interpretations in Medieval French Literature* (Stanford: Stanford University Press, 1997).
Boethius, *The Consolation of Philosophy*, trans. P.G. Walsh (Oxford: Oxford University Press, 1999).
Boffa, Sergio, *Warfare in Medieval Brabant, 1356–1406* (Woodbridge: Boydell, 2004).
Boffey, Julia. 'Chaucerian Prisoners: The Context of *The Kingis Quair*', in Julia Boffey and Janet Cowen (eds), *Chaucer and Fifteenth-Century Poetry* (London: King's College, 1991), 84–102.
————, 'Bodleian Library MS Arch. Selden. B. 24 and the Definitions of the "Household Book"', in A.S.G. Edwards, Vincent Gillespie and Ralph Hanna (eds), *The English Medieval Book: Studies in Memory of Jeremy Griffiths* (London: British Library, 2000), 125–34.
Boffey, Julia, and A.S.G. Edwards, *The Works of Geoffrey Chaucer and the* Kingis Quair*: A Facsimile of Bodleian Library, Oxford, MS Arch. Selden. B. 24* (Cambridge: Brewer, 1997).

Boffey, Julia, and A.S.G. Edwards, 'Bodleian MS Arch. Selden. B. 24 and the "Scotticization" of Middle English Verse', in Prendergast and Kline (eds), *Rewriting Chaucer*, 166–85.

Born, Lester Kruger, 'The Perfect Prince: A Study in Thirteenth- and Fourteenth-Century Ideals', *Speculum* 3 (1928): 470–504.

Bradley, Henry, 'Thomas Usk and the "Testament of Love"', *Englische Studien* 23 (1897): 437–8.

Bradwardine, Thomas, 'On Acquiring a Trained Memory', trans. Mary Carruthers, in Carruthers, *The Book of Memory*, 361–8.

Breisach, Ernst, *Historiography: Ancient, Medieval, and Modern*. 3rd edn (Chicago: University of Chicago Press, 2007).

Bressie, Ramona, 'The Date of Thomas Usk's "Testament of Love"', *Modern Philology* 26.1 (1928): 17–29.

Brown, J.T.T., *Authorship of* The Kingis Quair*: A New Criticism* (Glasgow: MacLehose, 1896).

Brown, Michael, *James I*, rev. edn (East Linton: Tuckwell, 2000).

Brown, Peter, *The Body and Society: Men, Women, and Sexual Renunciation in Early Christianity* (New York: Columbia University Press, 1988).

———, 'Bodies and Minds: Sexuality and Renunciation in Early Christianity', in David M. Halperin, John J. Winkler, and Froma I. Zeitlin (eds), *Before Sexuality: The Construction of Erotic Experience in the Ancient Greek World* (Princeton: Princeton University Press, 1990), 479–90.

Brownlee, Kevin, 'Orpheus Song Re-sung: Jean de Meun's Reworking of *Metamorphoses*, X', *Romance Philology* 36 (1982): 201–9.

———, *Poetic Identity in Guillaume de Machaut* (Madison: University of Wisconsin Press, 1984).

———, 'Ovide et le Moi poétique "moderne" à la fin du Moyen Âge: Jean Froissart et Christine de Pizan', in Brigitte Cazelles and Charles Méla (eds), *Modernité au moyen âge: Le défi du passé* (Geneva: Droz, 1990), 153–73.

———, 'Pygmalion, Mimesis, and the Multiple Endings of the *Roman de la Rose*', *Yale French Studies* 95 (1999): 193–211.

Buñuel, Luis, *My Last Breath*, trans. Abigail Israel (London: Vintage, 1994).

Burnley, J.D. 'Late Medieval English Translation: Types and Reflections', in Ellis (ed.), *The Medieval Translator*, 37–53.

Busby, Keith, 'Froissart's Poetic Prison: Enclosure as Image and Structure in the Narrative Poetry', in Maddox and Sturm-Maddox (eds), *Froissart Across the Genres*, 81–100.

Butterfield, Ardis, *Poetry and Music in Medieval France: From Jean Renart to Guillaume de Machaut* (Cambridge: Cambridge University Press, 2002).

———, *The Familiar Enemy: Chaucer, Language and Nation in the Hundred Years War* (Cambridge: Cambridge University Press, 2003).

Calin, William. *A Poet at the Fountain: Essays on the Narrative Verse of Guillaume de Machaut* (Lexington: University Press of Kentucky, 1974).

————, '*La Fonteinne amoureuse* de Machaut: son or, ses oeuvres-d'art, ses mises en abyme,' in *L'Or au Moyen âge (monnaie–métal–objets–symbole)* (Aix-en-Provence: C.U.E.R. M.A., 1983), 75–87.

————, *The French Tradition and the Literature of Medieval England* (Toronto: University of Toronto Press, 1994).

————, 'The French Presence in Medieval Scotland: Le roi René and *King Hart*', *Florilegium* 24 (2007): 11–20.

————, 'The *dit amoureux* and the Makars: an Essay on *The Kingis Quair* and *The Testament of Cresseid*', *Florilegium* 25 (2008): 217–50.

————, 'The *dit amoureux*, Alain Chartier, and the *Belle Dame sans mercy* Cycle in Scotland: John Rolland's *The Court of Venus*', in Emma Cayley and Ashby Kinch (eds), *Chartier in Europe* (Cambridge: Brewer, 2008), 149–64.

Carlson, David R., 'Chaucer's Boethius and Thomas Usk's *Testament of Love:* Politics and Love in the Chaucerian Tradition,' in R.A. Taylor et al. (eds), *The Centre and its Compass: Studies in Medieval Literature in Honor of Professor John Leyerle*, (Kalamazoo: Western Michigan University, 1993), 29–70.

Carretta, Vincent, '*The Kingis Quair* and the *Consolation of Philosophy*', *Studies in Scottish Literature* 16 (1981): 14–28.

Carruthers, Mary, *The Craft of Thought: Meditation, Rhetoric and the Making of Images, 400–1200* (Cambridge: Cambridge University Press, 1998).

————, *The Book of Memory: A Study of Memory in Medieval Culture*, 2nd edn (Cambridge: Cambridge University Press, 2008).

Carruthers, Mary, and Jan M. Ziolkowski, eds. *The Medieval Craft of Memory: An Anthology of Texts and Pictures* (Philadelphia: University of Pennsylvania Press, 2002).

Cazelles, Raymond, *Société politique, noblesse et couronne sous Jean le Bon et Charles V* (Geneva: Droz, 1982).

Cerquiglini, Jacqueline, 'Tension sociale et tension d'écriture au XIVème siècle: les dits de Guillaume de Machaut,' in Danielle Buschinger, ed. *Littérature et société au moyen âge*, Actes du colloque d'Amiens des 5 et 6 mai 1978 (Paris: Champion, 1978), 111–29.

————, '*Un Engin si soutil*': Guillaume de Machaut et l'écriture au XIVe siècle* (Geneva: Slatkine, 1985).

————, 'Écrire le temps: Le lyrisme de la durée aux XIVe et XVe siècles', in Yvonne Bellenger (ed.), *Le Temps et la durée dans la littérature au Moyen Âge et à la Renaissance* (Paris: Nizet, 1986), 103–14.

————, 'Fullness and Emptiness: Shortages and Storehouses of Lyric Treasures in the Fourteenth and Fifteenth Centuries', trans. Christine Cano and John Jay Thompson, *Yale French Studies* (special edition), *Contexts: Style and Values in Medieval Art and Literature* (1991): 224–39.

————, *La Couleur de la mélancolie: La fréquentation des livres au XIVe siècle 1300–1415* (Paris: Haiter, 1993).

Chaucer, Geoffrey. *The Riverside Chaucer*. Gen. ed. Larry D. Benson. 3rd edn (Oxford: Oxford University Press, 1988).

Cherniss, Michael D., *Boethian Apocalypse: Studies in Middle English Vision Poetry* (Norman: Pilgrim, 1986).

Colunga, Alberto, and Laurentio Turrado (eds), *Biblia Sacra Iuxta Vulgatem Clementinam*, (Madrid: Bibliotheca de Autores Christianos, 1985).

Cooper, Lane, *A Concordance of Boethius: The Five Theological Tractates and the* Consolation of Philosophy (Cambridge, MA.: Medieval Academy of America, 1928).

Copeland, Rita, *Rhetoric, Hermeneutics, and Translation in the Middle Ages* (Cambridge: Cambridge University Press, 1991).

Courcelle, Pierre, 'L'Âme en Cage', in Kurt Flasch (ed.), *Parusia: Studien zur Philosophie Platons und zur Problemgeschichte des Platonismus. Festgabe für Johannes Hirschberger* (Frankfurt: Minerva, 1965), 103–16.

———, 'Tradition platonicienne et traditions chrétiennes du corps-prison (*Phédon* 62b; *Cratyle* 400c)', *Revue des études latines*, 43 (1965): 406–43.

———, *La Consolation de Philosophie* dans la tradition littéraire (Paris: Etudes augustiniennes, 1984).

Cowling, David. *Building the Text: Architecture as Metaphor in Late Medieval and Early Modern France* (Oxford: Clarendon, 1998).

Crabbe, Anna, 'Literary Design in the *De Consolatione Philosophiae*', in Gibson (ed.), *Boethius*, 237–77.

Cropp, Glynnis M., 'Le Prologue de Jean de Meun et *Le Livre de Boece de Consolacion*', *Romania* 103 (1982): 278–98.

———, 'Les Manuscrits du *Livre de Boece de Consolacion*', *Revue d'histoire des textes* 12–13 (1982–1983): 263–352.

———, 'Boèce et Christine de Pizan', *Le Moyen Age* 87 (1981), 387–417.

———, 'The Medieval French Tradition', in Maarten J.F.M Hoenen and Lodi Nauta (eds), *Boethius in the Middle Ages: Latin and Vernacular Traditions of the* Consolatio Philosophiae (Leiden: Brill, 1997), 243–65.

———, (ed.), *Le Livre de Boece de Consolacion* (Geneva: Droz, 2006).

———, 'An Italian Translation of *Le Livre de Boece de Consolacion*', in Noel Harold Kaylor, Jr., and Philip Edward Phillips (eds), *New Directions in Boethian Studies* (Kalamazoo: Medieval Institute Publications, 2007), 75–82.

———, 'Boethius in Translation in Medieval Europe', in Harald Kittel et al., *Traduction: Ein internationales Handbuch zur Übersetzungsforschung*, 2 (Berlin: de Gruyter, 2007), 1329–37.

———, (ed.), *Böece de Confort remanié*, MHRA European Translations 1 (London: Modern Humanities Research Association, 2011).

Curry, Anne, *The Hundred Years War*, 2nd edn (Houndmills: Palgrave, 2003).

Curtius, Ernst Robert, *European Literature and the Latin Middle Ages*, trans. Willard R. Trask (London: Routledge, 1953).

Dante Alighieri, *The Banquet*, trans. Christopher Ryan (Saratoga: Anma Libri, 1989).

———, *The* Divine Comedy *of Dante Alighieri III:* Paradiso, trans. John D. Sinclair (Oxford: Oxford University Press, 1961).

Davis, Isabel, *Writing Masculinity in the Later Middle Ages* (Cambridge: Cambridge University Press, 2006).

Dedeck-Héry, L.V., (ed), 'Boethius' *De Consolatione* by Jean de Meun', *Mediaeval Studies* 14 (1952): 162–275.

Delachenal, R., *Histoire de Charles V.* 5 vols (Paris: Picard, 1909–1931).

Deschaux, Robert, 'Consolateur d'illustres exclus: Guillaume de Machaut', *Exclus et systèmes d'exclusion dans la littérature et la civilisation médiévales*. Actes du colloque organise par le C.U.E.R. M.A. à Aix-en-Provence, les 4–5–6 mars 1977 (Paris: Champion, 1978), 59–67.

Douzinas, Costas, and Slavoj Žižek (eds), *The Idea of Communism* (London: Verso, 2010).

Dronke, Peter, *Verse with Prose from Petronius to Dante: The Art and Scope of the Mixed Form* (Cambridge, MA: Harvard University Press, 1994).

Dunbabin, Jean, *Captivity and Imprisonment in Medieval Europe 1000–1300* (Houndmills: Palgrave, 2002).

Duval, Frédéric, and Françoise Vielliard, *Miroir des classiques*, Éditions en ligne de l'École des chartes, 17 (Paris, École nationale des chartes, 2007–), http://elec.enc.sorbonne.fr/miroir/boece/traduction/para=françaises.html, consulted 10 July 2011.

Dwyer, Richard, *Boethian Fictions: Narratives in the Medieval French Versions of the Consolatio Philosophiae* (Cambridge, MA: The Medieval Academy of America, 1976).

Eakin, Paul John, *Fictions in Autobiography: Studies in the Art of Self Invention* (Princeton: Princeton University Press, 1985).

Earp, Lawrence, *Guillaume de Machaut: A Guide to Research* (New York: Garland, 1995).

Ebin, Lois A., 'Boethius, Chaucer and *The Kingis Quair*', *Philological Quarterly* 53 (1974): 321–41.

Ehrhart, Margaret J., 'Machaut's *Dit de la fonteinne amoureuse*, the Choice of Paris, and the Duties of Rulers', *Philological Quarterly* 59 (1980): 119–39.

———, *The Judgment of the Trojan Prince Paris in Medieval Literature* (Philadelphia: University of Pennsylvania Press, 1987).

Elliott, Elizabeth, 'The Counsele of Philosophy: The *Kingis Quair* and the Medieval Reception History of the *Consolation of Philosophy* in Vernacular Literature', PhD Diss., University of Edinburgh, 2006.

———, 'The Open Sentence: Memory, Identity and Translation in the *Kingis Quair*', in Sarah Carpenter and Sarah M. Dunnigan (eds), *'Joyous Sweit Imaginatioun': Essays on Scottish Literature in Honour of R. D. S. Jack*, SCROLL (Amsterdam and New York: Rodopi, 2007), 23–39.

Ellis, Roger, (ed.), *The Medieval Translator: The Theory and Practice of Translation in the Middle Ages* (Cambridge: Brewer, 1989).

Enders, Jody, 'Music, Delivery, and the Rhetoric of Memory in Guillaume de Machaut's *Remède de Fortune*', *PMLA* 107 (1992): 450–64.

————, *Rhetoric and the Origins of Medieval Drama* (Ithaca: Cornell University Press, 1992).

————, 'Memory, Allegory, and the Romance of Rhetoric', *Yale French Studies* 95 (1999): 49–64.

————, *The Medieval Theatre of Cruelty: Rhetoric, Memory, Violence* (Ithaca: Cornell University Press, 1999).

Epstein, Robert, 'Prisoners of Reflection: The Fifteenth-Century Poetry of Exile and Imprisonment', *Exemplaria* 15 (2003): 159–98.

Figg, Kristen M., 'The Narrative of Selection in Jean Froissart's Collected Poems: Omissions and Additions in BN MSS fr. 830 and 831', *Journal of the Early Book Society*, 5 (2002): 37–55.

Foer, Joshua, *Moonwalking with Einstein: The Art and Science of Remembering Everything* (London: Allen Lane, 2011).

Fradenburg, Louise Olga, *City, Marriage, Tournament: Arts of Rule in Late Medieval Scotland* (Madison: University of Wisconsin Press, 1991).

Fulgentius, *Mitologiarum Libri Tres, Opera*, ed. R. Helm (Leipzig: Teubner, 1898).

Fuog, Karin E.C., 'Placing Earth at the Center of the Cosmos: *The Kingis Quair* as Boethian Revision', *Studies in Scottish Literature* 32 (2001): 140–49.

Galloway, Andrew, 'Private Selves and the Intellectual Marketplace in Late Fourteenth-Century England: The Case of the Two Usks', *New Literary History* 28.2 (1997): 291–318.

Gauvard, Claude, 'Portrait du prince d'après l'oeuvre de Guillaume de Machaut: étude sur les idées politiques du poète', in *Guillaume de Machaut, Poète et compositeur*, Actes et Colloques no. 23 (Paris: Klincksieck, 1982), 23–39.

Geoffrey of Vinsauf, *Poetria Nova*, in Edmond Faral (ed), *Les Arts poétiques du XIIe et du XIIIe siècle: recherches et documents sur la technique littéraire du moyen âge* (Paris: Champion, 1962).

Gibson, Margaret, (ed.), *Boethius: His Life, Thought and Influence* (Oxford: Blackwell, 1981).

Goff, Jacques Le, 'Head or Heart? The Political Use of Body Metaphors in the Middle Ages', trans. Patricia Ranum, in Michel Feher (ed.), *Fragments for a History of the Body*, vol. 3 (New York: Zone, 1989), 13–56.

Goldberg, Jonathan, *Writing Matter: From the Hands of the Renaissance* (Stanford: Stanford University Press, 1990).

Goris, Mariken, and Wilma Wissink, 'The Medieval Dutch Tradition of Boethius' *Consolatio philosophiae*', in Hoenen and Nauta (eds), *Boethius in the Middle Ages*, 121–65.

Greenfield, Concetta Carestia, *Humanist and Scholastic Poetics, 1250–1500* (Toronto: Associated University Presses, 1981).

Guillaume de Lorris, and Jean de Meun, *Le Roman de la Rose*, ed. Félix Lecoy, 3 vols (Paris: Editions Champion, 1965–70).

————, *The Romance of the Rose*, trans. Frances Horgan (Oxford: Oxford University Press, 1994).

Guillaume de Machaut, *Le Jugement du roy de Behaigne* and *Remede de Fortune*, ed. and trans. James I. Wimsatt and William W. Kibler (Athens: University of Georgia Press, 1988).

———, *Le Confort d'ami (Comfort for a Friend)*, ed. and trans. R. Barton Palmer (New York: Garland, 1992).

———, *The Fountain of Love (La Fonteinne Amoureuse) and Two Other Love Vision Poems*, ed. and trans. R. Barton Palmer (New York: Garland, 1993).

———, *Le livre de la Fontaine amoureuse*, ed. Jacqueline Cerquiglini-Toulet (Paris: Stock, 1993).

———, *Le Livre dou Voir Dit (The Book of the True Poem)*, ed. Daniel Leech Wilkinson, trans. R. Barton Palmer (New York: Garland, 1998).

———, *Le Livre du Voir Dit*, ed. and trans. Paul Imbs, rev. Jacqueline Cerquiglini-Toulet, Lettres Gothiques (Paris: Livre de Poche, 1999).

Gvillelmi de Conchis, *Glosae svper Boetivm*, ed. L. Nauta (Turnhout: Brepols, 1999).

Gybbon-Monypenny, G.B., 'Guillaume de Machaut's Erotic "Autobiography": Precedents for the Form of the *Voir-Dit*', in William Rothwell et al. (eds), *Studies in Medieval Literature and Languages in Memory of Frederick Whitehead* (Manchester: Manchester University Press, 1973), 133–52.

Hallmundson, May Newman, 'The Community of Law and Letters: Some Notes on Thomas Usk's Audience,' *Viator* 9 (1978): 357–65.

Hanrahan, Michael, 'The Seduction of *The Testament of Love*', *Literature and History* 7.1 (1998): 1–15.

Hardman, Phillipa, 'Chaucer's Muses and His "Art Poetical",' *Review of English Studies*. n.s. 37 (1986): 478–94.

Hayles, N. Katherine, *How We Became Posthuman: Virtual Bodies in Cybernetics, Literature, and Informatics* (Chicago: University of Chicago Press, 1999).

Hayton, Heather Richardson, '"Many privy thinges wimpled and folde": Governance and mutual obligation in Usk's *Testament of Love*', *Studies in Philology* 96.1 (1999): 22–41.

Hector, L.C., and B.F. Harvey (eds and trans.), *The Westminster Chronicle, 1381–1394*, (Oxford: Clarendon Press, 1982).

Heinrichs, Katherine, 'Lovers' "Consolations of Philosophy" in Boccaccio, Machaut, and Chaucer', *Studies in the Age of Chaucer* 11 (1989): 93–115.

———, *The Myths of Love: Classical Lovers in Medieval Literature* (Pennsylvania: Pennsylvania University Press, 1990).

Higden, Ranulph, *Polychronicon Ranulphi Higden monachi Cestrensis; Together with the English Translations of John Trevisa and of an Unknown Writer of the Fifteenth Century*, ed. Churchill Babington, vol. 1 (London: Longman, 1865).

Hoenen, Maarten J.F.M., and Lodi Nauta (eds), *Boethius in the Middle Ages: Latin and Vernacular Traditions of the* Consolatio Philosophiae (Leiden: Brill, 1997).

Hœpffner, Ernest (ed.), *Œuvres de Guillaume de Machaut*, 3 vols, SATF (Paris: Firmin Didot, 1908–1921).

Holy Bible, The; Translated from the Latin Vulgate and Diligently Compared with Other Editions in Divers Languages (Douay, AD 1609, Rheims, AD 1582) (London: Washbourne, 1914).

Hugh of St Victor, *Didascalicon*, ed. C.H. Buttimer (Washington, D.C.: Catholic University Press, 1939).

———, 'The Three Best Memory-Aids for Learning History', trans. Mary Carruthers, in Carruthers, *The Book of Memory*, 339–44.

Huot, Sylvia, *From Song to Book: The Poetics of Writing in Old French Lyric and Lyrical Narrative Poetry* (Ithaca: Cornell University Press, 1987).

———, 'The Daisy and the Laurel: Myths of Desire and Creativity in the Poetry of Jean Froissart', *Yale French Studies* (special edn), *Contexts: Style and Values in Medieval Art and Literature* (1991): 240–51.

———, 'Guillaume de Machaut and the Consolation of Poetry', *Modern Philology* 100 (2002): 169–95.

———, 'Reading the Lies of Poets: The Literal and the Allegorical in Machaut's *Fonteinne amoureuse*', *Philological Quarterly* 85 (2006): 25–48.

Jaeger, C. Stephen, *Ennobling Love: In Search of a Lost Sensibility* (Philadelphia: University of Pennsylvania Press, 1999).

James, Clair F., '*The Kingis Quair*: The Plight of the Courtly Lover', in David Chamberlain (ed.), *New Readings of Late Medieval Love Poems* (Lanham: University Press of America, 1993): 95–118.

Jameson, Fredric, *The Political Unconscious: Narrative as a Socially Symbolic Act* (London: Routledge, 1981).

Jean Froissart, *Chronicles*, trans. Geoffrey Brereton (Harmondsworth: Penguin, 1978).

———, *Chroniques*, ed. J.A.C. Buchon (Paris: A. Desrez, 1835).

———, *L'Espinette amoureuse*, ed. Anthime Fourrier (Paris: Klincksieck, 1963).

———, *La Prison amoureuse*, ed. Anthime Fourrier (Paris: Klincksieck, 1974).

———, *'Dits' et 'Débats'*, ed. Anthime Fourrier (Geneva: Droz, 1979).

Jeffrey, C.D., 'Anglo-Scots Poetry and the *Kingis Quair*', in Jean-Jacques Blanchot and Claude Graf (eds), *Actes du 2ᵉ colloque de langue et de littérature écossaises (Moyen Âge et Renaissance)*, Université de Strasbourg 5–11 Juillet 1978 (Strasbourg: Université de Strasbourg, 1979), 198–206.

Jellech, Virginia Bording, '*The Testament of Love* by Thomas Usk: A New Edition,' D. Phil. Diss., St Louis: Washington University, 1970).

Julian of Norwich, *A Revelation of Love*, ed. Marion Glasscoe (Exeter: University of Exeter Press, 1976).

Kay, Sarah, '"Le moment de conclure": Initiation as Retrospection in Froissart's *Dits amoureux*', in Nicola F. McDonald and W.M. Ormrod (eds), *Rites of Passage: Cultures of Transition in the Fourteenth Century* (York: York Medieval Press, 2004), 153–71.

———, *The Place of Thought: The Complexity of One in Late Medieval French Didactic Poetry* (Philadelphia: University of Pennsylvania Press, 2007).

————, 'Touching Singularity: Consolation, Philosophy, and Poetry in the French *Dit*', in Léglu and Milner (eds), *The Erotics of Consolation*, 21–38.

————, 'Legible Skins: Animals and the Ethics of Medieval Reading', *Postmedieval: A Journal of Medieval Cultural Studies* 2 (2011): 13–32.

Kaylor, Noel Harold, Jr., *The Medieval* Consolation of Philosophy: *An Annotated Bibliography* (New York: Garland, 1992).

Kaylor, Noel Harold, Jr., and Philip Edward Phillips (eds), '*The Boke of Coumfort of Bois* [Bodleian Library, Oxford MS Auct. F.3.5.]: A Transcription with Introduction', in Kaylor and Phillips (eds), *New Directions in Boethian Studies*, 223–79.

Kaylor, Noel Harold, Jr., and Philip Edward Phillips (eds), *New Directions in Boethian Studies* (Kalamazoo: Medieval Institute Publications, 2007).

Kelly, Douglas, *Medieval Imagination: Rhetoric and the Poetry of Courtly Love* (Madison: University of Wisconsin Press, 1978).

————, 'Les inventions ovidiennes de Froissart: Reflexions intertextuelles comme imagination', *Littérature*, 41 (1981): 82–92.

————, 'Imitation, Metamorphosis, and Froissart's use of the exemplary *Modus tractandi*', in Maddox and Sturm-Maddox (eds), *Froissart Across the Genres*, 101–18.

Kerby-Fulton, Kathryn, and Steven Justice, 'Langlandian Reading Circles and the Civil Service in London and Dublin, 1380–1427,' *New Medieval Literatures* 1 (1997): 59–83.

Kibler, William W., 'Poet and Patron: Froissart's *Prison amoureuse*', *L'Esprit Créateur*, 19 (1978): 32–46.

Kolve, V.A., *Chaucer and the Imagery of Narrative: The First Five Canterbury Tales* (London: Arnold, 1984).

Kottler, Barnet, 'The Vulgate Tradition of the *Consolatione Philosophiae* in the Fourteenth Century', *Mediaeval Studies* 17 (1955): 209–14.

Leach, Elizabeth Eva. *Guillaume de Machaut: Secretary, Poet, Musician* (Ithaca: Cornell University Press, 2011).

Lechat, Didier, *'Dire par fiction'*: *Métamorphoses du je chez Guillaume de Machaut, Jean Froissart et Christine de Pizan* (Paris: Champion, 2005).

Lees-Jeffries, Hester, *England's Helicon: Fountains in Early Modern Literature and Culture* (Oxford: Oxford University Press, 2007).

Léglu, Catherine E., and Stephen J. Milner (eds), *The Erotics of Consolation: Desire and Distance in the Late Middle Ages* (Houndmills: Palgrave, 2008).

————, 'Introduction: Encountering Consolation', in Léglu and Milner (eds), *The Erotics of Consolation*, 1–18.

Lehoux, Françoise, *Jean de France, duc de Berri: Sa vie, son action politique, 1340–1416*, 4 vols (Paris: Picard, 1966–68).

Lerer, Seth, *Boethius and Dialogue: Literary Method in* The Consolation of Philosophy (Princeton: Princeton University Press, 1985).

————, *Courtly Letters in the Age of Henry VIII: Literary Culture and the Arts of Deceit* (Cambridge: Cambridge University Press, 1997).

Leupin, Alexandre, 'The Powerlessness of Writing: Guillaume de Machaut, the Gorgon, and Ordenance', trans. Peggy McCracken, *Yale French Studies* 70 (1986), 127–49.

Lewis, Lucy, 'Langland's Tree of Charity and Usk's Wexing Tree', *Notes and Queries*, 42 (1995): 429–33.

———, 'The Identity of Margaret in Thomas Usk's *Testament of Love*', *Medium Aevum* 68 (1999): 63–72.

———, 'British Boethianism 1380–11436, PhD. Diss., University of London, 2000.

Lochrie, Karma, *Margery Kempe and Translations of the Flesh* (Philadelphia: University of Pennsylvania Press, 1991).

Looze, Laurence de, '"Mon nom trouveras': a New Look at the Anagrams of Guillaume de Machaut. The Enigmas, Responses, and Solutions', *Romanic Review* 79.4 (1988): 537–57.

———, (ed. and trans.), *Jean Froissart: La Prison amoureuse (The Prison of Love)* (New York: Garland, 1994).

———, *Pseudo-Autobiography in the Fourteenth Century: Juan Ruiz, Guillaume de Machaut, Jean Froissart, and Geoffrey Chaucer* (Gainesville: University of Florida Press, 1997).

Lothario dei Segni (Pope Innocent III), *De miseria condicionis humane*, ed. and trans. Robert E. Lewis (Athens: University of Georgia Press, 1978).

Love, Harold, *Attributing Authorship: An Introduction* (Cambridge: Cambridge University Press, 2002).

Lynch, Kathryn L., *The High Medieval Dream Vision: Poetry, Philosophy, and Literary Form* (Stanford: Stanford University Press, 1988).

Machabey, Armand, *Guillaume de Machault 130?–1377: La vie et l'œuvre musical*, 2 vols (Paris: Richard-Masse, 1955).

Machan, Tim William, (ed., with the assistance of A.J. Minnis), *Sources of the Boece* (Athens: University of Georgia Press, 2005).

———, *Techniques of Translation: Chaucer's* Boece (Norman: Pilgrim, 1985).

———, 'Chaucer as Translator', in Ellis (ed.), *The Medieval Translator*, 55–67.

Maddox, Donald, and Sara Sturm-Maddox (eds), *Froissart Across the Genres* (Gainesville: University of Florida Press, 1998).

Maguire, Eleanor A. et al., 'Routes to Remembering: The Brains Behind Superior Memory', *Nature Neuroscience* 6.1 (2003): 90–95.

Mapstone, Sally, 'Kingship and the *Kingis Quair*', in Helen Cooper and Sally Mapstone (eds), *The Long Fifteenth Century: Essays for Douglas Gray* (Oxford: Clarendon, 1997), 51–69.

———, 'Introduction: Older Scots and the Fifteenth Century', in Sally Mapstone (ed.), *Older Scots Literature* (Edinburgh: Birlinn, 2005), 3–13.

Marcus, Laura, *Auto/biographical Discourses: Theory, Criticism, Practice* (Manchester: Manchester University Press, 1994).

Marenbon, John, (ed.), *The Cambridge Companion to Boethius* (Cambridge: Cambridge University Press, 2009).

Martin, Ellen E., 'Chaucer's Ruth: An Exegetical Poetic in the Prologue to the *Legend of Good Women*', *Exemplaria* 3.2 (1991): 467–90.

Martin, Joanna, 'The Translations of Fortune: James I's *Kingis Quair* and the Rereading of Lancastrian Poetry', in Nicola Royan (ed.), *Langage Cleir Illumynate: Scottish Poetry from Barbour to Drummond, 1375–1630* (Amsterdam: Rodopi, 2007), 43–60.

———, *Kingship and Love in Scottish Poetry, 1424–1540* (Aldershot: Ashgate, 2008).

Matzke, John E. (ed.), *Les œuvres de Simund de Freine* (Paris: Société des Anciens Textes Français, 1909), 1–60.

McCrillis, Maury, III, 'Narrative Subjectivity and Narrative Distancing in James I of Scotland's *Kingis Quair*.' in G. Caie et al. (eds), *The European Sun: Proceedings of the Seventh International Conference on Medieval and Renaissance Scottish Language and Literature* (East Linton: Tuckwell, 2001), 202–10.

McDiarmid, Matthew P., (ed.), *The* Kingis Quair *of James Stewart* (London: Heinemann, 1973).

McGrady, Deborah, *Controlling Readers: Guillaume de Machaut and his Late Medieval Audience* (Toronto: University of Toronto Press, 2006).

———, '"Tout son païs m'abandonna": Reinventing Patronage in Machaut's "Fonteinne amoureuse"', *Yale French Studies*, 110 (2006): 19–31.

Medcalf, Stephen, 'Transposition: Thomas Usk's *Testament of Love*', in Ellis (ed.), *The Medieval Translator*, 181–95.

———, 'The World and Heart of Thomas Usk', in Minnis, Morse and Turville-Petre (eds), *Essays on Ricardian Literature*, 222–51.

Middleton, Anne, 'The Idea of Public Poetry in the Reign of Richard II', *Speculum* 53.1 (1978): 94–114.

———, 'Thomas Usk's "Perdurable Letters": The *Testament of Love* From Script to Print', *Studies in Bibliography* 51 (1998): 63–116.

Miller, Mark, *Philosophical Chaucer: Love, Sex, and Agency in the* Canterbury Tales (Cambridge: Cambridge University Press, 2004).

Mills, Robert, *Suspended Animation: Pain, Pleasure and Punishment in Medieval Culture* (London: Reaktion, 2005).

Minnis, A.J., 'Aspects of the Medieval French and English Traditions of the *De Consolatione Philosophiae*', in Margaret Gibson (ed.), *Boethius: His Life, Thought and Influence* (Oxford: Blackwell, 1981), 312–61.

———, (ed.), *The Medieval Boethius: Studies in the Vernacular Translations of* De Consolatione Philosophiae (Cambridge: Brewer, 1987).

———, *Medieval Theory of Authorship: Scholastic Literary Attitudes in the Later Middle Ages*, 2nd edn (Aldershot: Wildwood, 1988).

———, (ed.), *Chaucer's* Boece *and the Medieval Tradition of Boethius* (Cambridge: Brewer, 1993).

———, 'Looking for a Sign: The Quest for Nominalism in Chaucer and Langland', in Minnis, Morse and Turville-Petre (eds), *Essays on Ricardian Literature*, 142–78.

————, *Magister amoris: The* Roman de la Rose *and Vernacular Hermeneutics* (Oxford: Oxford University Press, 2001).

————, 'Medieval Imagination and Memory', in Alastair Minnis and Ian Johnson (eds), *The Cambridge History of Literary Criticism. Vol. II. The Middle Ages* (Cambridge: Cambridge University Press, 2005), 239–74.

————, *Fallible Authors: Chaucer's Pardoner and Wife of Bath* (Philadelphia: University of Pennsylvania Press, 2008).

Minnis, A.J., Charlotte C. Morse and Thorlac Turville-Petre (eds), *Essays on Ricardian Literature in Honour of J.A. Burrow* (Oxford: Clarendon, 1997).

Minnis, A.J., and Tim William Machan, 'The *Boece* as Late-Medieval Translation', in A.J. Minnis (ed.), *Chaucer's* Boece *and the Medieval Tradition of Boethius* (Cambridge: Brewer, 1993), 167–88.

Mühlethaler, Jean-Claude, 'Entre amour et politique: métamorphoses ovidiennes à la fin du Moyen Âge: la fable de Céyx et Alcyoné de l'*Ovide moralisé* à Christine de Pizan et Alain Chartier', *Cahiers de Recherches Médiévales*, 9 (2002): 143–56.

Nancy, Jean-Lucy, *The Inoperative Community*, ed. Peter Connor, trans. Peter Connor et al. (Minneapolis: University of Minnesota Press, 1991).

Nauta, Lodi, 'The *Consolation*: The Latin Commentary Tradition, 800–1700', in Marenbon (ed.), *The Cambridge Companion to Boethius*, 255–78.

Noest, Marcel, (ed.), 'A Critical Edition of a Late Fourteenth Century French Verse Translation of Boethius' *De Consolatione Philosophiae*: the *Boëce de Confort*', *Carmina Philosophiae: Journal of the International Boethius Society*, 8–9 (1999–2000).

Norton-Smith, John, (ed.), *James I of Scotland: The* Kingis Quair (Oxford: Clarendon).

Nouvet, Claire, 'Pour une économie de la dé-limitation: la *Prison amoureuse* de Jean Froissart', *Neophilologus*, 70 (1986): 341–56.

Oberman, Heiko A., *The Harvest of Medieval Theology: Gabriel Biel and Late-Medieval Nominalism* (Cambridge, MA.: Harvard University Press, 1963).

Oliver, Clementine, 'A Political Pamphleteer in Late Medieval England: Thomas Fovent, Geoffrey Chaucer, Thomas Usk, and the Merciless Parliament of 1388', *New Medieval Literatures* 6 (2003): 167–98.

————, *Parliament and Political Pamphleteering in Fourteenth-Century England* (Woodbridge: York Medieval Press, 2010).

Olney, James, *Autobiography: Essays Theoretical and Critical* (Princeton: Princeton University Press, 1980).

Panizza, Letizia A., 'Stoic Psychotherapy in the Middle Ages and Renaissance: Petrarch's *De Remediis*', in Léglu and Milner (eds), *The Erotics of Consolation*, 117–39.

Patch, Howard Rollin, *The Tradition of Boethius: A Study of His Importance in Medieval Culture* (New York: Oxford University Press, 1935).

Patourel, John Le, 'The Treaty of Brétigny, 1360', *Transactions of the Royal Historical Society*, 5th ser., 10 (1960): 19–39.

Patterson, Lee, *Chaucer and the Subject of History* (London: Routledge, 1991).

Pearsall, Derek, 'The English Chaucerians', in D.S. Brewer (ed.), *Chaucer and Chaucerians: Critical Studies in Middle English Literature* (London: Nelson, 1966), 201–39.

Peter of Ravenna, *The Art of Memory, that otherwise is called the Phenix, a boke very behouefull and profitable to all professours of science, grammaryens, rethoryciens, dialectyks, legystes, phylosophes and theologiens*, trans. Robert Copland [1545 (?)] STC 24112.

Petrina, Alessandra, *The* Kingis Quair *of James I of Scotland* (Padova: Unipress, 1997).

————, *Cultural Politics in Fifteenth-Century England: The Case of Humfrey, Duke of Gloucester* (Leiden: Brill, 2004).

Pickens, Rupert T., 'History and Narration in Froissart's *Dits*: The Case of the *Bleu Chevalier*', in Maddox and Sturm-Maddox (eds), *Froissart Across the Genres*, 119–52.

Poiron, Daniel, *Le Poète et le prince: l'évolution du lyrisme courtois de Guillaume de Machaut à Charles d'Orléans* (Paris: Presses Universitaires de France, 1965).

————, 'Narcisse et Pygmalion dans le *Roman de la Rose*', in Raymond J. Cormier and Urban T. Holmes (eds.), *Essays in Honor of Louis Francis Solano* (Chapel Hill: University of North Carolina Press, 1970), 153–65.

Porter, Elizabeth, 'Gower's Ethical Microcosm and Political Macrocosm', in A.J. Minnis (ed), *Gower's* Confessio Amantis: *Responses and Reassessments* (Cambridge: Brewer, 1983), 135–62.

Prendergast, Thomas A.,'Chaucer's Doppelgänger: Thomas Usk and the Reformation of Chaucer', in Prendergast and Kline (eds), *Rewriting Chaucer: Culture*, 258–69.

Prendergast, Thomas A., and Barbara Kline (eds), *Rewriting Chaucer: Culture, Authority, and the Idea of the Authentic Text, 1400–1602* (Columbus: Ohio State University Press, 1999).

Quinn, William, 'Memory and the Matrix of Unity in *The Kingis Quair*.' *Chaucer Review* 15 (1981): 332–55.

Relihan, Joel C., *The Prisoner's Philosophy: Life and Death in Boethius's* Consolation (Notre Dame: University of Notre Dame Press, 2007).

Ricklin, Thomas, '…Quello non conosciuto da molti libro di Boezio. Hinweise zur *Consolatio philosophiae* in Norditalien', in Maarten J.F.M. Hoenen and Lodi Nauta (eds), *Boethius in the Middle Ages: Latin and Vernacular Traditions of the* Consolatio Philosophiae (Leiden: Brill, 1997), 267–86.

Robertson, D.W., Jr., 'The Pearl as a Symbol', *Modern Language Notes* 65 (1950): 155–61.

Rockwell, Paul Vincent, *Rewriting Resemblance in Medieval French Romance* (London: Garland, 1995).

Rose, Gillian, *Mourning Becomes the Law: Philosophy and Representation* (Cambridge: Cambridge University Press, 1996).

Rosenfeld, Jessica, 'The Doubled Joys of *Troilus and Criseyde*', in Léglu and Milner (eds), *The Erotics of Consolation*, 39–59.

———, *Ethics and Enjoyment in Late Medieval Poetry: Love after Aristotle* (Cambridge: Cambridge University Press, 2011).

Rossi, Paolo, *Logic and the Art of Memory: The Quest for a Universal Language*, trans. Stephen Clucas (London: Continuum, 2000).

Rundle, David, 'On the Difference between Virtue and Weiss: Humanist Texts in England during the Fifteenth Century,' in D.E.S. Dunn (ed.), *Courts, Counties, and the Capital in the Later Middle Ages* (New York: St Martins Press, 1996), 181–203.

———, 'Humanism before the Tudors: On Nobility and the reception of *Studia Humanistas* in Fifteenth-Century England', in J. Woolfson (ed.), *Reassessing Tudor Humanism* (Basingstoke: Palgrave Macmillan, 2002), 22–42.

———, 'Habits of Manuscript Collecting: The Dispersals of the Library of Humfrey, Duke of Gloucester,' in James Raven (ed.), *Lost Libraries: The Destruction of Great Book Collections since Antiquity* (London: Palgrave Macmillan, 2004), 106–23.

Rutledge, Monica, 'Dante, the Body and Light', *Dante Studies*, 113 (1995): 151–65.

Salutati, Coluccio, *De fato et fortuna*, ed. Concetta Bianca (Florence: Olschki, 1985).

Sammut, Alfonso, *Unfredo duca di Gloucester e gli umanisti italiani* (Padova: Antenore, 1980).

Sanderlin, George, 'Usk's *Testament of Love* and St. Anselm', *Speculum* 17 (1942): 69–73.

Sawday, Jonathan, *Engines of the Imagination: Renaissance Culture and the Rise of the Machine* (London: Routledge, 2007).

Schreiber, Earl G., and Thomas E. Maresca, trans. *Commentary on the First Six Books of Virgil's Aeneid* (Lincoln: University of Nebraska Press, 1979).

Shears, F.S., *Froissart: Chronicler and Poet* (London: Routledge, 1939).

Siennicki, Barbara Lorraine, 'No Harbour for the "Shippe of Traveyle": A Study of Thomas Usk's *Testament of Love*', unpublished D. Phil. Thesis (Ontario: Queen's University, 1984).

Skeat, W.W., *The Complete Works of Chaucer: Chaucerian and Other Pieces*, vol. 7 (Oxford: Clarendon, 1897).

———, (ed), *The* Kingis Quair: *Together with* A Ballad of Good Counsel: *by King James I. of Scotland* 2nd edn Scottish Text Society, n.s. 1 (Edinburgh: Blackwood, 1911).

Skura, Meredith Anne, *Tudor Autobiography: Listening for Inwardness* (Chicago: University of Chicago Press, 2008).

Sleiderink, Remco, *De stem van de meester: De hertogen van Brabant en hun rol in het literaire leven (1106–1430)* (Amsterdam: Prometheus, 2003).

Smalley, Beryl, *English Friars and Antiquity in the Early Fourteenth Century* (Oxford: Oxford University Press, 1960).

Smith, Janet M., *The French Background of Middle Scots Literature* (Edinburgh: Oliver and Boyd, 1934).

Smith, Lesley, ed. and trans., *Medieval Exegesis in Translation: Commentaries on the* Book of Ruth (Kalamazoo: Medieval Institute Publications, 1996).

Smith, Sidonie, and Julia Watson, *Reading Autobiography: A Guide for Interpreting Life Narratives*. 2nd edn (Minneapolis: University of Minnesota Press, 2010).

Smyth, Adam, *Autobiography in Early Modern England* (Cambridge: Cambridge University Press, 2010).

Spargo, John Webster, 'Chaucer's Love-Days', *Speculum* 15.1 (1940): 36–56.

Spearing, A.C., 'Dreams in the *Kingis Quair* and the Duke's Book', in Mary-Jo Arn (ed.), *Charles d'Orléans in England (1415–1440)* (Cambridge: Brewer, 2000), 123–44.

Spencer, Alice, *Dialogues of Love and Government: A Study of the Erotic Dialogue Form in some Texts from the Courtly Love Tradition* (Newcastle: Cambridge Scholars Publishing, 2007).

Spicer, Jakki, 'The Author Is Dead, Long Live the Author: Autobiography and the Fantasy of the Individual', *Criticism* 47.3 (2005): 387–403.

Steiner, Emily, *Documentary Culture and the Making of Medieval English Literature* (Cambridge: Cambridge University Press, 2003).

Stockton, Eric W., (ed. and trans.), *The Major Latin Works of John Gower: The Voice of One Crying and the Tripartite Chronicle* (Seattle: University of Washington Press, 1962).

Strohm, Paul, 'Politics and Poetics: Usk and Chaucer in the 1380s', in Lee Patterson (ed.), *Literary Practice and Social Change in Britain, 1380–1550* (Berkeley: University of California Press, 1990), 83–112.

——, *Hochon's Arrow: The Social Imagination of Fourteenth-Century Texts* (Princeton: Princeton University Press, 1992).

Summers, Joanna, 'Gower's *Vox Clamantis* and Usk's *Testament of Love*', *Medium Ævum* 68.1 (1999): 55–62.

——, *Late-Medieval Prison Writing and the Politics of Autobiography* (Oxford: Oxford University Press, 2004).

Sutton, John, 'Porous Memory and the Cognitive Life of Things', in Darren Tofts, Annemarie Jonson, and Alessio Cavallaro (eds), *Prefiguring Cyberculture: An Intellectual History*, (Cambridge, MA: MIT Press, 2002), 130–41.

Swift, Helen J., '*Tamainte Consolation / me fist lymagination*: A Poetics of Mourning and Imagination in Late Medieval *dits*' in Léglu and Milner (eds), *The Erotics of Consolation*, 141–64.

Tatlock, John S.P., *A Concordance to the Complete Works of Geoffrey Chaucer and to the* Romaunt of the Rose (Washington: Carnegie, 1927).

Taylor, Paul Beekman, and Sophie Bordier, 'Chaucer and the Latin Muses', *Traditio* 47 (1992): 215–32.

Thiry, Claude, 'Allégorie et histoire dans la *Prison amoureuse* de Froissart', *Studi Francesi* 61–2 (1977): 15–29.

Thomas, Antoine, and Mario Roques, 'Traductions françaises de la *Consolatio Philosophiae* de Boèce', *Histoire littéraire de la France* 37 (1938), 419–88.

Thynne, William, *The Workes of Geffray Chaucer newly printed with dyuers workes whiche were neuer in print before* (London: Thomas Godfray 1532), STC 5068.

Trevisa, John, *The Governance of Kings and Princes: John Trevisa's Middle English Translation of the* De regimine principium *of Aegidius Romanus*, ed. David C. Fowler, Charles F. Briggs and Paul G. Remley (New York: Garland, 1997).

Turner, Marion, '"Certaynly His Noble Sayenges Can I Not Amende": Thomas Usk and *Troilus and Criseyde*', *Chaucer Review* 37 (2002): 26–39.

———, *Chaucerian Conflict: Languages of Antagonism in Late-Fourteenth Century London* (Oxford: Oxford University Press, 2007).

———, 'Usk and the Goldsmiths', *New Medieval Literatures* 9 (2008): 139–77.

Usk, Thomas, 'The Appeal of Thomas Usk against John Northampton', in R.W. Chambers and Marjorie Daunt (eds), *A Book of London English 1384–1425* (Oxford: Clarendon Press, 1967), 22–31.

———, *The Testament of Love*, ed. R. Allen Shoaf (Kalamazoo: Medieval Institute Publications, 1998).

———, *Testament of Love*, ed. Gary W. Shawver (Toronto: University of Toronto Press, 2002).

Vance, Eugene. *Mervelous Signals: Poetics and Sign Theory in the Middle Ages* (Lincoln: University of Nebraska Press, 1986).

Wailes, Stephen L., 'Potency in *Fortunatus*', *The German Quarterly* 59.1 (1986): 5–18.

———, *Medieval Allegories of Jesus' Parables* (Berkeley: University of California Press, 1987).

Walker, Greg, *Plays of Persuasion: Drama and Politics at the Court of Henry VIII* (Cambridge: Cambridge University Press, 1991).

Wallen, Martha, 'Biblical and Mythological Typology in Machaut's *Confort d'Ami*', *Res Publica Litterarum* 3 (1980): 191–206.

Wetherbee, Winthrop, 'The *Consolation* and medieval literature', in Marenbon (ed.), *The Cambridge Companion to Boethius*, 279–302.

Wilkins, Nigel, 'A Pattern of Patronage: Machaut, Froissart and the Houses of Luxembourg and Bohemia in the Fourteenth Century', *French Studies*, 37 (1983): 256–84.

Wogan-Browne, Jocelyn et al. (eds), *The Idea of the Vernacular: An Anthology of Middle English Literary Theory, 1280–1520* (Exeter: University of Exeter Press, 1999).

Wolfe, Jessica, *Humanism, Machinery, and Renaissance Literature* (Cambridge: Cambridge University Press, 2004).

Yates, Frances A., *The Art of Memory* (London: Pimlico, 1992).

Zink, Michel, 'The Allegorical Poem as Interior Memoir', trans. Margaret Miner and Kevin Brownlee, *Yale French Studies* 70 (1986): 100–126.

————, *Froissart et le temps* (Paris: Paris: Presses Universitaires de France, 1998).

Žižek, Slavoj, *Did Somebody Say Totalitarianism? Five Interventions in the (Mis) use of a Notion* (London: Verso, 2001).

————, *The Plague of Fantasies*, 2nd edn (London: Verso, 2008).

————, *The Ticklish Subject: The Absent Centre of Political Ontology* (London: Verso, 2008).

Index

For Product Safety Concerns and Information please contact our EU
representative GPSR@taylorandfrancis.com Taylor & Francis Verlag GmbH,
Kaufingerstraße 24, 80331 München, Germany

Batch number: 08158427

Printed by Printforce, the Netherlands